Regional Wage Inflation and Unemployment

Edited by R L Martin

Pion Limited, 207 Brondesbury Park, London NW2 5JN

ISBN 0 85086 090 3

Printed in Great Britain by Page Bros (Norwich) Limited.

Regional Wage Inflation and Unemployment

Preface

The period since the mid-1960s has witnessed the emergence of persistent though varying wage inflation, while at the same time unemployment has risen to record postwar levels. For their part, economists have in general tended to ignore the geography of inflation and unemployment, being preoccupied with the problem of linking microeconomic theory with econometric aggregates in an attempt to find the basis for effective policy prescription. The myth that characterises much of this approach is that economy-wide relations amongst wages, employment, and unemployment are simply enlarged analogues or consistent summations of relationships amongst corresponding variables for individual households and firms within a single, homogeneous labour market. The shortcomings of such a view are obvious. In contrast, the underlying premise of the present volume is that consideration of the regional dimensions of the labour market can make an important contribution to understanding aggregate trends in wages and unemployment.

On the one hand, there is a small but rapidly-growing interest amongst regional economists in the spatial labour-market aspects of wage determination and unemployment dynamics, not only in order to help explain the observed behaviour of regional earnings and unemployment in a number of industrial economies, but also because an explicit regional or subregional perspective on labour-market issues may serve to reveal the potentialities and limitations of alternative policy formulations. On the other, within geography there is a substantial body of literature, much of it developed during the 1970s, dealing with the regional unemployment problem. Although the earlier work was overly descriptive and tended to treat unemployment simply as a statistical 'indicator' of regional economic fluctuation, more recent studies in this area have been increasingly concerned with identifying the causes of regional unemployment differentials and with the nature and functioning of regional labour markets. Allied to this, there has been a growing awareness of the need to take account of the monetary side of labour-market adjustments. The purpose of this volume is to extend these convergent lines of interest by bringing together a number of studies selected from, but hopefully representative of, the research currently being conducted in this field. By combining contributions from geographers and economists, and by drawing on empirical examples from the United Kingdom, the USA, and Canada, the various essays illustrate the ways in which wages and unemployment in the spatially disaggregated labour market are determined both by the external forces generated by the different networks of economic, social, institutional, and political linkages between regions, and by the internal forces that operate within individual labour-market areas themselves. Not only do these studies provide additional viewpoints from which to examine the prolonged inflationary recession of recent years, they also point conclusively to the relevance of the regional and local labour market as a conceptual and empirical category, and to the importance of the labour market itself in regional and urban analysis.

Since the themes covered by these essays relate to some of the central policy conflicts currently facing governments in several industrial countries, and since regional problems are inextricably linked with labour-market issues, the book should be of interest not only to geographers and economists generally, but also to a variety of specialists concerned with particular theoretical or applied aspects of the modern labour market or space economy, from labour economists to regional analysts. Thus the book should appeal to students and researchers alike in university departments of geography, economics, regional science and urban studies, and equally to those working in government, and in other public bodies and associated research and advisory institutes which deal with or are responsible for regional economic planning, economic policy, or manpower programmes.

The compilation of a collected volume of this sort clearly depends on the successful collaborative effort of the various contributors. From the start each author was eager to participate in the project, and I owe a considerable debt of gratitude to them all for their constructive and sustained support. I also wish to thank John Ashby of Pion; for the enthusiasm that he displayed when I first put the idea to him, and for his editorial expertise that helped to bring the book to fruition. Responsibility for the views expressed and any errors of omission or comission remain, of course, with the authors.

Ron Martin
St Catherine's College
Cambridge
May 1981

Contributors

C L Carmichael — *Manpower Services Commission, Selkirk House, 166 High Holborn, London WC1V 6PF, England*

H Chang — *Department of Geography, University of Oklahoma, 455 West Lindsey, Norman, Oklahoma 73019, USA*

P C Cheshire — *Department of Economics, Faculty of Urban and Regional Studies, University of Reading, Whiteknights, Reading RG6 2BU, England*

G L Clark — *Department of City and Regional Planning, John F Kennedy School of Government, Harvard University, Cambridge, Massachusetts 02138, USA*

M Frost — *Department of Geography, King's College, University of London, Strand, London WC2R 2LS, England*

R Q Hanham — *Department of Geography, Portsmouth Polytechnic, Lion Terrace, Portsmouth PO1 3HE, England*

R A Hart — *International Institute of Management, Wissenschaftszentrum, Platz der Luftbrücke 1–3, D-1000 Berlin 42, FRG*

R L Martin — *Department of Geography, University of Cambridge, Downing Place, Cambridge CB2 3EN, England*

B Moore — *Department of Applied Economics, University of Cambridge, Sidgwick Avenue, Cambridge CB3 9DA, England*

J Rhodes — *Department of Applied Economics, University of Cambridge, Sidgwick Avenue, Cambridge CB3 9DA, England*

N Spence — *Department of Geography, London School of Economics and Political Science, University of London, Houghton Street, London WC2A 2AE, England*

R Tarling — *Department of Applied Economics, University of Cambridge, Sidgwick Avenue, Cambridge CB3 9DA, England*

F Wilkinson — *Department of Applied Economics, University of Cambridge, Sidgwick Avenue, Cambridge CB3 9DA, England*

Contents

1

Introduction

R L Martin

1.1 Context: wages, unemployment, and the labour market [1]

This book is concerned with certain regional aspects of what have become
two of the central domestic issues in the capitalist economy during the
1970s and 1980s: wages and unemployment. Stimulated by the widening
discrepancy between the predictions of competing explanations of
unemployment and wage determination on the one hand, and actual events
on the other, considerable economic and political debate has raged in
recent years over these two facets of the labour market. Up to the late
1960s, average rates of wage (and price) increase and unemployment in the
cyclical capitalist economy were generally low or moderate but also
variable, with a tendency for the rate of increase in wages to accelerate
when unemployment was low and to decelerate when unemployment was
high. This apparent inverse pattern led some economists to suggest the
existence of a policy choice or 'trade-off' between wage inflation and
unemployment: the maintenance of full employment would involve some
wage inflation, and conversely wage inflation was only likely to be reduced
at the cost of a higher rate of unemployment. For many Keynesians, this
'Phillips curve' supplied a much-needed theory of inflation to their model.
If a stable, downward-sloping relation existed between the rate of wage
increase and the level of unemployment, could not the government manage
aggregate demand in such a way as to be able to achieve a balance between
an 'acceptable' unemployment rate on the one hand and an 'acceptable'
rate of inflation on the other? Could not a positive rate of wage inflation
be regarded as the price which had to be paid for a policy of full
employment?

Not so, argued the neoclassical monetarists, for the Phillips curve is a
short-term phenomenon only, and in a given economy there will be an
infinity of such curves, each one corresponding to a different (constant)
expected rate of inflation. Moreover, because in the long run, workers'
expectations are in turn dependent on the unemployment rate, the Phillips
curve will shift until it becomes vertical at the 'natural' rate of unemployment
—that is at the level of unemployment due to 'frictional, structural and
institutional' factors in the labour market. The only result of attempts to
lower unemployment below this 'natural' rate by aggregate demand

[1] This introductory essay is intended to sketch some of the background and context
within which the following chapters might be located, and to convey the general
contribution that this volume seeks to make. It does not fully summarise the various
chapters; nor do the views expressed necessarily represent those of the individual
authors.

creation will be accelerating inflation. Thus, it was argued, in the long
run, fiscal and monetary expansion determines the rate of increase of wages
(and prices) but has no effect whatever on the level of unemployment;
there can be no justification for any policy other than one of restricting
growth of the money supply in accordance with a target for the rate of
inflation.

Whilst this Keynesian–Monetarist debate over the Phillips curve policy
locus deepened, the 'terms of trade' the curve purported to depict were
in any case being shattered by economic events. After about 1968, in the
United Kingdom, USA, Canada, Australia, and elsewhere, money-wage
movements ran contrary to Phillips curve pronouncements; higher rates of
wage increase were correlated with rising, not with declining, unemployment.
This 'stagflation' or 'slumpflation', the conjuncture of persistent inflation
and high and rising unemployment, is a new phenomenon, at least on its
present scale (Sherman, 1976; Haberler, 1977; Weintraub, 1978). The
debacle over short-run versus long-run relationships was soon redirected to
the problem of the collapsing or even disappearing Phillips curve. Never
very robust, the curve has recently become so weak that there is now
controversy whether it is merely comatose or actually dead. For some
the explanation of the 'breakdown' of the wage–unemployment relationship is to be found in increased cost-push forces in the labour market,
arising, in the view of 'pure' Keynesians, from an endogenous 'wage–wage'
spiral as different labour groups endeavour to preserve and improve their
relative wage positions, or, according to more radical theorists, from a yet
more fundamental class struggle and general 'crisis of capitalism'[2]. At
the other extreme, the explanation most frequently emphasised by the
monetarists is that the 'natural' rate of unemployment itself has been rising
as a result of changing conditions in the labour market (mainly increasing
'voluntary' and 'frictional' joblessness because of more 'liberal' unemployment benefits and social welfare payments), and of lags in the
adjustment of expectations and political institutions to high and volatile
inflation. Most eclectic Keynesians find themselves occupying the distinctly
uncomfortable middle ground between these two contrasting factions.

Now these differing interpretations of the problem of stagflation turn
essentially on a fundamental controversy about how labour markets
function in industrial economies. The currently fashionable 'monetarist'
position implicitly assumes that the labour market, apart from structural
and frictional problems, even in the short run functions in a competitive
manner. Wage changes are assumed to be determined by firms' offers and

[2] There is, of course, considerable diversity of opinion within these different schools.
Even amongst Marxian scholars there is disagreement over the determinants of wage
movements in the economy, not least perhaps because of the essentially demand-supply
explanation adopted by Marx himself:
"Taking them as a whole, the general movements of wages are exclusively regulated
by the expansion and contraction of the industrial reserve army, and these again
correspond to the periodic changes of the industrial cycle" (Marx, 1867, page 637).

workers' acceptance decisions as workers and vacancies flow through the market and as employed workers are granted wage increases to inhibit this flow. Neoclassical and Monetarist theorists like to picture the wage push by unions as a 'one-shot' transition from one equilibrium to another, with a higher rate of 'natural' unemployment, whenever monopolistic unions or other labour collectives are formed or when their 'market' power is increased. Attempts to maintain artificially high real wages must lead to an excess supply of labour, that is to a higher rate of unemployment. As regards unemployment, this theory has little to say on involuntary jobless-ness in the Keynesian sense of the term. Rather, most 'seemingly' involuntary unemployment is considered to be really voluntary, frictional-structural unemployment of the 'search' or 'waiting' kind, which cannot be eliminated in the long run by raising effective demand. It is assumed that workers choose to be unemployed in order to search for better job opportunities; it is even argued that it is desirable to be unemployed for the purpose of job search. However, the empirical fact that the majority of job-changers in the UK and USA experience no interim unemployment, but rather conduct job search whilst still employed, makes some of the grandiose mathematical models erected in the name of 'job search' theories of unemployment seem to be of dubious relevance to the real world.

Similarly, considerable doubt surrounds the concept of the 'natural' rate of unemployment. As defined by Friedman it is a condition of labour-market equilibrium in which there is neither excess demand for or excess supply of labour in the aggregate. It is that rate "which is consistent with the real forces and accurate perceptions" (M Friedman, 1977, page 15). By 'real forces' is meant how efficiently the labour market operates, the extent of competition or monopoly, the barriers or encouragements to working in various occupations, the degree of wage flexibility, and the relative level of unemployment benefits, whilst 'perceptions' relate to expectations and processes of adjustment to a given level of inflation. Thus defined, however, there can be no generally applicable or unique level of natural unemployment, but instead a host of rates dependent on the changing conditions in the labour market. And without knowing the expected rate of inflation, it is impossible to determine what the natural level of unemployment is at any particular time, let alone to test the hypothesis about its influence on the rate of change of money wages.

Pure Keynesians, institutionalists, and more radical theorists, on the other hand, all share a common rejection of this misleading conception of the labour market. In industrial economies the labour market is inherently imperfect and characteristically fragmented and segmented, where in many sectors wages are set by a cumbersome time-consuming process of collective bargaining and negotiation, made self-propelling by intergroup rivalries over real differentials and distributive justice. Even in nonunionised sectors, wages are set by custom and convention rather than by market forces. The social, often political, nature of wage determination, involving as it does many interacting segments of the labour force together with a general downward rigidity of wages, means that even without excess demand there could be an in-built inflationary bias in the modern labour market. In the Keynesian system, wage adjustments lag behind employment adjustments, so that in the face of labour-market disequilibrium the response is via the quantity adjustments of unemployment. Thus most unemployment is considered to be demand-deficient unemployment, the result of involuntary lay-offs of workers made by firms under conditions of deficient aggregate effective demand in the recessionary phase of the economic cycle. Such involuntary unemployment exists in the Keynesian labour market as long as there is any unemployment which can be reduced by raising aggregate demand without affecting the level of money wages. However, since the labour market is neither perfect nor homogeneous, and given the immobility of labour, no precise meaning can be given to the notion of a 'full employment' equilibrium. The essential difference between the 'natural' rate and Keynesian type theories of unemployment would then appear to be that whereas in the former a perpetuation of the disequilibrium level of unemployment with deficient aggregate demand seems to be impossible, except in the shortest of short runs, in the Keynesian system such an underemployment 'equilibrium' will persist unless the disequilibrating aggregate demand is cured (Lal, 1977, page 14).

Although for the most part these differing accounts have focused on the aggregate labour market, there has been a growing interest, both within the economic and the geographical literature, in the regional aspects of labour-market adjustment. Movements in wages, employment, and unemployment at the level of the national economy are but the outcome of adjustments within numerous underlying and interacting submarkets which vary in their occupational, industrial, and geographical coverage: in the actual labour market there is occupational, industrial, racial, sexual, and regional segmentation, with important real phenomena attached to each. Whereas there is no entirely adequate definition of sectoral labour markets on the basis of any one of these dimensions alone, at least one eminent labour economist has emphasised that "the most important boundaries between labour markets run along geographical lines" (Reynolds, 1951, page 41).

1.2 Regional perspectives
Within the economic literature, interest in the regional labour-market aspects of wage determination has centred on two main themes: (1) the derivation of a multimarket foundation for explaining aggregate Phillips-type relationships, and thence the implications for the national economy of changing conditions amongst individual submarkets; and (2) the process of money-wage-change transmission or spread between different sectors of the labour market. Through their somewhat distinct, though not unrelated, routes these two strands of work have begun to contribute significantly to

the development of a conceptual framework to account for the structure of regional wages and unemployment. Geographical study in this field has concentrated more on the empirical analysis of wage–unemployment relationships in specific spatial labour-market areas, although recently interest has shifted to the second of the above themes, that is to the nature and direction of wage transfers within the space eonomy [for brief reviews of this development see King (1976) and Martin and Spence (1981)].

The Phillips curve as such did not represent any radical change in the theory of unemployment; nor did it necessarily conflict with the analysis of involuntary, demand-deficient unemployment. But what it did signify was that other types of unemployment may have been underestimated, particularly the degree of frictional and structural maladjustment. The work of Lipsey (1960) was especially important in this respect, for he suggested that since the national labour market is the aggregate of a set of 'micro' markets, and since each of these was likely to have its own particular wage-change–unemployment relationship, changes in the distribution of unemployment between individual markets would influence the aggregate relationship and hence affect the macro trade-off. One of the implications of this hypothesis is that the average economy-wide rate of change of wages will depend not only on the total pressure of demand for labour but also on the way in which it is distributed amongst the different geographical regions of the country. In this way the regional structure of the labour market may be of crucial importance in the wage-inflation process. Given the policy dimension of this idea, it is not surprising that several writers have attempted to determine the extent of the influence on general wage movements of the degree of structural imbalance among regional unemployment rates (Archibald, 1969; Thirlwall, 1969a; Thomas and Stoney, 1971; Gordon, 1973; Higgins, 1973; Hewings, 1978). The underlying presumption is that the more even the distribution of unemployment across regions, the lower can be total national unemployment without inflationary consequences. That the issue has been of more than just academic interest is attested by the emphasis given to the argument in the proposal for the British regional employment premium:

"When the level of economic activity has been relatively high, the pressure of demand for labour in the centres of maximum employment, especially the South and Midlands, has built up from time to time to very high levels with consequent and well-known inflation effects and damage to the balance of payments ... . The more even the demand for labour, the higher can be total national employment without inflationary consequences and without prejudicing the balance of payments" (Department of Economic Affairs, 1967, paras 24–25).

In fact, the concept of the regional dispersion of unemployment has usually been implicit in most discussions of the case for and the composition of regional policies (for example, Moore and Rhodes, 1975).

   Notwithstanding that the hypothesis has been neither wholly rejected
nor confirmed empirically (see, for example, Hewings, 1978), conceptually
the proposition requires rather specific conditions concerning the nature
of the wage-change–unemployment relationship in each region, the extent
to which regional labour markets are independent of one another, and the
existence and pattern of interregional wage-transmission effects.   Whether
the required conditions are met, and hence whether policy conclusions of
the Lipsey type are relevant in practice, particularly in an era of high and
rising unemployment (cf Chisholm, 1976), is clearly a question that only
detailed analysis of regional labour-market adjustments can resolve.   The
economic and geographical studies that have been made of regional and
subregional wage determination indicate that wage–unemployment
functions in spatial labour markets are extremely diverse, suggesting not
only the importance of region-specific factors but also one possible
explanation of the observed instability of the aggregate relationship.
   At the same time, it is an established fact that the regional wages
structure in most industrial economies exhibits a remarkable rank-order
stability over time, with a tendency for the dispersion of wages within
such structures to narrow, in spite of persistent geographical differences in
unemployment.   This implies the operation of mechanisms that serve to
hold the wages structure together, irrespective of local labour-market
conditions.   Thus there is a growing body of literature concerned with
elucidating the processes of wage transfer and earnings spread at the
regional and subregional scale.   Various explanations of the interdependence
of regional wage movements have been formulated, ranging from hypotheses
that rely on the proposition that labour markets are noticeably less
efficient in areas of high unemployment because of frictional and structural
imbalances, through neoclassical models that stress the role of expected
(real) wages, job search, and potential migration, to theories of wage
spillover based on notions of national bargaining over wage rates, multilocational parity claims over earnings, and demonstration effects involving
regional wage leadership.   This area of enquiry would appear to be of
importance both for the light it may throw on the nature of wage
determination in a sectorally fragmented labour market, and as a factor
which may help to account for the geographical structure of unemployment
(see Williamson, 1975).
   In a similar way that the early work of Lipsey has stimulated an
expanding interest in the spatial labour-market aspects of inflation theory,
so perhaps Brechling's (1967) and Thirlwall's (1966; 1969b) studies of
British regional unemployment can be said to have been instrumental in
the recently burgeoning literature, particularly within economic geography,
on the causes and dynamics of regional unemployment disparities.   The
long-term persistence of pronounced unemployment differentials between
regions, at all stages of the economic cycle, represents one of the most
crucial problems confronting regional theory and regional policy, for the

continued existence of areas of high unemployment runs contrary to orthodox analysis (Dixon and Thirlwall, 1975; Holland, 1976; Stilwell, 1978). One school of thought on the question of regional unemployment disparities has argued that aggregate demand pressures are unevenly diffused across the space economy. Persistent differentials between regions are a reflection of differences in demand for products and labour. Accordingly, demand-deficient unemployment differentials can be reduced by stimulating overall economic activity. The proponents of this explanation would also suggest, however, that a national full-employment policy will be unable of itself to generate full employment in all regions simultaneously. That is, although the Keynesian technique of creating enough effective demand in the economy as a whole is a necessary condition of full employment in every part of the country, it is not a sufficient condition. Thus, it is contended, there may be a need for ancillary policies aimed at altering the regional distribution of product demand.

Another school of thought on the subject of regional unemployment gaps has argued that the persistence of these differentials reflects the existence of higher levels of non-demand-deficient unemployment in certain regions. The observed tendency, in the United Kingdom and the USA for example, for the regional dispersion of unemployment rates to vary inversely with the overall, national rate of unemployment suggests there are imbalances in the levels of structural joblessness. Structural unemployment is, in one sense, an extreme form of frictional unemployment, and some writers would appear to view the issue of regional differentials wholly in these terms, as simply frictional unemployment compounded by the geographical immobility of labour (Davies, 1967; Perlman, 1969; Lazar, 1977). Under this interpretation the appropriate policies would include improving information regarding job opportunities and assisting the migration of workers. However, this explanation ignores or conflates causes. Changes in the composition of the labour skills required in an economy can result from changes in the composition of final demand, changes in the location of industry, and changes in technology, the organisation of production, and the division of labour. Structural unemployment exists when these changes in labour-skill requirements are not matched by adaptations in the labour force, so that unemployment becomes concentrated for long periods of time in particular industries and regions. Typically, such dislocations in the labour market are reflected in long-term rising or falling trends in unemployment. The problem is not one essentially of lack of mobility as such, for many of the structurally unemployed in a given region will not be qualified for job opportunities existing elsewhere, even if these members of the labour force were prepared to relocate to those areas where such vacancies were available. The policies deemed appropriate to this view of the regional unemployment problem are selective, market-orientated, manpower programmes such as wage and employment subsidies, temporary job creation, and retraining schemes (Musgrave, 1980). Such programmes would be used in conjunction with a full-employment policy which includes measures directed at revitalising the industrial base of specific regions.

According to yet another approach, regional unemployment disparities, although structural, derive from a more basic dualism between capital and labour and the stratification both of the labour market and of the labour process that this dualism fosters. Characteristically, it is argued, the labour force is used to resolve the problems that shifts in demand and competition, and changes in technology and industrial organisation, pose for the economic system: labour is the variable factor of production, and as such can be freely hired—and fired—as productive activity fluctuates or is reorganised; being the residual factor in the planning of the productive process, labour is typically forced to adjust to other aspects of the economy, rather than the other way around; and the division and redivision of labour by skill, industry, and region is determined solely by the imperatives of capital and technology. Thus, workers and regions which were at one time 'central' to the economy may later become 'peripheral' (A Friedman, 1977, chapter 10). The emergence and persistence of areas of high unemployment is the result of an historical process in which the spatial division of labour called forth by the forces of production during one period is at some later date rendered 'obsolete' by changes in the conditions and development of production. Changing technology, changes in market structures, and changing political climates can all reduce the permanence of a region's central status. The centre–periphery distinction itself is not disturbed; rather the expendability of particular workers defined by skill, industry, and geographical location will change. In contrast, the permanence of a region's peripheral status, and accompanying high unemployment and underemployment, are not easily reduced. Depressed areas remain depressed for a long time. Workers' organisations, which were built up during periods of prosperity ('centrality'), are not easily broken down. It takes time for an area's normal relative wage to fall significantly; and it takes time for people to move out of the area. More vulnerable to unemployment, workers in high-unemployment regions will also be more likely to suffer the de-skilling which so often occurs with unemployment and reemployment (cf Massey, 1979), and whole areas may function essentially as secondary labour markets. The implication of this view is that it is misleading to attempt to separate demand-deficient from non-demand-deficient components in regional unemployment differentials: the problem is one of structural imbalance deriving from contradictions inherent in the system of production itself. Neither aggregate demand expansion nor regional policy instruments will be sufficient to remove regional inequalities.

As yet there is no fully articulated theory of spatial labour-market adjustment. However, the foregoing discussion has indicated the general range of factors and issues around which conceptual and empirical work has been developing. The aim of the present volume is to contribute to this development. The basic premise is that spatial disaggregation of the labour market provides additional insight into the observed behaviour of the economy-wide relations among wages, employment, and unemployment by revealing not only the external forces which are transmitted by the different economic, social, and political linkages between regional and subregional markets, but also the part played by internal forces generated within individual spatial labour-market areas themselves. At the very least, the essays emphasise the importance of a regional perspective for the construction of a detailed typology of labour markets which would reveal the principal structural and institutional characteristics of different markets and how these affect behaviour.

1.3 Overview
The contributions to this volume fall into two main groups. Chapters 2 to 6 are concerned with the interregional wage structure and the regional dimensions of the wage-determination process; the four remaining chapters on the other hand deal with different aspects of regional unemployment and employment adjustment. Although conceptual discussions occur at various points in the book, the overall emphasis is an empirical one with examples being drawn from a wide range of issues in the United Kingdom, the United States, and Canada.

In the first, and the only wholly theoretical, essay, Hart examines and develops the theory of spatial wage transfer as a basis for a consistent theory of the observed regional wage structure, which in its turn should provide important insights into the regional distribution of unemployment. The aim is to determine how far and in what ways market-adjustment mechanisms equilibrate regional wage differentials. The argument is developed in a number of stages: first, the concepts of the local labour market and the region are defined, great stress being placed on labour mobility, labour supply, and labour demand; second, the workings of the local labour market in terms of the dominant labour flows and employer adjustments are specified; and third, this framework is used to describe some of the interactions among local labour markets and regions. Then, against this background, a theory of spatial wage spread is formulated, based on labour migration, which extends and critiques the recent work of Brechling in this area. It is shown that, in most local labour markets, wages will be above their equilibrium, market-clearing levels because they are partly or mainly determined by market conditions elsewhere, through the process of wage-change transmission. The difference between actual and equilibrium clearing wages will be greater, as will the accompanying unemployment, in markets which possess the greatest structural problems, since many of their occupations will experience wage leadership from other markets within and/or outside their own region. The influence of quit-threat/migration on wage differentials is scale-dependent: it may be of relevance within local labour markets, but becomes largely ineffective at the interregional scale. Here the impact of other factors, such as national and multiplant bargaining, and regional policy are likely to be of greater significance.

It is with the assessment of such factors that the essays by Moore and Rhodes, and by Tarling and Wilkinson are concerned. The study by Moore and Rhodes reveals that there has been a gradual but persistent convergence in average earnings amongst the regions of the United Kingdom over the past two decades. The low relative wage, high-unemployment regions have experienced the highest growth in earnings, and vice versa, so that during the period from 1962 to 1979 the difference between the highest and lowest earnings regions was halved. The authors then attempt to disentangle the various influences which could be responsible for this convergence: these include regional differences in industrial structure, changes in the relative pressure of demand for labour, differential movements in labour productivity, changes in the size of industrial establishments, the regional distribution of foreign-owned firms, and the effects of regional policy. Of these, shifts in industry mix was found to be the most significant factor, although relative changes in labour demand, as measured by regional changes in vacancies as compared with those of the United Kingdom overall, and regional changes in productivity growth have also had an effect. Furthermore, the larger average plant size, the greater proportion of foreign enterprises, and the higher incidence of industrial stoppages in the depressed regions are all consistent with the faster growth of earnings in these areas. Tarling and Wilkinson extend this analysis in their study of the impact of national minimum-earnings agreements within the British engineering industry on the course of regional earnings differentials within this sector. They find that since the early 1960s, national agreements have become increasingly irrelevant as a determinant of relative earnings growth, although the substantial increases in minimum-earnings levels introduced under the 1972 agreement may have contributed a small part to the narrowing of regional differentials in the mid-1970s. Neither relative labour-market pressure nor regional policy seems to have played a major role, but regional variations in the size of industrial establishments do appear to be significantly correlated with relative movements in earnings. What these two studies of British regional wage trends indicate is that although there has been a steady narrowing of differentials in recent years, conventional hypotheses fail to supply an explanation. Both also point to the importance of changes in the structure of bargaining, particularly the continued trend away from the traditional multiemployer, industry-based structure to one of single-employer bargaining conducted at the company and plant level, as a factor requiring further investigation for its influence on regional wage differentials.

The next two chapters switch attention to regional wage determination in the US labour market. One of the most significant features of the US economy since about 1960 has been the dramatic shift in economic growth and development from the north and northeast to the south and west of the country. According to some, this realignment of the space economy has finally closed the longstanding, and much debated, north-south wage differential. For these reasons the USA provides an interesting environment in which to evaluate alternative hypotheses concerning the impact of regional conditions on wage movements. Hanham and Chang confine their analysis to individual urban labour markets in the Sunbelt states. Somewhat surprisingly, for the majority of the cities in this broad region excess demand for labour does not appear to have been a major determinant of relative wage inflation. Neither do local wage developments seem to follow at all closely changes in the (expected) cost of living. Rather, the principal causal mechanism is the wage spread amongst subregional groups of cities. Although levels of unionisation are low in this area, it is argued that the role of pattern-following wage-setting based on 'reference-group' comparisons is probably of central importance in many of the local labour markets. Certainly there is evidence to support this contention: for example, southern nonunionised textile firms are well-known for adopting union-like practices of coordinated wage rounds.

Martin's paper is directed more specifically to the question of wage-change interdependence amongst regional labour markets, and in particular to the so-called 'regional wage-leadership' hypothesis. According to this hypothesis, wage increases achieved by workers in one or more 'leading' regions effectively set the pace of wage growth in the rest of the economy. A crucial problem, however, is the definition of the 'leading' region(s). Martin critically reviews the various conceptual and empirical formulations of the hypothesis that have appeared in the recent literature, and argues that the specification of leading regions requires consideration of a much wider range of labour-market conditions, including structural and institutional characteristics, than has hitherto been the case. On the basis of this discussion, an exploratory analysis is then made of regional wage interactions in the US economy to test two alternative specifications of leading-region groupings. Although only tentative, the results suggest a general north-south wage-pattern structure with wage-transmission effects apparently more dominant from the south to the north than in the opposite direction. To the extent that wage increases in the high-growth regions of the south have spilled over to the declining and stagnating areas in the north and northeast, this may have intensified the deteriorating relative unemployment position of these latter regions that has occurred in recent years; and it is in such regions, therefore, that the current problem of stagflation is likely to be more pronounced.

In the first of the four chapters relating to the employment side of spatial labour markets, Clark examines this issue of the regional incidence of stagflation in some detail. He is concerned with analysing two possible mechanisms that account for the uneven impact of national stagflation on regional unemployment. A conceptual model is developed to show the possible causes of differential regional response to national demand fluctuations and general wage inflation, these causes relating primarily to variations in industrial structure (including the mix of high-growth and low-growth sectors) and the varying ability of firms to cope with and absorb wage increases transmitted, via institutional bargaining forces, from other labour markets. This model leads to the specification of an empirical relation designed to evaluate the impact of stagflation upon Canadian regional unemployment. The results from this indicate a distinct spatial polarisation of stagflation, particularly in the already designated high-unemployment depressed areas. There is a clear east–west dichotomy in the pattern of regional response: labour markets in the west of the country display a far greater ability to absorb national wage-rate increases, whereas in eastern markets wage inflation generates increases in unemployment. Findings such as these suggest that the manner in which governments approach wage inflation can have important implications for the problem of regional unemployment disparities. Wage controls imposed to lower the national rate of inflation may benefit depressed regions but could slow the growth of output in other regions: national economic stabilisation policies, therefore, require careful consideration of regional impacts and should be regionally disaggregated.

The study by Clark raises, in fact, the important question of how individual firms in a given local labour market adjust their workforces in response to changes in product demand. If firms have a known, desired level of labour demand, derived from output demand, any deviation of actual employment from this desired level will create a manpower imbalance, either a shortage or a surplus, to which firms will respond. But what are the strategies available to and actually used by employers in their attempts to maintain a reasonably efficient balance between desired and actual employment? To what extent and in what ways are these strategies used to achieve an equilibrium between the firm's internal labour market and the external labour market in which the firm is located and operates? Carmichael's chapter seeks to elucidate these and other aspects of employers' behaviour and the implications for employment change in firms and the local labour market. Some thirty-eight possible 'instruments' are identified as being available to firms to correct labour-force imbalances. This is a wide range of potential measures, which certainly casts doubt on traditional theories of price (wage) adjustment to disequilibrium in labour allocation between or within firms. The instruments fall into four main groups, namely desired total labour services, average hours worked per employee, labour outflows, and labour inflows. An attempt is made to quantify the relative role of these different adjustment methods amongst firms within a specific local labour-market area (Swindon). Survey data from seventy-four employers show that in the case of manpower shortages, most firms made adjustments by increasing labour inflows, and very little effort was made to reduce labour outflows. The main responses to a perceived labour surplus were to reduce average hours worked by employees and to increase labour outflows by introducing redundancies. The evidence is that changes in output demand only translate into external labour-market effects after a time lag, and only after a sustained rise or fall in demand.

This suggests that the spatial variation in unemployment fluctuation will depend in part upon whether firms make their adjustments internally or via the external labour market. And this in turn will depend upon labour-supply conditions in each of the external labour markets themselves. Further, these conditions will vary with the degree of interaction— particularly mobility—between local labour markets; and such interaction is itself a function of the overall level of demand. This intricate system of direct and indirect adjustment is an underlying theme in the contribution by Cheshire, who uses Oi's work on labour as a quasi-fixed factor of production to derive some novel propositions concerning the level of excess demand and the spatial distribution of unemployment. As is well-known, one of the implications of Oi's work is that qualities of labour with the highest 'degree of fixity' (high skills, high hiring and training costs, etc) will experience the lowest relative changes in employment due to any given change in product demand. Or, in other words, the incentive for employers to hoard skilled labour in a cyclical downturn and to work this labour overtime in the upturn will be greater than is the case with unskilled labour. Cheshire shows, however, that in addition, as the mean unemployment rates of a particular quality of worker rise, employers increasingly treat such labour as a variable factor of production. The implication for regional labour markets is that employers in high-unemployment regions should hoard less labour on average, so that for a given change in output there should be a larger change in employment in high-unemployment regions than in low-unemployment areas. Also, the labour hoarding that does occur in high-unemployment regions is likely to be more in the form of 'unpaid-for' hoarding (that is, short-time working). Thus in spatial labour markets with different long-run expected levels of unemployment, employers have different attitudes to labour hoarding: employment will be much more sensitive to output changes in high-unemployment regions than in low, and employers will have greater recourse to the external labour market in such areas. These hypotheses are supported by evidence from the British regions. What this interesting analysis implies is that high-unemployment regions will tend to have more 'frictional-structural' unemployment at any given level of excess demand. This additional frictional-structural unemployment is not a primary cause of labour-market inefficiency, however; it is the result of the long-run level of excess demand itself being lower in these regions.

The final chapter in this volume seeks to link the relative sensitivity to unemployment of different regions to spatial variations in the dynamic behaviour of unemployment response. The identification of regional lead–lag structures in unemployment change has attracted considerable attention in economic geography, particularly in the form of Brechling's 'decomposition equation' (see the review by Martin and Spence, 1981). In their essay, Frost and Spence pinpoint a number of difficulties in attempting to detect differences in the timing characteristics of regional unemployment fluctuations, especially using Brechling's approach in isolation, and they achieve a more detailed analysis through the application of multivariate procedures. From an analysis of unemployment time-series for the British subregions and travel-to-work areas, the authors conclude that there is no evidence to suggest any consistent differences in the timing of local unemployment response across the country. A subsequent factor analysis, however, reveals a distinct spatial ordering of areas that show similar responses to specific aggregate fluctuations. In particular, there is a significant north–south division of local labour markets, in that those in the north of the country (most of the high-unemployment areas) overreacted to the 1971–1972 recession but have underreacted to recent events, and vice versa for labour markets in the south. In addition, there appears to be a discernible cycle of employment advantage–disadvantage running through time in the economy, with first the north and then the south experiencing a period of relative advantage followed by one of relative disadvantage in terms of national events. Superimposed on this general north–south structure, there are also several subregional groups of local areas which share a common pattern either of late or of early changes in unemployment. The actual causes of these various responses remain elusive; but this study by Frost and Spence does indicate clearly the complexity of local unemployment movements, particularly in terms of very different responses to individual national fluctuations and developments. This highlights the need to monitor continually the changing map of unemployment, not only so that incipient 'distressed' areas can be identified, but also so that decisions to de-schedule 'assisted' areas might be made on the basis of informed judgment rather than of political expediency.

The issues examined and the questions raised in the ensuing chapters are numerous, but not comprehensive. They are, however, representative of much of the converging interest within geography and regional economics in this field of enquiry. Most of the essays cover events which extend up to the end of the 1970s. Current developments, particularly the worsening unemployment situation, in some cases intensified by the rigid pursuance of monetarist policies to combat inflation, emphasise rather than diminish the need for regional analysis. If the present studies stimulate further research and debate on the regional dimensions of wages and unemployment, the aims of this volume will have more than served their purpose.

References

Archibald G C, 1969 "The Phillips curve and the distribution of unemployment" *American Economic Review* **59** 124-134

Brechling F P R, 1967 "Trends and cycles in British regional unemployment" *Oxford Economic Papers* **19** 1-21

Chisholm M, 1976 "Regional policies in an era of slow population growth and higher unemployment" *Regional Studies* **10** 201-213

Davies G, 1967 "Regional unemployment, labour availability, and redeployment" *Oxford Economic Papers* **19** 59-74

Department of Economic Affairs, 1967 *The Development Areas: A Proposal for a Regional Employment Premium* (HMSO, London)

Dixon R J, Thirlwall A P, 1975 *Regional Growth and Unemployment in the United Kingdom* (Macmillan, London)

Friedman A, 1977 *Industry and Labour: Class Struggle at Work and Monopoly Capitalism* (Macmillan, London)

Friedman M, 1977 *Inflation and Unemployment: The New Dimensions of Politics* Institute of Economic Affairs, London

Gordon R A, 1973 "Some macroeconomic aspects of manpower policy" in *Manpower Programs in the Policy Mix* Ed. L Ulman (The Johns Hopkins University Press, Baltimore) pp 14-50

Haberler G, 1977 "Stagflation: an analysis of its causes and cures" in *Economic Progress, Private Values and Public Policy* Eds B Balassa, R Nelson (North-Holland, Amsterdam) pp 311-329

Hewings G J D, 1978 "The trade-off between aggregate national efficiency and inter-regional equity: some empirical evidence" *Economic Geography* **54** 254-263

Higgins B, 1973 "Trade-off curves and regional gaps" in *Development and Planning* Eds J N Bhagwati, R S Eckaus (MIT Press, Cambridge, Mass) pp 152-177

Holland S, 1976 *Capital versus the Regions* (Macmillan, London)

King L J, 1976 "Alternatives to a positive economic geography" *Annals of the Association of American Geographers* **66** 293-308

Lal D, 1977 *Unemployment and Wage Inflation in Industrial Economies* (OECD, Paris)

Lazar F, 1977 "Regional unemployment rate disparities in Canada: some possible explanations" *Canadian Journal of Economics* **10** 112-129

Lipsey R G, 1960 "The relation between unemployment and the rate of change of money wage rates in the United Kingdom, 1862-1957: a further analysis" *Economica* **27** 1-31

Martin R L, Spence N, 1981 "Some recent developments in quantitative economic geography: a review" in *Quantitative Geography in Britain: Retrospect and Prospect* Eds N Wrigley, R J Bennett (Routledge and Kegan Paul, Henley-on-Thames, Oxon) chapter 5.2.2

Marx K, 1867 *Capital* Volume I (Foreign Languages Publishing House, Moscow, 1961)

Massey D, 1979 "In what sense a regional problem?" *Regional Studies* **13** 233-243

Moore B, Rhodes J, 1975 "The economic and exchequer implications of British regional economic policy" in *Economic Sovereignty and Regional Policy* Ed. J Vaisey (Gill and Macmillan, Dublin) pp 80-102

Musgrave R S, 1980 *Abolishing Unemployment* Research Study 7, Economic Research Council, London

Perlman R, 1969 *Labor Theory* (John Wiley, New York)

Reynolds L G, 1951 *The Structure of Labor Markets* (Harper and Row, New York)

Sherman H J, 1976 *Stagflation: A Radical Theory of Unemployment and Inflation* (Harper and Row, New York)

Stilwell F J B, 1978 "Competing analyses of the spatial aspects of capitalist development" *Review of Radical Political Economics* **10**(3) 18-27

Thirlwall A P, 1966 "Regional unemployment as a cyclical phenomenon" *Scottish Journal of Political Economy* **13** 205-219

Thirlwall A P, 1969a "Demand disequilibrium in the labour market and wage rate inflation in the United Kingdom" *Yorkshire Bulletin of Economics and Social Research* **21** 65-76

Thirlwall A P, 1969b "Types of unemployment: with special reference to 'non-demand-deficient' unemployment in Great Britain" *Scottish Journal of Political Economy* **16** 20-49

Thomas R L, Stoney P J M, 1971 "Unemployment dispersion as a determinant of wage inflation in the United Kingdom, 1925-66" *The Manchester School* **39**(2) 83-116

Weintraub S, 1978 *Capitalism's Inflation and Unemployment Crisis* (Addison-Wesley, Reading, Mass)

Williamson J, 1975 "The implications of European monetary integration for the peripheral areas" in *Economic Sovereignty and Regional Policy* Ed. J Vaizey (Gill and Macmillan, Dublin) pp 105-121

2

Regional wage-change transmission and the structure of regional wages and unemployment

R A Hart

2.1 Introduction

Interest in the spatial labour-market aspects of inflation theory has grown at an accelerating rate since Lipsey's (1960) development of a sectoral dimension to the aggregate Phillips curve. Although much of the literature has attempted to establish a microfoundation to the aggregate-inflation-excess-demand trade-off, it has necessarily given rise to offshoots which have important implications for other fields of study. In particular the work has provided a significant breakthrough towards the development of a theory to explain the structure of regional wages and unemployment, and it is on this aspect which the present chapter concentrates.

Since one author (Tobin, 1972, page 9) has described the aggregate Phillips curve as an "empirical finding in search of a theory, like Pirandello characters in search of an author", it may be permissible to present, in similar vein, some empirical evidence on the regional wage and unemployment structure before embarking on theoretical constructs. As with the Phillips study, attention is confined to the case of Britain.

Long historical time-series data of wages[1] by specific regions[2] of Britain exist only for the engineering industry, although, given both the central significance and breadth of activity such an industry envelops, it is not unreasonable to surmise that such data serve as an indicator of sectoral wages within a much wider industrial context. A series of wage earnings for the British engineering industry over the period 1914–1968 together with comparable unemployment data has recently been published (Hart and MacKay, 1975). The series refers to the two key groups in the industry, skilled fitters and labourers, and information is presented for twenty-eight major towns, cities, and labour-market areas across the whole geographical space of Britain. The empirical findings of this study may be summarised as follows:

(a) Over the period 1925–1939 and especially over the period 1951–1968 there is substantial wage drift (where wages both include and exclude overtime payments).

(b) In the interwar period regional wage differentials are stable, but these narrowed appreciably in the postwar period.

[1] Unless stated otherwise, 'wages' in this study refer to wage earnings; that is, including all payments over and above standard rates.

[2] The term 'region' is used quite loosely here; it will be important at a later stage to give a reasonably precise definition.

(c)   The regional wage hierarchy (ranking) is very stable over time.

(d)   Regional unemployment differences persist throughout both periods, exhibiting a high degree of stability in the year-to-year coefficients of variation (see also Brechling, 1967).

(e)   Throughout both periods, certain regions emerge both as wage leaders and areas of relatively low unemployment.

(f)   Despite (e) there is no systematic relationship between regional wage changes and unemployment.

An explanation of persistent differences among regional unemployment rates, observed in many countries, provides one of the greatest challenges to regional economists, since conventional theory of long-run spatial market behaviour would predict that labour and capital flows would adjust to, and thereby eliminate, such differences.   However, the above observation of the long-run stability (or even narrowing) of the regional wage structure would suggest that the operation of an equilibrating price mechanism is impeded in some way and that the market price of labour in high unemployment regions lies somewhat above its shadow price (see Archibald, 1972).

Hence a consistent theory of the observed regional wage structure should provide important insights into the regional unemployment structure.

The aim of this chapter is to examine and develop the theory of spatial wage transfer in an attempt to gain some stronger appreciation of the above empirical phenomena.   In section 2.2 a brief summary of related work to date is undertaken.   Three necessary conditions for the theoretical development of the present paper are:

(1)   a reasonably strict definition of local labour-market areas and regions, with particular emphasis on how a given market area may be realistically demarcated from comparable areas;

(2)   a description of the specific construction and working of a local labour market;   and

(3)   a discussion of the interactions among local labour markets and regions.

Such constructs are attempted in section 2.3.   Against this background, a theory of wage-change transfer is developed in section 2.4 and a discussion of the implications for regional wage and unemployment structures is contained in section 2.5.   Brief conclusions are given in section 2.6.

2.2 Recent research on the relationship between regional and national aggregate wage changes

The regional dimension to the study of wage inflation has manifested itself in three distinct ways.   The first springs directly from Lipsey's (1960) work on the Phillips relationship and has become known as the nonlinear aggregation hypothesis.   The second, which may be broadly termed the common-national-influence category, has viewed local changes in wages as a response to changes in minimum wage rates which are negotiated nationally and/or to expected national aggregate changes in the cost of living.

The third has been linked to much earlier work, viz Samuelson's (1948) concept of dynamic market interdependence, and views local wage changes as a response to wage changes in alternative localities, the vehicle of transfer is variously argued as being institutional or related to market forces; such a process is popularly termed the wage-spread hypothesis.

Imagine a situation where wage changes in a given region are independent of wage changes in any other region. Then it has been well established theoretically that differences in regional excess labour demands may still hold important implications for the aggregate Phillips curve trade-off. This has been illustrated in its purest form by Lipsey's own aggregation hypothesis, which suggests that if there exists an identical and convex Phillips curve for all regions then the greater the disparity of unemployment rates among regions, and/or the greater the degree of convexity of the curve itself then the greater will be the displacement of aggregate observations above the individual regional curves. As shown by Archibald (1969), however, the assumption of identical regional curves is not a necessary condition and the assumption of strict convexity of the aggregate curve is neither a necessary nor a sufficient condition for upward displacement to result from a greater variance of unemployment rates. The more general upward displacement condition derived by Archibald is that regions with relatively low unemployment rates should have steeper Phillips curves (convex or linear) than do other regions.

Theory apart, Lipsey's hypothesis is inconsistent with the observation in the interwar period [see finding (b), section 2.1] that regional wage differentials are stable despite substantial and persistent differences in unemployment[3], and Archibald's hypothesis, although consistent with this evidence, has policy implications which are remote from reality (see Burns, 1972). Moreover, the empirical evidence for the above aggregation phenomena has been very weak; Archibald (1969) and Thomas and Stoney (1971) give it *highly* qualified support, Thirlwall (1970) and Brechling (1973) have found some support but attribute to it only a minor role as a potential policy means of regulating aggregate inflation. Accordingly this aspect of the regional dimension to aggregate wage changes will be ignored in the development of this chapter.

Equally, the development below will discount the importance of the national bargaining (over wage rates) hypothesis, one of the two common-national-influence categories. Although several authors (Thirlwall, 1970; Metcalf, 1971; and Archibald, 1972) have concluded that bargaining over rates conducted within a national framework is an important explanation of the regional wage structure over time, other empirical investigations (Hart and MacKay, 1976) have found no support for this contention. Indeed, such an hypothesis is diametrically opposed to the finding [see finding (a),

---

[3] Hence, different regions can only have the same Phillips curve if it is U-shaped!

section 2.1] of substantial wage drift in Britain in the prewar and postwar periods. Given such drift, it would be expected that if national bargaining over wage rates is the prime determinant of the regional wage structure, then regional wage differentials would widen or certain regions, especially those with high unemployment, would show relatively slow increases in wages. Neither expectation is confirmed by the evidence. Instead, postwar regional wage differentials have narrowed [see finding (b), section 2.1] and there is no significant relationship between regional wage changes and unemployment rates [see finding (f), section 2.1 and also Lerner and Marquand (1963)—a similar finding is recorded by Brechling (1973) for the USA].

On the other hand, the role of price expectations as a determinant of wage changes, developed by Phelps (1970) and Friedman (1968), would seem to have important regional implications (see, especially, Williamson, 1975). Thus, within a monetary union where inflation expectations are equalised among regions, regional wage changes may be kept roughly in line by similar reactions to expected changes in the national cost-of-living index. Indeed, if the famous monetarist prediction of a long-run coefficient of unity on the price-change coefficient is found to apply to each and every individual region's wage-change equation, then a powerful theory which predicts stable structures both for regional wages and for unemployment could be devised. However, empirical evidence is far from convincing concerning similar long-term regional reactions to price-change coefficients (see Hart and MacKay, 1976) and although such explanations will not be dismissed in this chapter, it is not proposed to pursue them in any depth.

The institutional interpretation of the wage-spread hypothesis, whereby wage inflation in one region may be transmitted to other regions, has been widely accepted by researchers (see, for example, Lerner and Marquand, 1963; Cowling and Metcalf, 1967; and Thirlwall, 1970). However, effects on the regional wage structure through wage transmission can also be given an equilibrium interpretation. "Potential mobility", wrote Hicks (1932, page 79) "is the ultimate sanction for the interrelation of wage rates." Taking this view, the existing structure of wage differentials may reflect nonpecuniary elements, and the cost of movement and other barriers to geographical mobility. Changes in regional wages would be interlinked because of competition, real or potential, between firms operating in different regions (Brechling, 1973).

A common strand running both through the institutionalists and through the equilibrium-theorists arguments is that wage transfer under the wage-spread hypothesis follows a scheme whereby, in any given time period, the flow of interregional wage transmission is in one direction, from 'leading' to other regions (see Thomas and Stoney, 1971; Brechling, 1973). A recent argument has been advanced, however, that the transmission process is essentially simultaneous in nature and that recursive systems belie the inherent complexities (see Hart and MacKay, 1977).

In general, it will be argued that the wage-spread hypothesis contains propositions most consistent with the observed empirical phenomena outlined in section 2.1 and, in particular, that it is the simultaneous, rather than the recursive, wage-change transmission model which provides the stronger set of predictions.

2.3 Aspects of local labour markets and regions
2.3.1 Some definitions
Definitions of what constitutes a local labour market vary considerably (see Goodman, 1970)[4] and range from precise mathematical formulations of market areas under strict assumptions to somewhat loose descriptions which are more amenable to empirical investigation. A reasonably self-contained definition is important as a means of describing both the interaction within a given market and the interrelations among markets.

Here, the (popular) view is taken that the main lines of demarcation between local boundaries should be viewed in terms of labour mobility frictions; thus most workers in most occupations seek to maximise their utility with respect to residence by minimising their pecuniary and their psychic daily travel-to-work costs, and also their employment search costs. Arising from this, four key considerations would seem to be important when forming a general definition of a local labour market; (1) the travel-to-work costs within the market, (2) the composition of the market's labour force, (3) the market's employment possibilities, and (4) the accessibility to market information concerning actual and potential wages as well as job vacancies. If we adopt this framework, a definition of a local labour market may be derived by using a somewhat amended version of definitions advanced by Goodman (1970, pages 184–185).

A local labour market is defined to be a spatially delineated area which fulfils simultaneously the following boundary requirements[5]:
(a) an insignificant proportion of daily travel-to-work journeys are made across the boundary;
(b) any given employment opportunity within the market boundary does not discriminate significantly, in pecuniary or psychic daily travel costs, among any potential unit of labour supply within the same boundary;
(c) search unemployment within the boundary is negligible since each unit of the labour force has (almost) complete information concerning the market's wage and employment opportunities;

---

[4] A special acknowledgement should be made to Goodman's paper on local labour-market definitions (which provides an excellent survey and appraisal of the literature) since this subsection borrows heavily from his work.

[5] For convenience, local labour-market (and regional) boundaries are taken to be fixed rather than adopting the more realistic, though analytically more intractable concept [of such writers as Kerr (1950)] which portrays the boundaries as bands which mark various levels of resistance (or friction) to labour mobility.

(d) firms are located so that they can obtain the major proportion of their potential labour supply within their own boundary;

(e) as a result of (d), the composition of the enclosed firms is such that workers view a significant number of firms as providing close substitutes for their labour services.

In order to be reasonably explicit about what is meant by a region, a definition is used which is closely akin to the above requirements for a local labour market but where labour migration replaces daily travel-to-work. Consider an economy split into n elements called local labour markets. These elements are now divided into $m(m < n)$ mutually exclusive and exhaustive regions where each region contains at least one local labour market. (Where two or more local labour markets form a region, they may not necessarily comprise a contiguous area.)

Each region, comprising a given set of local labour markets, is defined to be a spatially delineated area which fulfils simultaneously the following boundary requirements:

(1') the pecuniary and psychic migration costs within the boundary of any given region are significantly less than the comparable costs of interregional migration between that region and any other region of the economy;

(2') although information concerning a given region's wages and employment opportunities is imperfect for that region's labour force, search costs are significantly less than those for searching in an alternative region;

(3') the level of intraregional migration [which results partially from requirements (1') and (2') and from arguments and evidence to be given later] is significantly higher than the level of interregional migration.

2.3.2 Short-run employment demand in the local labour market

Consider the short-run demand for effective labour services, L, in a local market where it is postulated, conventionally, that L is a function of desired sales and planned stock changes, $Q^{*\,(6)}$, which are assumed to be exogenously determined, as well as the capital stock, K, and the state of technology, T, significant changes in which are perceived over longer time horizons. Thus

$$L = f(Q^*, K, T); \quad f_Q > 0, \quad f_K < 0, \quad f_T < 0. \tag{2.1}$$

In accordance with such writers as Brechling (1965), Feldstein (1967), and Rosen (1968), effective labour services are functionally related to the actual number of workers, E, and their level of utilisation as measured by average hours worked per person, H; that is

$$L = g(E, H), \quad g_E, g_H > 0; \quad g_{EE} < 0, \quad g_{HH} < 0. \tag{2.2}$$

---

[6] Conventionally, and throughout what follows, the desired levels of variables are assumed to define their equilibrium values.

Average hours are divided into average standard hours, H_s, which are assumed to be exogenously determined, and average premium hours, H_p, which are endogenous, hence

$$H = H_s + H_p . \qquad (2.3)$$

It is hypothesised that the market's short-run strategy consists of minimising total costs, C, by means of an optimum allocation of labour services between E and H in equation (2.2). The total wage bill to the market is defined as

$$C = (H_s W_s + H_p W_p + C_1 + C_2 + C_3)E \qquad (2.4)$$

where W_s is the average standard wage rate, W_p is the average premium wage rate, and the C_i are 'fixed' employment costs with C_1 the average 'recurring' fixed employment costs (such as employers' medical insurance contributions and paid holidays), and

$$C_i = (q+I)C_i' , \qquad i = 2, 3 , \qquad (2.5)$$

where q is the quit rate, I is the rate of interest, C_2' is the average 'once-over' fixed employment costs related to hiring and firing workers, C_3' is the average 'once-over' fixed employment costs related to training labour; thus 'once-over' costs, referred to by Rosen (1968) and by Nadiri and Rosen (1969) as 'under costs', are adjusted by the quit rate and discounted at a suitable rate of interest to reflect the opportunity cost of capital.

As a simplifying assumption, but without critically affecting later arguments, it is assumed that

$$W_p = \alpha W_s , \qquad \alpha = \text{constant} > 1 , \qquad (2.6)$$

that is, premium rates are determined as some fixed proportion of standard rates.

Thus the problem is one of constrained minimisation of expression (2.4), subject to equation (2.2), which may be expressed for a given basic wage rate, W_s, in the following manner [using equations (2.3) and (2.6)]:

$$\text{minimise } \frac{C}{W_s} = H_s E + \alpha(H - H_s)E + \frac{C_1 E}{W_s} + \frac{C_2 E}{W_s} + \frac{C_3 E}{W_s} , \qquad (2.7\text{a})$$

subject to

$$L = g(E, H) . \qquad (2.7\text{b})$$

This yields the marginal conditions (where μ is a Lagrangian multiplier)

$$H_s + \alpha(H - H_s) + \frac{C_1}{W_s} + \frac{C_2}{W_s} + \frac{C_3}{W_s} + \mu g_E = 0 , \qquad (2.8\text{a})$$

$$\alpha(E) + \mu g_H = 0 , \qquad (2.8\text{b})$$

$$g(E, H) - L = 0 . \qquad (2.8\text{c})$$

Conditions (2.8a)–(2.8c) implicitly determine the equilibrium values of workers and hours (E^*, H^*) as functions of all the parameters of the model, that is,

$$E^* = F_1\left(H_s, \frac{C_1}{W_s}, \frac{C_2}{W_s}, \frac{C_3}{W_s}, L\right), \tag{2.9}$$

$$H^* = F_2\left(H_s, \frac{C_1}{W_s}, \frac{C_2}{W_s}, \frac{C_3}{W_s}, L\right). \tag{2.10}$$

Although explicit expressions for the values of the partial derivatives of functions (2.9) and (2.10) may be derived formally (see Hart, 1978), it will suffice here to report the expected sign, and the intuitive reasoning behind it, for each partial (see table 2.1).

Before proceeding to discuss intramarket labour flows within the structure of this framework, it is important to mention briefly a restriction introduced by Hart and Sharot (1978) and developed further by Hart (1978) and Kirwan (1979). Equations (2.9) and (2.10) define the local labour market's cost-minimum, comparative static equilibrium levels of the number of workers employed, E^* and their average rate of utilisation, H^* in the local labour market. Thus, the excess demand for labour services is defined as the difference between the desired level and the actual level of the two components, men and hours, that is $E^* - E$ and $H^* - H$. Actual and desired levels can both be expressed as functions of Q^*, K, and T using equations (2.1) and (2.2), that is

$$L = g(E, H) = g(E^*, H^*) = f(Q^*, K, T). \tag{2.11}$$

Now suppose firms in the local labour market wish to substitute between H and E because of a change in one or more explanatory variables in equations (2.9) and (2.10). Equation (2.11) implies that such substitution will be governed by

$$(H^* - H) = \Gamma(E^* - E); \qquad \Gamma' < 0. \tag{2.12}$$

Table 2.1. Signs of partial derivatives in equations (2.9) and (2.10).

Sign	Reason
$\dfrac{\partial E^*}{\partial H_s} > 0$, $\dfrac{\partial H^*}{\partial H_s} < 0$	Here it is assumed (not unreasonably—see Ehrenberg, 1971) that in equilibrium, $H_p > 0$. Thus, for example, a fall in H_s will increase the marginal cost of new workers, and induce the market to substitute H^* for E^*.
$\dfrac{\partial E^*}{\partial C_i} < 0$, $\dfrac{\partial H^*}{\partial C_i} > 0$ $i = 1, 2, 3$	Since each C_i is independent of hours worked, an increase in such costs relative to wage costs will lead the market to substitute H^* for E^*.
$\dfrac{\partial E^*}{\partial L} > 0$, $\dfrac{\partial H^*}{\partial L} \geqslant 0$	As emphasised by Ehrenberg (1971), the effect on H^* of an increase in L depends as much on intuitive reasoning as on explicit derivation, but somewhat restrictive assumptions lead to the conclusion that H^* is invariant to scale (see Ehrenberg's appendix to chapter 2).

However, with regard to the right-hand side of equation (2.12), it is well established both in the theoretical and in the empirical literature [for example, see Oi (1962), Brechling (1965), and Soligo (1966)] that, given transaction cost impediments, E adjusts only sluggishly to E^*. The adjustment of H to H^*, on the other hand, is likely to be relatively speedy, particularly if it largely involves the manipulation of H_p.

The adjustment pattern of E to E^* may be represented by the well-known partial adjustment scheme,

$$E - E_{-1} = \lambda(E^* - E_{-1}); \qquad 0 < \lambda < 1 . \tag{2.13}$$

On substituting from equation (2.13) into equation (2.12), it is possible to examine the implications of differential adjustment possibilities for workers and for hours worked per worker; this is shown in figure 2.1.

Suppose, as in figure 2.1, that the local labour market is in long-run equilibrium with $L = L_0$; L_0 is the amount of labour services produced by H_0^* and E_0^* at the combination of average hours and workers given by point s. In the usual fashion, such an optimum point is given at the tangent of $L = L_0$ with the relevant isocost line. Two possibilities are now considered [7].

First, for $L = L_0$ [that is with Q^*, K, and T fixed in equation (2.1)], the equilibrium position will change to H_1^*, E_1^* at t, as a result of, for example, an increase(s) in C_i/W_s ($i = 1, 2, 3$) and/or a fall in H_s in equations (2.9) and (2.10) (see table 2.1). Because of equation (2.13), the actual fall in the size of the workforce is only a proportion, λ, of the desired fall. Moreover, the new combination H, E (that is, H_1, E_1 at u) determined

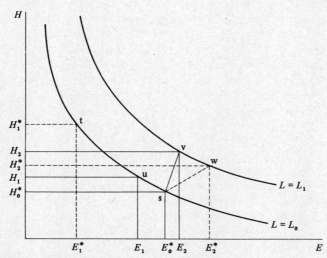

Figure 2.1.

[7] The following analysis is discussed in greater detail in Hart (1978).

by the partial adjustment of E (that is, by the size of λ), is achieved by an offsetting increase in average hours. Because of equation (2.12), $E^* - E$, is accommodated by $H^* - H$, so that the excess in the stock of workers $(E_1^* < E_1)$ is compensated by a shortfall of actual to desired labour utilisation $(H_1^* > H_1)$. We may term the reaction just described as a *pure adjustment effect*.

Alternatively, again starting from long-run market equilibrium at s, suppose there is a permanent increase in Q^*, in equation (2.1), producing a desired increase in labour services from $L = L_0$ to $L = L_1$. However, the short-run adjustment impediments represented by equation (2.13) may prevent the market from achieving the new equilibrium H_2^*, E_2^* at w along the optimum expansion path s–w. Instead the new equilibrium is achieved along the path s–v–w. In this situation, the change in the proportions of labour inputs may be divided as the result of two effects. First the *shift effect*, which consists principally of a highly elastic response of average hours to an increase in output expectations in order to achieve a new labour services requirement. Second, the *adjustment effect*, which consists of a partial reduction of the gap between the desired and actual workforce, with an offsetting decrease in average hours. After the initial period, H_2 ($>H_2^*$) accommodates E_2 ($<E_2^*$) through equation (2.12).

2.3.3 Intramarket labour flows

Figure 2.2 depicts the stocks and flows of a closed local labour market by using a modification to a schematic originally proposed by Holt (1970). The modifications arise from the discussion in the previous subsection. Thus, labour services are viewed in terms of man-hours rather than the number of workers. Further, the fact that available man-hours differ from utilised man-hours to the extent of the degree of nonutilisation of man-hours in the external labour market *and* within firms themselves (the internal labour market) is explicitly incorporated into the flow diagram.

Consider, in figure 2.2, an arbitrary percentage increase in production, arising from an exogenous upturn in the demand for goods and services, which renders man-hours required to be in excess of man-hours available. This in turn will generate an increase in new dishoarding, D, and new vacancies, V, as employers adjust their man-hours requirements to fill the gap. The resulting implications for the external market have been analysed in some detail by Holt (1970, pages 58–59). A strong tendency for the system to display negative feedback produces the net result of a small percentage fall in unemployment relative to the large flow into and out of the stock of unemployment.

Initially the stock of unemployed workers falls and the stock of employed workers rises as the increase in the stock of vacancies improves the worker–job match. This is followed by a partial restoration of the initial stock levels through an increase in quits induced by a rise in the duration of vacancies relative to unemployment. The process is retriggered, however, since the probability of worker–job matches rises as the quits create increases both in the duration of vacancies and in the stock of unemployed. At the same time, in a climate of an increase in the demand for man-hours, a lengthening duration of vacancies, and an increase in

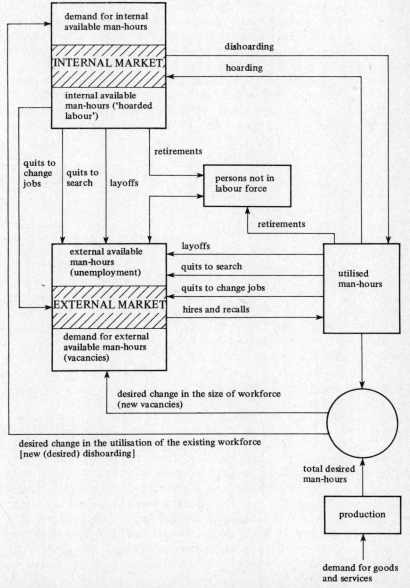

Figure 2.2. A modified Holt schematic for a local labour market.

quit-threats, employers will be induced to reduce layoffs. More quits will follow, as the reduction in layoffs will lead to an increase in the stock of employed workers and a reduction in the stock of unemployed workers (also reducing new hires), which again increases the duration of vacancies relative to unemployment.

Although the above argument implies an overall tendency for the stock of unemployment to decline, the degree of decline will also be determined by two important factors. First, by the degree to which inflows of 'new' workers both from the indigenous secondary labour force and from other local labour markets take advantage of the new job opportunities [8]. Second, by the local labour market's propensity to convert excess man-hours into an increased flow of new vacancies, V, as opposed to new dishoarding, D. The relative weight of this response is best viewed by relating V and D to the excess demand for labour services as defined in subsection 2.3.2, thus

$$V = h_1(E^* - E), \qquad h_1' > 0, \tag{2.14}$$

$$D = h_2(H^* - H), \qquad h_2' > 0. \tag{2.15}$$

In other words, V and D are functions of all independent variables specified in equations (2.9) and (2.10), and so subject to the restrictions in equations (2.12) and (2.13). For example, some markets will exhibit relatively sluggish employment adjustment [low values of λ in equation (2.13)] to a change in sales expectations, owing to, say, relatively high human-capital investments with accompanying high recruitment, training costs, etc. As illustrated in figure 2.1, the short-run external market effects will be reduced in such markets by a tendency to utilise the internal labour market in order to overcome restrictions in employment adjustment; D will vary more than proportionately to V. As another example, the desire to substitute hours for workers in certain markets, owing to increases in fixed employment costs and/or falls in normal hours, may be greater than the desire to employ new workers for a contemporaneous increase in sales expectations, with the result that D and V move in *opposite* directions; here the adjustment effect overwhelms the shift effect.

2.3.4 Intermarket labour flows

Consider an economy comprising an indecomposable intermarket trading system. Each local market is assumed to possess a labour structure similar to that shown in figure 2.2 but the scale size of the rectangles will vary from market to market according to the size of the production sector. An increase in aggregate demand for goods and services will stimulate production in all markets (given the assumed trading structure) although the degree of such a stimulus will vary from market to market, given

---

[8] Migration effects are discussed in subsection 2.3.4.

differences in structural characteristics. Further, as just discussed in relation to equations (2.14) and (2.15), the response of V relative to D will vary among markets, given differences in employment adjustment, and relative strengths of economic stimuli and such variable responses will represent changes in employment opportunities among markets. It is now proposed to examine the implications of such changes, together with other factors, in the following simple sketch of the factors which influence intermarket labour migration.

In the ith local labour market let

L_{ij}^{d} be the desired labour-migration flow from market i to market j,

W_i^e be the expected present value of real wages in market i,

u_i^e be the expected utility derived from present value of nonpecuniary returns and, for simplicity[9], let V_i and D_i represent expected employment opportunity in the external and internal labour markets, respectively. Further, let

$$\theta_{ij} = \frac{u_i^e}{u_j^e} . \tag{2.16}$$

The general formulation relating to L_{ij}^{d} may now be written as

$$L_{ij}^{d} = \phi_{ij}\left(\frac{W_i^e}{W_j^e}, \frac{V_i}{V_j}, \frac{D_i}{D_j}\right)\theta_{ij} \tag{2.17}$$

where

$$\frac{\partial L_{ij}^{d}}{\partial(W_i^e/W_j^e)} < 0 , \qquad \frac{\partial L_{ij}^{d}}{\partial(V_i/V_j)} < 0 , \qquad \frac{\partial L_{ij}^{d}}{\partial(D_i/D_j)} < 0 , \qquad \frac{\partial L_{ij}^{d}}{\partial \theta_{ij}} = < 0 .$$

The first argument in equation (2.17) is based on individual maximising behaviour under the assumption that a potential migrant (employed or unemployed) searches to find an alternative local market which maximises the difference between expected wages in his present market and expected wages in an alternative market (after subtracting migration costs). Excepting the unrealistic assumption of homogeneous labour and capital, then different labour units, depending on such factors as skill level, occupation, type of industry, etc, will have different markets which satisfy this maxim. Therefore, the smaller the ratio W_i^e/W_j^e, the greater the number of potential migrants who view the jth market as possessing the highest expected wages. Of course, search activity based solely on pecuniary considerations is suboptimal, since expected pecuniary gains from migration are subject to relative employment prospects in the market of residence and the potential market of destination. The ratio V_i/V_j represents relative employment opportunity in the external market with, ceteris paribus, a rise in this ratio reducing desired migration from the ith market. However, the term 'employment opportunity' represents more than the relative flow of new vacancies between pairs of markets. Although vacancies may be of

[9] A more dynamic specification would be more appropriate here, but the adopted simplicity does not detract from the central arguments.

critical importance to those potential migrants who are unemployed, potential migrants who search for alternative employment while still employed[10] presumably require employment opportunities which go beyond merely finding a new job. The ratio D_i/D_j represents the relative flow of new dishoarding between pairs of markets. Attempts to increase the labour-service flow on the internal market would be reflected by employers both increasing average hours worked, by the use of more overtime per worker, and increasing the average product of existing hours, through such devices as higher bonus and piecework payments. Thus, ceteris paribus, it is expected that an increase in the ratio D_i/D_j will reduce L_{ij}^d since the relatively higher internal pressure will enhance the bargaining position of employees in the ith market for premium and other payments.

Finally, the whole function describing L_{ij}^d is multiplied through by the relative expected utilities derived from nonpecuniary returns between the ith and jth markets, θ_{ij}. Ceteris paribus, the higher the value of θ_{ij}, the lower, in proportion, will be the potential migration between any i, j pair of markets. The view is taken, therefore, that the reaction of potential migrants to relative pecuniary returns and employment opportunities is modified by their subjective evaluation of relative nonpecuniary returns, which embrace a broad spectrum of sociological, environmental, climatic, geographical, etc considerations. To illustrate this point, let such an expected utility for potential migrants in market i be represented by

$$u_i^e = E\{u[B_i(0)]\} = \int_0^\tau \exp(-\Psi_i t)u[B_i(t)]\,\mathrm{d}t \,, \tag{2.18}$$

where $B_i(t)$ are mean net psychic returns discounted over the interval 0 to τ years at a mean subjective discount rate Ψ_i. Further let

$$u[B_i(t)] = k_i[B_i \exp(-d_i t)] \,, \qquad 0 < k_i \leqslant 1 \,, \tag{2.19}$$

that is utility is given by some mean proportion, k_i, of the psychic returns and, moreover, such returns are deemed to decline continuously and exponentially at the rate d_i per year[11]. Substituting from equation (2.19) into (2.18), and evaluating the integral for $\tau \to \infty$, gives

$$u_i^e = \frac{k_i B_i}{\Psi_i + d_i} \,, \tag{2.20}$$

and so θ_{ij} in equation (2.16) becomes,

$$\theta_{ij} = \frac{k_i B_i(\Psi_j + d_j)}{k_j B_j(\Psi_i + d_i)} \,. \tag{2.21}$$

---

[10] The quantitative importance of on-the-job employment search is probably quite high (see Tobin, 1972).

[11] Here, it is assumed that potential migrants take the risk-averse precaution of assessing how the psychic returns currently enjoyed may deteriorate.

Thus in the simple case where $i = j$ for k, Ψ, and d; potential migrants compare the expected psychic returns in the two markets although there is no a priori reason to reject the hypotheses that $i \neq j$ for any of the right-hand side expressions in equation (2.21). Indeed, it is quite plausible that risk will be discounted more heavily and the returns anticipated to decline at a faster rate in the less well-known region, j (that is, $\Psi_j > \Psi_i$, $d_j > d_i$), thereby increasing θ_{ij} and reducing the migrant responsiveness to the pecuniary stimuli.

A region was earlier defined [see definition (1′), section 2.3.1] to comprise a group of labour markets where psychic (and pecuniary) migration costs were significantly less than elsewhere. The identification with a social culture or a particular environment may not be, and probably is not, constrained by the boundary of a local labour market which has been demarcated along strictly economic lines; it may well straddle several such markets[12]. Such a distinction between the economic and psychic domains has important implications for the expected performance of equation (2.17) as well as for its role in the process of wage transmission (see below).

Suppose a given economy can be divided into local labour markets, l_i ($i = 1, ..., n$) and regions, r_j ($j = 1, ..., m$; $m < n$) according to the criteria laid out in section 2.3.1. Suppose further that the n markets are ordered and grouped into m kinds ($n_1, ..., n_m$, where $n_1 + ... + n_m = n$) subject to $n_1 \in r_1, ..., n_m \in r_m$. Now consider equation (2.17) in the form $L_{ij}^d / \theta_{ij} = \phi_{ij}[(W_i^e/W_j^e), (V_i/V_j), (D_i/D_j)]$, with m given sample values of the right-hand side variables. The above regional definition would result

$$L_{ij}^d \, (i, j \in n_i) > L_{ij}^d \, (i \in n_i, j \in n_j, i \neq j) \,,$$

which would be manifested in a statistical model by larger regression coefficients (on average) on the independent variables. Another important difference in the two cases concerns the relationship between L_{ij}^d and L_{ij}. If we assume a migration adjustment scheme similar to equation (2.13) for employment (see Hart, 1975), then the lower intraregional pecuniary migration costs and search costs [see definitions (1′) and (2′), section 2.3.1] would lead to the expectation that $L_{ij} \rightarrow L_{ij}^d$ $(i, j \in n_i)$ faster than $L_{ij} \rightarrow L_{ij}^d$ $(i \in n_i, j \in n_j, i \neq j)$.

The sense of the foregoing distinctions vis-à-vis equation (2.17) is supported by the actual migration pattern. In the UK, intraregional migration is significantly larger than interregional migration (seven or eight times greater, on average), a factor which would not be predicted by a model that excluded psychic considerations, since the size of wage and employment-opportunity differences tends to correlate positively with distance.

[12] This is almost certainly the case for the United Kingdom, where individual's strong cultural ties with Scotland, N Ireland, SW England, etc embrace a number of local labour markets within those regions.

2.4 Wage-change transmission

The standard neoclassical microframework for the discussion of the inter-market migration decision given in section 2.3.4 is that the potential migrant, after discounting expected migration costs, searches for the local market which, compared to his present location, maximises the difference between the expected present value of the pecuniary returns and employment opportunity, subject to an evaluation of expected psychic returns. Since labour is heterogeneous, information flows are imperfect and, in particular, there are divergent subjective estimates of psychic returns; several different markets will be expected to satisfy the maxim for different individuals in a given market.

Against this background, Brechling (1973) has sketched a theory to explain the spatial transmission of wage changes. After allowing for migration costs, employment opportunity, and psychic returns, the minimum wage acceptable to an employee working in a given occupation in local labour market i would be the wage which equals the highest perceived wage in a similar occupation in an alternative market. Suppose a group of employees in a given occupation in market i receive such a wage, based on a comparison with a similar occupation in market j. Now, ceteris paribus, if the wage improves in j relative to i, the employer in i may be faced with potential quit threats and may be induced to make a 'neutralising' wage offer, thereby raising the wage in i. Even if the employer does not respond and some employees migrate, wages in i may still rise, given conventional neoclassical profit maximisation assumptions concerning the marginal productivity of labour, and equilibrium wages (see Hart, 1975; Kim, 1977). Thus, threatened or realised migration may effectively provide an argument for the interdependence of market wage changes. Further, in the light of the discussion in section 2.3.2, it may be expected that the higher the quasi-fixity of labour, the stronger will be the effect of threatened migration since employers will be more inclined to protect their human capital investments. In this section it is argued that both the strength of Brechling's theory and its implications for the structure of wage-level transfer depend essentially on the level of spatial aggregation. Accordingly, wage-change transmission is examined in local, regional, and national market perspectives.

2.4.1 The closed local labour market

It is postulated that, within each closed ith local labour market, real anticipated average-wage changes are functionally related to the excess demand for labour services, thus

$$\dot{w}_i^e = f(x_i), \qquad f'(x_i) > 0, \qquad i = 1, ..., n, \tag{2.22}$$

where

$$\dot{w}_i^e = \frac{1}{W_i}\frac{\mathrm{d}W_i}{\mathrm{d}t} - \frac{1}{P_i^e}\frac{\mathrm{d}P_i^e}{\mathrm{d}t},$$

and W_i, P_i^e, and x_i refer to, respectively, wages, anticipated prices, and the excess demand for labour services. Further, in accordance with the development in section 2.3.2,

$$x_i = g(E_i^* - E_i, H_i^* - H_i) .\tag{2.23}$$

Brechling's analysis is most helpful in supporting the relatively simple structure embodied in equation (2.22)[13]. The equation represents aggregation across firms and occupations in the ith market and implicitly allows complete and instantaneous wage-change transmission among firms and occupations. Recall that, in the definition of a local labour market [definitions (a)–(e), section 2.3.1], pecuniary and psychic costs of job search are insignificant [definition (b)], market information is near perfect [definition (c)], and occupational variation is relatively narrow [definitions (d) and (e)][14]. Thus, given a differential impact of demand change among firms, near frictionless market conditions will permit almost instantaneous employee reactions both through quit threats and through job changes, which, in turn, will eradicate potential fluctuations in wage relativities. Indeed, the specification of aggregate equations similar to equation (2.22), which are common in macroeconomics literature, imply this somewhat 'pure' special case of wage transfer[15].

2.4.2 The closed regional labour market
At the regional level of aggregation [see definitions (1′)–(3′), section 2.3.1], significantly greater labour-market frictions become apparent for two main reasons. First, job search between pairs of local labour markets within the regional boundary now involves migration and psychic cost considerations as well as an evaluation of employment opportunities. Second, a greater variation in capital endowment and job skills across regional markets will lead to market differences in (external) employment responses to changes in demand expectations. For example, in line with the analyses in sections 2.3.2 and 2.3.3, markets with relatively high skill levels may be expected to exhibit relatively greater propensities to hoard/dishoard labour, given variations in demand expectations, whereas markets with relatively low skill levels may be expected to exhibit more elastic external employment responses.

[13] The model incorporated in equations (2.22) and (2.23) is analysed in some detail in Hart (1978).

[14] The skill mix would be expected to be narrow since, where there are many close substitute firms [definition (e)], there would tend to be a similar distribution of human capital attributes within each firm. In turn, this would tend to narrow the mix in the composition of $E^* - E$ and $H^* - H$ in equation (2.23) across firms.

[15] An interesting paper by Bell (1979) has revealed certain equation biases in aggregate specifications which omit the possibility of wage transfer. For example, an upward bias on the coefficient of price change would seem to render tests of unity coefficients, given long-term monetarist assumptions, even more hazardous than has already been recognised.

It should be emphasised that the difference between the closed local and closed regional labour markets is one of degree, although in the latter case the higher frictions may permit short-run wage-leading markets to emerge. In other words, some markets may possess perceived earnings/employment advantages for some given occupation and may thus feature in the bargaining process for significant groups of workers from other markets through the processes of actual and threatened migration.

If we accept the assumptions concerning the constitution of a local labour market, it would be surprising if, given market frictions, pure lagging markets did not emerge. A high level of market integration of wage costs, psychic costs, and employment opportunity would lend support to the view that a market with relatively weak structural characteristics would experience such disadvantages reflected in relatively low wage expectations and employment opportunities across the whole market occupational structure. In a given time period, therefore, a pure lagging market is defined as a market in which no key bargains are struck. Occupational wage changes in such markets may be influenced by wage-change transmission from comparable occupations in external markets where wage leadership is exhibited by their ability to induce realised or threatened migration.

In other markets, however, it is multidirectional, not unidirectional, wage-change transfer which is most likely to be experienced, since key bargains will be struck from within and outside market boundaries. Two supporting arguments are advanced for this proposition.

First, given a greater heterogeneity of labour and occupational composition at the regional as opposed to the individual local labour-market level of aggregation, there may well be two or more markets in a given region which possess at least one occupational category which exhibits regional wage leadership. The fact that wage leadership exists in one occupation in a given market does not preclude lagging wage expectations in other comparable occupations.

Second, there is an unfounded assumption in the literature that key bargains necessarily occur in relatively 'tight' labour markets (Thomas and Stoney, 1971) or markets with highest-ranking wage expectations (Brechling, 1973). The sort of labour-market pressures which permit relatively high wage expectations may also generate wage bargains which seek to maintain differentials over those markets where such pressures are not so apparent. For example, workers in tight markets may view their wage differential as compensation for the relatively high psychic costs associated with the pressures in the workplace and within the social environment, which may not be so apparent among comparable workers in other markets. Thus, workers in such markets may regard key bargains to be those struck elsewhere which threaten to erode their differentials. As emphasised in section 2.3.4, the general importance of psychic costs considerations in the migration decision should not be underrated. From a

limited pecuniary perspective, a given market may not be regarded as a
wage leader, but when its relative psychic advantages (for example, scenic
beauty) are taken into account then the adjusted calculations may reveal
that it is an important wage setter for certain occupations in the region;
a positive change in its wages, although perhaps still leaving expected wages
below those of other markets, may nevertheless render its pecuniary *and*
psychic returns greater than all other markets[16].

The implications of the above wage-transfer possibilities for the regional
version of equation (2.22) are as follows. Suppose there are k local labour
markets in the jth region and, for simplicity but without loss of generality,
assume that the basic inflation model in equation (2.22) can be represented
by the system of linear stochastic equations:

$$\beta w_t^e + \Gamma x_t = \epsilon_t , \tag{2.24}$$

$$
\begin{bmatrix}
1 & -\beta_{12} & \cdots & -\beta_{1k} \\
-\beta_{21} & 1 & \cdots & -\beta_{2k} \\
\vdots & \vdots & & \vdots \\
-\beta_{k1} & -\beta_{k2} & \cdots & 1
\end{bmatrix}
\begin{bmatrix}
\dot{w}_{1jt}^e \\
\dot{w}_{2jt}^e \\
\vdots \\
\dot{w}_{kjt}^e
\end{bmatrix}
$$

$$
+
\begin{bmatrix}
\gamma_{10} & \gamma_{11} & 0 & \cdots & 0 \\
\gamma_{20} & 0 & \gamma_{22} & \cdots & 0 \\
\vdots & \vdots & \vdots & & \vdots \\
\gamma_{k0} & 0 & 0 & \cdots & \gamma_{kk}
\end{bmatrix}
\begin{bmatrix}
1 \\
x_{1jt} \\
\vdots \\
x_{kjt}
\end{bmatrix}
=
\begin{bmatrix}
\epsilon_{1jt} \\
\epsilon_{2jt} \\
\vdots \\
\epsilon_{kjt}
\end{bmatrix} . \tag{2.25}
$$

At one extreme, if β in equation (2.24) is a unit matrix then, as in the local
labour-market equation (2.22), no wage-change transmission is implied. At
the other extreme, a full β matrix implies that each and every local labour
market in region j contains at least one key bargain, in period t, which
influences bargaining in all other markets. A unidirectional wage-transfer
structure implies that it is meaningful to rank the wage-change vector in
equation (2.25), starting, for example, with the highest anticipated wage
market, and then to impose the restriction that the β matrix is lower
triangular—that is, wage-change transmission follows a recursive pattern.

Recall, the excess-demand matrix in equation (2.25) refers both to the
external and to the internal markets. This is in contrast to the work of
Thomas and Stoney (1971), who use relative employment rates as a proxy
for 'the degree of tightness'. Unfortunately their measure constitutes a
serious specification error since it omits excess demand in the internal
market. A particularly serious problem arises if, given the analysis

[16] It is noted here that although Brechling's theoretical discussion of dynamic market
interdependence is couched in terms both of psychic and of pecuniary wage expectations,
his subsequent empirical analysis ranks expected wages only in terms of pecuniary
returns.

surrounding figure 2.1, section 2.3.2, a negative (positive) excess demand in the external market contrasts with a positive (negative) excess demand internally. It is noted that Brechling's (1973) use of unemployment rankings as a basis of wage leadership provides poor results. However, in his final specifications, regional employment opportunity is represented as 1− (unemployment rate), which again omits the problem of differential, internal market excess demand.

2.4.3 The national labour market

Consider an economy divided into local labour markets l_i ($i = 1, ..., n$) and then, as in section 2.3.4, further divided into regions r_j ($j = 1, ..., m$; $m < n$). Further let the n markets be ordered into m kinds ($n_1, ..., n_m$, where $n_1 + ... + n_m = n$) subject to $n_1 \in r_1, ..., n_m \in r_m$. In equation (2.24), $\beta \dot{w}_t^e$ may now be extended to the form

$$
\begin{bmatrix}
\beta_{11} & \beta_{12} & \cdots & \beta_{1m} \\
\beta_{21} & \beta_{22} & \cdots & \beta_{2m} \\
\cdot & \cdot & & \cdot \\
\cdot & \cdot & & \cdot \\
\cdot & \cdot & & \cdot \\
\beta_{m1} & \beta_{m2} & \cdots & \beta_{mm}
\end{bmatrix}
\begin{bmatrix}
\dot{w}_t^{e(1)} \\
\dot{w}_t^{e(2)} \\
\cdot \\
\cdot \\
\cdot \\
\dot{w}_t^{e(m)}
\end{bmatrix} . \qquad (2.26)
$$

Thus, in the jth region, $\dot{w}_t^{e(j)}$ is an ($n_j \times 1$) vector of anticipated wage changes, and β_{ij} is a corresponding ($n_j \times n_j$) square matrix of coefficients for the ith local labour market. Γx_t may be ordered equivalently so as to conform for each jth region with the scheme given in system (2.25).

If there is no intermarket wage transmission, for $i = j$ the β_{ij} are unit matrices, and for $i \neq j$ the β_{ij} are all zeroes. At the other extreme, if all the β_{ij} are full matrices then the system is generally interdependent.

The fact that interregional migration flows are significantly smaller than intraregional flows has been accommodated both in the definition of a region employed in this paper and in the brief analysis of interregional migration. It has been argued that such a discrepancy results from significantly higher psychic and pecuniary costs of movement as well as from other market frictions at the regional level. Now, if the interregional frictions are so high that no short-run change in any ith local labour market in any jth region could induce an actual or threatened move from any other local market in any other region, then β in matrix (2.26) would reduce to a block-diagonal matrix with wage transmission confined strictly within each jth region. A block-recursive pattern would result under the assumption of unidirectional wage transfer mechanism, combined with the somewhat arbitrary process of forming weighted averages of the $\dot{w}_{it}^e$ across regions and then ranking in, say, descending order [this β in matrix (2.26) is lower triangular]. Simple recursivity would result from the unidirectional transfer inference after ranking the $\dot{w}_{it}^e$ ($i = 1, ..., n$) *irrespective* of regions.

Although it might be expected that, owing to high interregional market frictions, the national β matrix in system (2.26) would be considerably sparser than the equivalent jth regional matrix in system (2.25), for the same arguments presented for the regional composition of β the likely national structure is one of nonrecursivity lying somewhere between a block diagonal and a generally independent system[17]. Indeed the view that there is no a priori reason to support unidirectional wage transfer is strongly supported by the British evidence (Hart and MacKay, 1977).

2.5 The long-run structure of regional wages and unemployment

2.5.1 The wage-change transmission process

A useful background against which to examine some long-run implications of spatial wage transmission is Oi's (1962) framework of profit-maximising behaviour by firms combined with quasi-fixity of labour. This approach involves diverging somewhat from the cost-minimising assumptions of section 2.3.2. However, the two behavioural patterns are roughly compatible if the restriction is imposed that there is zero elasticity of substitution between workers and hours worked per worker (see Briscoe and Peel, 1975), and although such a restriction weakens the earlier analysis, it does not affect general long-run conclusions.

Profits in the ith local labour market are maximised in period t at the point where the total discounted cost of employing an additional worker equals the total discounted revenue, that is

$$\sum_{j=2}^{3} C_{ij} = \int_0^{\tau_i} (M_{i(t)} + \delta M_{i(t)} - W_{i(t)}^e - C_{1i(t)}) \exp(-\phi_i t) , \qquad (2.27)$$

where the C_{ij} are the fixed employment costs outlined in section 2.3.2, M is the worker's marginal value product, δM is the increment in the marginal value product resulting from investment in training, W^e is the expected wage, τ is the worker's expected period of employment, and ϕ is the rate of discount.

If we assume that the local labour market forms single-valued expectations such that

$$M_{i(t)} = M_i^* , \quad \delta M_{i(t)} = \delta M_i^* , \quad W_{i(t)} = W_i^* , \quad C_{1i(t)} = C_{1i} , \quad t = 0, ..., \tau, \qquad (2.28)$$

then substituting these values into system (2.27) gives the long-run equilibrium condition

$$R_i + W_i^* = M_i^* + \delta M_i^* , \qquad (2.29)$$

[17] At a regional level of aggregation, the argument that there will be a significant number of markets which possess at least one leading-wage occupational group is well supported by the evidence. A detailed study of the regional wage and employment structure among occupations in the British engineering industry in 1962 revealed that *all* regions achieved first or second rankings in two or more occupations and, if the Northern region is excluded, all remaining regions achieved such rankings in five or more occupations (see Lerner and Marquand, 1963, table XI).

where

$$R_i = \frac{1}{1 - \exp(-\phi_i \tau_i)} \phi_i \left(\sum_{j=2}^{3} C_{ij} \right) + C_{1i} .$$ (2.30)

R_i is the periodic rent or "the surplus that must be earned by each worker in order to amortise the initial fixed employment costs over the expected period of employment ..." (Oi, 1962, page 541).

In order to simulate the implications of unidirectional wage transfer for the long-run regional wage and unemployment structure, consideration is given to the simplest possible case of a two-region economy where each region consists of only one local market; that is $r_1 = l_1$, and $r_2 = l_2$. The production activity of each region is defined over a similar vector of goods and services and also each region is assumed to possess a similar distribution of labour fixity. Initially, both regions are in long-run equilibrium, with region 1 possessing lower expected wages and higher unemployment compared to region 2 in *all* occupations. In terms of equation (2.29) for $i = 1, 2$,

$$R_1 + W_1^* = M_1^* + \delta_1 M_1^* , \quad R_2 + W_2^* = M_2^* + \delta_2 M_2^* .$$ (2.31)

Long-run equilibrium in the context of equation (2.31) implies that there is zero mobility of labour and capital between regions. Thus, the gap between W_2^* and W_1^* is compatible with zero economic migration after account has been taken of the expected cost of moving from region 1 to 2 and the relative discounted psychic costs and employment opportunities.

Starting in such long-run equilibrium, suppose there is a rise in nominal aggregate demand for all goods and services owing to, say, a once-for-all expansion in the supply of money. This is equivalent to assuming a rise in each element of the expected price vector in each region and, therefore, an increase in the expected marginal-value product. Assuming, in equation (2.22), that price expectations exhibit a lag adjustment to actual price changes, there will be a short-run Phillips-type trade-off between inflation and unemployment (Friedman, 1968). Equilibrium will be restored through the dual process of increases in wages, in order to induce a greater short-run supply of labour, and a probable lowering of the marginal value product as employment adjusts to the new desired level. Of course, in the longer term, the *aggregate* unemployment rate may return to its natural level as actual and expected price changes coincide. Of particular interest here, however, are the implications for the *relative* wage and unemployment structure between the two regions.

On fairly standard Phillips-curve assumptions, the demand increase will result in wages being bid-up at a faster rate in region 2 than in region 1 because, by assumption, it lies nearer its short-run capacity limit for all occupations. The implied increasing wage differential over the whole occupational structure will induce actual and threatened migration from region 1. Actual migration will produce falls in unemployment, over and above those induced by demand, both through migration of unemployed persons and through job creation resulting from the migration of employed persons [18]. Such falls will be offset, however, to the extent that wage-change transmission, induced by quit-threat, succeeds in creating unemployment by pricing region 1's expected wage above its expected marginal-value product. The migration flow will eventually be choked-off through (1) wage transmission restoring interregional wage differentials, (2) the possibility that the migration process will produce a lowering of the marginal-value product of region 2 relative to region 1, and (3) a worsening of relative employment opportunity in region 2 relative to region 1 through migration. In the long run, when anticipated price changes have adjusted to actual price changes, premigration real wages will be restored in each region with employment cut back to its former levels. However, in the absence of strong assumptions concerning return migration, the actual migration flows from region 1 to 2 will result in a narrowing of unemployment differences between the two regions, a result generally at odds with observation (d), section 2.1. Such an unemployment prediction is mitigated, on the other hand, to the extent that the demand change contains a permanent real component. Here, the reduction in unemployment resulting from actual migration from and (real) job creation in region 1 would be permanently offset to the extent that the part of wage-change transmission representing the differential real impact on wage changes creates unemployment by forcing up wages above 'indigenous' equilibrium levels.

The regional structure of wages in the above process is stable in the long run because it is assumed that wage-change transmission is unsustained. This is equivalent to describing a discrete sequence in the unidirectional model, where wage leadership is established and then eroded before a further shock to the system produces a new scheme of wage transmission, possibly involving a different leading region(s). However, it is typically claimed in empirical work directed towards testing the unidirectional hypothesis that wage changes are transmitted continuously from wage-leading regions and, moreover, that the *same* regions act as leaders for

---

[18] Reductions in unemployment of this latter type are inversely related to the degree of success achieved by employees' quit-threats. This, in turn, is related to the degree of labour fixity; the higher the fixed element, the more successful the quit-threat because of potentially greater loss of human-capital investment. In other words, the degree to which employers will attempt to minimise the increase in periodic rent in equation (2.30) (which has resulted from the fact that quit-threat reduces the expected period of employment, τ_i) will be directly related to the degree of fixity.

significant *long-run* periods of time[19] (see, for example, Brechling, 1973; Thomas and Stoney, 1971).

Using the same equilibrium starting point as in the previous example, let us now assume that wage leadership is maintained on a continuous basis in region 2 by a long-term nominal aggregate-demand stimulus and/or a long-term real growth in the economy. In this event, the prediction would apparently follow that not only unemployment but also wage differentials would diverge rather than, as in observation (b), section 2.1, remain stable or narrow. The equilibrating forces of migration and quit-threat would constantly be adjusting to rising wage targets, with resulting widening of regional wage gaps given such adjustment, through information and mobility frictions, is likely to be only partial in any given time period.

Note, however, that the above prediction of divergent long-run wage differentials is dependent on the dual assumption that region 2 is the wage-leading region as well as being a relatively tight labour market over a long-run period of time. If, on the other hand, long-run wage-leading regions are identified as regions which do not possess relatively tight labour markets [a possibility consistent with observation (f), section 2.1], then an unsupportable prediction would result from the (long-run) unidirectional model. Regional wages would still tend to diverge but with lagging regions becoming more wealthy than leading regions, since both types would have roughly similar wage changes arising from local excess demand conditions, but the lagging regions would also benefit from transmitted wage changes.

If the more realistic assumptions are now imposed that a subset of occupations in region 1 experience 'tighter' demand conditions and higher expected wages than equivalent occupations in region 2, and that workers in leading occupations in both regions attempt to preserve their wage differentials, then structural stability may be, at least partially, restored. Long-run regional unemployment differences are more compatible with a pattern of actual migration which exhibits strong flows in *both* directions and, therefore, where the stock of unemployed in the external market is being constantly replenished by search quits both from within and from without the region. This, of course, is more in line with the observed migration pattern which does not consist of large net movements of population between given pairs of regions but rather comprises relatively small net changes representing the residual in the balance of much larger countervailing gross flows (see Hart, 1970). Again, the rate of divergence of regional wage differentials under the assumption of long-run unidirectional

[19] Long-term wage leadership may occur in specific occupations which possess, for example, (1) an established trade-union organisation which has achieved a permanent impact on wage differentials, (2) distinct locational advantages (such as high accessibility to other markets or an indigenous labour force with a long history of acquiring relevant skills) and (3) a technological back-up and know-how which ensures long-term productive advantage.

regional wage leadership will be reduced if offsetting leadership occurs in the opposite direction for several occupations.

2.5.2 Regional policy

Under a multidirectional wage-change transmission system, differences in the strength of change transmission among markets and regions are likely to occur. Markets with the highest proportions of leading wage occupations may be expected to exert the greatest impact on other markets. If such relative strengths of leadership remain into the long term then, given partial adjustment through intermarket frictions, the prediction would remain that regional wage differentials would widen although at a some-what slower rate than under a unidirectional system. However, another important influence on the more disadvantaged regions, with the smallest proportions of leading occupations, is government intervention through regional policy. Intervention enables such regions to increase wages beyond those determined by changes in demand and by wage transmission.

Returning to the two-region example, consider the equilibrium equation for the more depressed region, region 1;

$$\frac{\phi_1(C_{12} + C_{13})}{1 - \exp(-\phi_1 \tau_1)} + C_{11} + W_1^* = M_1^* + \delta M_1^* . \tag{2.32}$$

If such an equilibrium is again disturbed, but this time by a rise in aggregate demand combined with a government 'package' of regional subsidies, wages in the region would rise through the impacts of demand, wage transmission, and the effect of the subsidies themselves. Without attempting an exhaustive list, regional subsidies could raise W_1 in the following ways.

(a) *Direct employment grants.* Here W_1 is raised directly if part of the subsidy can be passed on in the form of higher wages.

(b) *Subsidies to marginal value product.* The value of M_1 to the firms in the region may be increased (with, therefore, an extra potential for increasing W_1) if, for example, capital subsidies are made available, prices of final output are subsidised, and grants are given to improve the social infrastructure.

(c) *Training grants.* Two effects are possible here. First, if the government pays for all or part of the training that would have been undertaken by firms in any case, then C_{13} is directly reduced to the firm (allowing, ceteris paribus, a rise in W_1). Second, if all or part of the training grants are provided for training in addition to that intended by firms themselves, then increases in δM and, given some degree of job specificity in the training, τ_1, would be experienced, again allowing extra increases in W_1.

In a more dynamic setting, any tendency for divergence in the regional wage structure owing to maintained differentials in the strengths of wage leadership may be offset partially, fully, or more than fully by a growth in the monetary value of the government's regional policy instruments.

2.5.3 Regional differential fixed-employment costs

As stated earlier, the potency of a given labour unit's quit-threat is related to the degree of fixity of the unit. Employers are more likely to react to a threatened quit with an improved wage offer, if the potential shortening of the expected employment duration involves a significant loss of human capital investment. The fact that an occupation in a given local labour market is a wage leader at regional and/or national level is likely, in many cases, to be significantly correlated with the fact that it belongs to an enterprise which enjoys a technological advantage over its competitors. In part, the high wage expectations reflect the skill endowment of the occupational labour force. At the same time, such occupations may be expected to have a higher fixity component in their total wage bills compared to similar occupations in other markets. This will arise, for example, from higher hiring and training costs associated with the higher skills, and the subsequent inducements, such as fringe benefits, which are designed to protect relatively high human capital investment by inducing longer terms of employment.

If the assumption of a similar regional distribution of labour fixity is dropped, to allow for the strong possibility that relatively prosperous regions with relatively high proportions of leading occupations have higher-than-average fixed employment costs[20], then two important modifications to the foregoing discussion arise.

First, the argument given in section 2.4, that the national matrix of transmission coefficients in system (2.26) is likely to be sparse relative to its regional equivalent, is reinforced by the likelihood that several markets will not respond to transmission to any significant extent. There is little impetus for employers to respond to quit threats in markets with a predominantly unskilled labour force and high unemployment. Of course, regional policy may still maintain wages above their 'natural' equilibrium levels in such markets. Moreover, the argument supporting nonrecursivity of the matrix is also reinforced, since although relatively prosperous regions may be expected to have fewer quit-threats, an average threat is relatively more effective owing to the potentially higher human-investment losses.

---

[20] The likelihood of relatively high fixed employment costs in the more prosperous regions is strengthened in Britain for another reason. Many enterprises, both in the public and in the private sector, locate their administrative headquarters and a large proportion of their managerial workforce in the most prosperous markets. For a variety of reasons (see, especially, Soligo, 1966) it is the employees who work in such headquarters who incur the highest fixed employment costs of all. For direct econometric evidence to support differences in fixed labour costs between prosperous and other regions, see Bell and Hart (1980).

Second, arguments that migration may be relatively ineffective as a means of changing the long-term structure of regional unemployment, because of (a) the relatively low numbers of migrants involved (especially owing to high psychic costs)[21], and (b) the even lower net migration magnitudes owing to offsetting counter-flows, are also reinforced. As discussed with reference to figure 2.2, section 2.3.3, the importance of the internal market in meeting fluctuations in market demand is enhanced where high degrees of labour fixity are involved and thus significant levels of hoarding and dishoarding take place. If a relatively high propensity to operate through the internal market is apparent in more prosperous regions, then this will serve to depress the employment opportunities of potential migrants who, of course, operate through the external market.

2.6 Conclusions

This chapter has concentrated on analysing the wage-spread hypothesis since, apart from its moderately successful statistical validation, it appears to provide a set of arguments which are reasonably consistent with the long-run structure of regional wages and unemployment.

In most local labour markets any tendency for market clearing wages to be reached is constrained by the fact that many wage bargains are in part determined by market conditions elsewhere, through the process of wage-change transmission. In effect, transmission maintains unemployment above natural market levels[22] by keeping real wages above those which would have been determined by excess demand conditions in the market. The difference between actual wages and equilibrium clearing wages will be most pronounced, as will be the associated unemployment, in markets which, for whatever historical reasons, possess the greatest structural problems, since most or all of their occupations will experience effective leadership from other markets from within and/or outside their own region. However, the propensity of market forces to erode such differences is prevented by the very process which has helped to establish them in the first place. First, the integration of market wages provides an impediment to the mobility of capital, other than that directed by government, which seeks to combine with relatively cheap labour and thus improve future regional prosperity. Second, the already weak tendency of interregional migration to erode differences in regional wages and unemployment is further limited by a process which either prevents the attainment of market clearing wages for lagging occupations, or accentuates the importance of

[21] It is perhaps ironic that the vast amount of academic effort devoted to the analysis of regional migration has been expended on a subject whose quantitative importance is highly questionable. Perhaps journal editors in future should less readily accept papers purporting to answer the question, "Why do people migrate?" but rather show much greater sympathy to attempts at answering the more important question, "Why do so few people migrate?".

[22] The natural unemployment rate is determined by the market frictions inherent in the local labour market itself.

internal markets for leading occupations. In any event, such equilibrating migration flows that do occur have a minor impact on differentials, since they occur in reasonably similar magnitudes in both directions between given pairs of regions.

Although such arguments support a high degree of sluggishness in the ability of market forces to eradicate economic disparities, they perhaps stop short at explaining long-term stability in the regional wage structure, and certainly at explaining the narrowing of wage differences in the post-war era. One further argument presented here is that the growth of regional subsidies in this era may have enabled wages in poorer regions to move appreciably nearer the national average wage. However, in this latter respect, it would be wrong to underestimate the growth of multi-plant firms, in the private sector and public sector enterprises in general, that have formed national uniform-wage agreements which have transcended all regional and local market boundaries.

It is clear that many important questions are involved in this area of regional economics and although, at best, this chapter, has opened a few avenues for discussion, it at least points firmly to the conclusion that there is room for much important new research work.

References

Archibald G C, 1969 "The Phillips curve and the distribution of unemployment" *American Economic Review, Papers and Proceedings* **59** 124–134

Archibald G C, 1972 "On regional economic policy in the United Kingdom" in *Essays in Honour of Lord Robbins* Eds B Corry, M Peston (Weidenfeld and Nicolson, London) pp 224–245

Bell D N F, 1979 "Wage transmission and price expectations" Fraser Institute, University of Strathclyde, Glasgow (mimeographed)

Bell D N F, Hart R A, 1980 "The regional demand for labour services" *Scottish Journal of Political Economy* **27** 140–151

Brechling F P R, 1965 "The relationship between output and employment in British manufacturing industries" *Review of Economic Studies* **32** (July) 187–216

Brechling F P R, 1967 "Trends and cycles in British regional unemployment" *Oxford Economic Papers* **19** 1–21

Brechling F P R, 1973 "Wage inflation and the structure of regional unemployment" *Journal of Money, Credit and Banking* **5** 355–384

Briscoe G, Peel D A, 1975 "The specification of the short-run employment function" *Bulletin of the Oxford University Institute of Economics and Statistics* **37** 115–142

Burns M E, 1972 "Regional Phillips curves: a further note" *Bulletin of the Oxford Institute of Economics and Statistics* **34** 295–307

Cowling R, Metcalf D, 1967 "Wage–unemployment relationships: a regional analysis for the UK, 1960–65" *Bulletin of the Oxford University Institute of Economics and Statistics* **29** 31–39

Ehrenberg R G, 1971 *Fringe Benefits and Overtime Behaviour* (D C Heath, Lexington, Mass)

Feldstein M S, 1967 "Specification of the labour input in the aggregate production function" *Review of Economic Studies* **34** 375–386

Friedman M, 1968 "The role of monetary policy" *American Economic Review* **58** 1–17

Goodman J F B, 1970 "The definition and analysis of local labour markets: some empirical problems" *British Journal of Industrial Relations* **8** 179–196

Hart R A, 1970 "A model of inter-regional migration in England and Wales" *Regional Studies* 4 279-296

Hart R A, 1975 "Interregional economic migration: some theoretical considerations (Part 1)" *Journal of Regional Science* 15 127-138

Hart R A, 1978 "Short-run earnings changes and the excess demand for labour services" Discussion Paper, Department of Economics, University of Strathclyde, Glasgow

Hart R A, MacKay D I, 1975 "Engineering earnings in Britain, 1914-1968" *Journal of the Royal Statistical Society* Series A, General 138 32-50

Hart R A, MacKay D I, 1976 "Wage inflation and regional policy" Discussion Paper, Department of Economics, University of Strathclyde, Glasgow

Hart R A, MacKay D I, 1977 "Wage inflation, regional policy and the regional earnings structure" *Economica* 44 267-281

Hart R A, Sharot T, 1978 "The short-run demand for workers and hours: a recursive model" *Review of Economic Studies* 45 299-309

Hicks J R, 1932 *The Theory of Wages* (Macmillan, London)

Holt C C, 1970 "Job search, Phillips' wage relations, and union influence: theory and evidence" in *Microeconomic Foundations of Employment and Inflation Theory* Eds E S Phelps and others (W W Norton, New York) pp 53-123

Kerr C, 1950 "Labour markets, their character and consequences" *American Economic Review* 40 278-291

Kim S, 1977 "Interregional economic migration: some theoretical considerations: comment" *Journal of Regional Studies* 17 117-124

Kirwan F X, 1979 "Non-wage costs, employment and hours of work in Irish manufacturing industry, 1969-77" *Economic and Social Review* 10 231-254

Lerner S W, Marquand J, 1963 "Regional variations in earnings, demand for labour and shop stewards combine committee in the British engineering industry" *Manchester School of Social and Economic Studies* 31 261-296

Lipsey R G, 1960 "The relation between unemployment and the rate of change of money wage rates in the United Kingdom, 1862-1957: A further analysis" *Economica* 27 1-31

Metcalf D, 1971 "The determinants of earnings changes: a regional analysis for the UK, 1960-68" *International Economic Review* 12 273-282

Nadiri M I, Rosen S, 1969 "Interrelated factor demand functions" *American Economic Review* 59 457-471

Oi W Y, 1962 "Labour as a quasi-fixed factor" *Journal of Political Economy* 70 538-555

Phelps E S, 1970 "Money wage dynamics and labour market equilibrium" in *Microeconomic Foundations of Employment and Inflation Theory* Eds E S Phelps and others (W W Norton, New York) pp 124-166

Rosen S, 1968 "Short-run employment variation on Class-I railroads in the US, 1947-1963" *Econometrica* 36 511-529

Samuelson P A, 1948 *Foundations of Economic Analysis* (Harvard University Press, Cambridge, Mass)

Soligo R, 1966 "The short-run relationship between employment and output" *Yale Economic Essays* 6 160-216

Thirlwall A P, 1970 "Regional Phillips curves" *Bulletin of the Oxford University Institute of Economics and Statistics* 32 19-32

Thomas R L, Stoney P J M, 1971 "Unemployment dispersion as a determinant of wage inflation in the UK, 1925-66" *Manchester School of Social and Economic Studies* 39 83-116

Tobin J, 1972 "Inflation and unemployment" *American Economic Review* 62 1-18

Williamson J, 1975 "The implications of European monetary integration for the peripheral areas" in *Economoc Sovereignty and Regional Policy* Ed. J Vaizey (Gill and Macmillan, Dublin) pp 105-121

The convergence of earnings in the regions of the United Kingdom

B Moore, J Rhodes

3.1 The convergence of earnings in regions of the United Kingdom

There is a substantial amount of evidence which shows that in the last two decades there has been a steady convergence of earnings across the regions of the United Kingdom (DEm, 1979).

Several possible factors influencing regional wage differentials have been suggested, notably industry mix, pressure of demand in the labour market, changes in productivity, and degree of unionisation (Batra and Scully, 1972). In the UK, emphasis has been placed on assessing the importance of industry mix and of differences in the pressure of demand for labour in explaining regional differentials in earnings (see, for example, Thirlwall, 1970; Hart and MacKay, 1977). But only at the national level have factors such as productivity growth, degree of unionisation, and size of firm been evaluated for their impact on earnings change between industries (Ball and Skeach, 1980).

The purpose of this study is firstly to show the degree of convergence in regional earnings amongst UK regions, then to quantify how all these possible causal factors have varied differentially across regions and hence assess their potential contribution to the process of convergence. There are, of course, serious problems in disentangling the relative importance of each of these factors (Bradfield, 1976). But before any attempt can be made to identify their role and to test alternative theories of regional wage convergence, it is necessary to develop quantitative indicators of how the possible explanatory factors have changed differentially across regions. The main emphasis of the study is to establish the extent of these regionally differentiated changes, but we also present some preliminary tests of their relative importance.

It is essential that we understand more about the factors which are bringing about convergence in regional earnings, because such convergence could make it more difficult to achieve a balanced growth of output and employment across the country. From a neoclassical perspective, in circumstances where 'exchange rates' are fixed between regions, flexibility of wages and prices are required to bring about labour market adjustments which reduce regional unemployment disparities. Even outside the neoclassical paradigm the convergence of earnings could reduce the competitiveness of the labour-surplus regions, thus exacerbating the regional problem. But convergence need not be damaging to the problem regions if relative increases in earnings are accompanied by relative increases in productivity such that competitiveness is not eroded.

From the regional policy perspective, however, convergence of earnings could offset any advantages to the firm arising from regional policy subventions such as a regional employment premium. On the other hand, regional policy has as one of its objectives the reduction of regional earnings disparities. Insofar as regional policy generates an improvement in productivity associated with an increase in earnings, the aims of regional policy are being achieved without a deterioration in the competitive position of the problem regions.

We first examine, in section 3.2, the changes in weekly earnings for male and female manual workers in all industries in the regions between 1962 and 1979, highlighting the relative movements between each area and the UK as a whole.

Section 3.3 begins to disentangle some of the factors which could be responsible for the convergence in regional earnings. These possible causal factors include differences in industrial structure amongst the regions, changes in relative labour demand as reflected in unfilled vacancies, national wage policies (for example, with respect to low pay, which affect regions differently), and the record of industrial relations in the regions. Other factors, which are investigated for manufacturing industry in selected regions, include differential movements in labour productivity, changes in the size of industrial plants, the incidence of foreign-owned firms in the regions, and regional policy.

3.2 Measurement of the degree of convergence in regional earnings
The analysis begins by presenting average weekly earnings levels and growth rates for the standard regions on an all industry basis. Table 3.1 shows this separately for male and female manual workers.

In 1962, average weekly earnings for male manual workers in the South East were 5·7% above the GB average whereas those in Northern Ireland were 21% below the GB figure. But other regions differed from Great Britain by typically less than 5%. Earnings for female manual workers, which are given for 1970, showed a similar pattern of deviation from the national average.

The general pattern is one of convergence, with regions having relatively low earnings experiencing the highest growth in earnings and vice versa. There are some exceptions to this general rule, notably male and female earnings in the North West after 1970, and male earnings in the South West. By 1979 the effect of the convergence was to reduce the difference between the highest and lowest regions by half. In addition, some regions, notably Scotland and the Northern region, which traditionally have had low earnings levels had risen above average by 1979, whereas the West Midlands, a traditionally high-wage area for men, had fallen below average by 1979.

Although the evidence establishes some presumption of convergence, comparability of earnings growth amongst regions should ideally be made after various adjustments have been applied to the basic data series.

Table 3.1. Annual percentage growth in average weekly earnings by region, 1962–1979. Full time male and female manual workers, for all industries.

Region	Male		Female	Wage levels, £ per week			
				male		female	
	1962–1970	1970–1979	1970–1979	1962	1979	1970	1979
Northern Ireland	8·7	15·2[a]	na	12·4	na	na	na
Scotland	7·6	15·4	17·1	14·3	93·6	13·1	54·3
North	7·2	15·4	17·6	15·2	95·5	12·6	54·0
North West	7·3	14·7	17·0	15·2	92·2	13·2	54·2
Wales	6·9	14·9	17·9	15·8	94·1	12·8	56·4
West Midlands	na	13·9	16·7	na	93·1	13·8	55·3
Yorkshire and Humberside	6·9	15·5	17·3	15·1	94·3	12·6	53·0
East Anglia	na	15·5	17·9	14·3[b]	89·3	12·4	54·5
South West	6·9	14·5	17·4	14·6	84·0	12·5	52·8
East Midlands	na	15·3	16·6	na	92·3	13·5	53·9
South East	6·7	14·6	17·0	16·6	94·8	14·2	58·1
Great Britain	7·0	14·8	17·0	15·7	93·0	13·4	55·2

[a] 1970–1978. [b] estimated.
Sources: *Department of Employment Gazette* and *New Earnings Surveys*, various issues (HMSO, London).

Table 3.2. Differences in the average annual growth of actual and 'expected' hourly earnings for male manual workers in manufacturing and nonmanufacturing industries, 1962–1978.

Region	Difference in average annual growth rate (%)	
	manufacturing	nonmanufacturing
Northern Ireland	+0·8	+0·5
Scotland	+0·5	+0·5
North	+0·4	+0·2
North West	+0·3	0·0
Wales	−0·3	0·0
West Midlands	−0·2	−0·1
Yorkshire and Humberside	+0·3	0·0
East Anglia[a]	+0·6	0·0
South West	+0·1	−0·2
East Midlands[a]	0·0	−0·1
South East	−0·1	−0·2

[a] Index based on the rate for 1967 being set at 100.
Sources: *Department of Employment Gazette* and *New Earnings Surveys*, various issues (HMSO, London).

One factor which may introduce distortion in the comparisons is that differences in the growth of weekly earnings may be affected by regional variations in the numbers of hours worked. These regional variations in hours worked are quite small in practice, and tables 3.2 and 3.3 below confirm that earnings convergence between regions is found when hourly earnings, rather than weekly earnings, are compared.

Tables 3.2 and 3.3 also show an adjustment for a second important complicating factor, namely regional variations in industrial structure. The impact of this factor has been investigated by many studies, including Bell (1967), Mayhew (1976), Malizia (1978), and Tarling and Wilkinson (1978). Variations in industrial structure could be important if industries in which earnings are growing relatively rapidly are concentrated heavily in some regions and not in others.

There are several ways of removing any possible distortions introduced by regional variations in industrial structure. The method used here is to compare actual earnings changes in the region with changes occurring nationally, weighted to take account of the industrial structure of the region (termed the 'expected' earnings). Employment in each industry in the region (SIC order number level) in June 1972 was used to weight together earnings change in each industry[1]. Figure 3.1 shows the ratio of the actual growth of hourly earnings and the 'expected' growth of hourly earnings in each region, having removed the impact of variations in industrial structure.

Clearly industrial structure as measured at the order number level was not the major cause of any convergence in hourly regional earnings.

Table 3.3. Differences in the average annual growth of actual and 'expected' hourly earnings for female manual workers in manufacturing and nonmanufacturing industries 1970–1978.

Region	Difference in average annual growth rates (%)	
	manufacturing	nonmanufacturing
Scotland	+0·4	+0·6
North	+0·2	+0·1
North West	−0·1	+0·2
Wales	+0·5	na
West Midlands	0	−0·7
Yorkshire and Humberside	+0·5	+0·5
East Anglia	na	na
South West	−0·7	−0·7
East Midlands	−0·2	+0·9
South West	−0·5	−0·2

[1] Changes in the degree of industrial disaggregation and in base year could affect the magnitude of the adjustment made for variations in industrial structure, but in the case of the UK, where industries are widely dispersed throughout the region and where wages do not vary much between industries, the impact is very small.

The structural adjustment has made little difference to the relationship between the level of earnings in the base year and the subsequent change in hourly earnings. Low-earnings regions such as Northern Ireland and Scotland show a persistent rise in actual earnings relative to 'expected' earnings, whilst high-earnings regions such as the South East and West Midlands show a steady fall in actual relative to 'expected' earnings.

Tables 3.2 and 3.3 and figure 3.1 show clearly that after making adjustments to take account of regional variations in hours worked and industrial structure, strong evidence remains for persistent convergence in regional earnings. This applies both to male and female earnings and to manufacturing and nonmanufacturing activities, and leads to a strong presumption that factors other than hours worked, sex, and industry composition are responsible for the convergence in regional earnings.

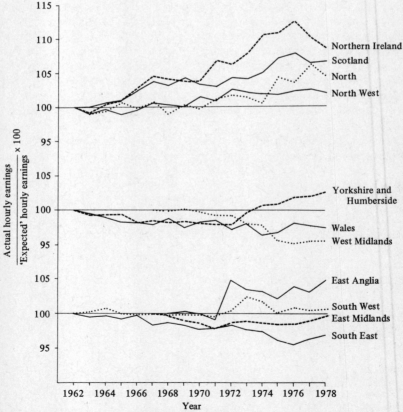

Figure 3.1. Ratio of actual to 'expected' regional average hourly earnings for male manual workers, all industries, 1962–1968 (ratio for 1962 = 100).

3.3 Explanation of movements in regional earnings

3.3.1 Relative changes in the pressure of demand

Previous attempts to explain differential changes in regional earnings invariably included a measure of levels and changes in the regional pressure of demand for labour [see, for example, Cowling and Metcalf (1967), Thirlwall (1970), Hart and MacKay (1977), and Webb (1974)]. This work suggests that regional differences in the pressure of demand for labour, when measured by unemployment rates, has little or no impact on the rates of earnings change in the regions. However, the evidence does suggest that *changes* in unemployment and more particularly changes in vacancies may have some influence on changes in regional earnings. Our own work on the period 1966–1978 broadly supports the results of earlier studies.

The relationship estimated was the logarithmic regression

$$\ln W_{it} = \alpha_{i1} + \alpha_{i2} \ln \hat{W}_{it} + \alpha_{i3} \ln \Delta V_{i/\text{UK},\,t} + \alpha_{i4}t + \epsilon_{it}\,, \qquad t = 1, ..., 13 \qquad (3.1)$$

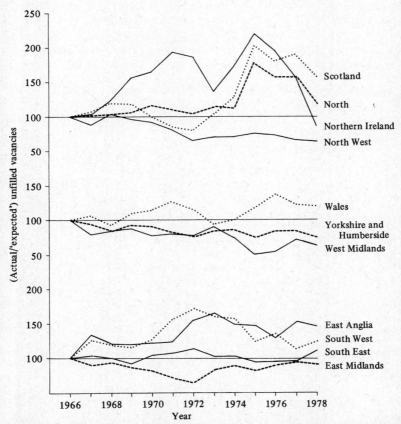

Figure 3.2. Ratio of changes in regional vacancies to changes in vacancies in the UK (ratio for 1962 = 100).

where

W_i are the actual earnings for male manual workers in region i;

$\hat{W_i}$ are the 'expected' earnings in region i (that is, national earnings after taking account of the region's industrial structure);

$\Delta V_{i/UK,t}$ are the changes in vacancies in region i relative to changes in vacancies in the UK (see figure 3.2);

t is a time trend;

ϵ is a stochastic error.

The term $\hat{W}$ reflects the changes in a region's earnings which arise from factors common to all industries and all regions, and if variables such as ΔV were to explain the differential movements between $\hat{W}$ and W, then the coefficient for $\hat{W}$ should be 1. The inclusion of the $\hat{W}$ term is important insofar as there is likely to be great similarity across the country in the response of money wages to, for example, the rate of price inflation and changes in national productivity.

The variable, $\hat{W}$, should also reflect the institutional system of wage bargaining in the UK whereby, in many industries, wage rates in each region are agreed at the national level. Also, $\hat{W}$ allows the differential impact of industrial structure to be taken into account—a feature in general not present in earlier studies. A further important aspect of the

Table 3.4. Parameter estimates and t-ratios for the estimating equations.

Region	Constant a	$\hat{W_t}$	$\Delta V_{i/UK,t}$	Time trend, t	$\bar{R}^2$	DW[a]
Northern Ireland	−0·63* (2·5)	1·11* (22·1)	0·03* (2·5)	−0·01 (1·2)	0·999	2·03
Scotland	−0·17 (1·3)	1·02* (29·1)	0·02* (2·2)	0·0002 (0·5)	0·999	2·73
North	−0·41* (2·20)	1·06* (21·8)	0·03 (1·0)	−0·004 (0·7)	0·999	2·26
North West	0·24* (2·4)	0·99* (50·9)	−0·04* (2·4)	−0·002 (1·0)	0·999	2·86
Wales	0·06 (0·4)	0·99* (34·8)	0·02 (0·8)	0·0 (0·0)	0·999	2·76
West Midlands	1·05* (8·5)	0·80* (39·5)	−0·03* (2·4)	0·02* (8·08)	0·999	2·66
Yorkshire and Humberside	−0·67* (5·7)	1·08* (56·1)	0·06* (2·9)	−0·005* (1·9)	0·999	1·23
East Anglia	−0·34 (0·9)	0·99* (14·5)	0·08* (2·1)	0·005 (0·5)	0·999	3·18
East Midlands	−0·20 (1·6)	1·01* (32·5)	0·03* (2·2)	−0·002 (0·6)	0·999	1·48
South West	−0·21 (0·9)	1·02* (25·8)	0·03 (1·5)	0·001 (0·3)	0·999	1·58
South East	−0·22 (1·1)	0·99* (39·6)	0·05* (1·9)	−0·002 (0·6)	0·999	2·05

[a] DW Durbin–Watson.   * Significant at the 90% level.

specification of the equation is the use of the growth of vacancies in the region *relative* to that for the UK (see figure 3.2). This is adopted because the impact of changes in vacancies nationally will be captured in $\hat{W}$. Hence $\Delta V_{i/UK}$ is included to assess whether the regionally differentiated demand for labour explains the regionally differentiated part of the change in regional earnings. The coefficient $\Delta V_{i/UK}$ should be positive. Preliminary results are presented in table 3.4.

As expected, the coefficients on $\hat{W}$ are statistically significant for all regions and, with the exception of the West Midlands, are very close to 1. With respect to relative vacancies, nine out of eleven regions show the expected positive sign, but only in eight regions is the relationship statistically significant. Even in these regions the contribution of demand pressure as measured by relative vacancies is quite small. In most cases the time trend is not significant. It should be emphasised that these results are provisional and further work needs to be undertaken.

3.3.2 Relative changes in productivity growth
It could be expected that regions experiencing the most rapid increases in productivity growth would also experience the larger increases in earnings. Some of the productivity gains are likely to be distributed to other regions through lower prices as argued by those favouring a normal cost pricing hypothesis (Coutts et al, 1977), but it is also likely, particularly in oligopolistic markets where firms are more apprehensive about price cutting, that some of the gains from increases in productivity will increase wages insofar as trade unions react to any marked rise in profits (Eatwell et al, 1974; Kuh, 1967). Moreover, productivity clauses in wage bargains are not uncommon. A recent study by Ball and Skeach (1980) provides some empirical support for the significance of productivity in wage determination at the plant level. In view of these arguments, if there are regional differences in productivity growth, they should in part be reflected in regionally differentiated earnings.

For only three regions in the UK is it possible to obtain reliable time-series data on productivity growth, namely Northern Ireland, Scotland, and Wales[2]. Output was measured using indices of production which are published separately for these regions.

Table 3.5 shows comparisons in productivity growth in manufacturing industry between the regions (actual) and the UK (expected) after taking account of differences in industrial structure. For all periods since 1950 actual productivity growth in Scotland and Northern Ireland exceeded 'expected' productivity growth. It will be recalled that these two regions have also experienced a relative increase in the growth of earnings.

[2] We do not regard Census of Production data for English regions as sufficiently reliable for this purpose, particularly in recent years, because of the growing incidence of "combined returns" and the difficulty of "brought-in-services" being included in net output.

On the other hand, Wales has experienced productivity growth which in some periods has been below that of the UK and this has been associated with below average growth in earnings.

Since pressure of demand and productivity growth are *both* quantifiable, at least for three regions, it seemed worthwhile conducting a few preliminary experiments to appraise the possible significance of the two factors. It should be emphasised that the results presented below should be treated with caution because of their provisional nature.

The estimated equation for the manufacturing sector only becomes

$$\ln W_{it} = \alpha_{i1} + \alpha_{i2} \ln \hat{W}_{it} + \alpha_{i3} \ln \Delta V_{i/UK,t} + \alpha_{i4} \ln \dot{y}_{i/UK,t} + \alpha_{i5} t + \epsilon_{it} , \qquad (3.2)$$

where

$\dot{y}_{i/UK,t}$ is the productivity growth in the region relative to productivity growth in the UK.

As before, the major determinant of the pace at which regional earnings grow would be expected to be the rate of increase of earnings in the UK (structurally adjusted) because of the overwhelming importance of common factors across industries, including trends in national wage bargaining. This is measured by $\hat{W}$, for which we expect the coefficient to be close to 1. The coefficients on $\Delta V_{i/UK}$ and $\dot{y}_{i/UK}$ should be positive and that on $\dot{y}_{i/UK}$ should be less than 1.

Scotland 1962-1976

$$\ln W_t = 0 \cdot 36 + 0 \cdot 93 \ln W_t + 0 \cdot 05 \ln \Delta V_{i/UK,t} + 0 \cdot 25 \ln \dot{y}_{i/UK,t} + 0 \cdot 01 t ;$$
$$\quad (4 \cdot 2) \quad (61 \cdot 6) \qquad (4 \cdot 8) \qquad\qquad (2 \cdot 6) \qquad\qquad (5 \cdot 7)$$

when estimated by ordinary least squares,

$$R^2 = 1 \cdot 00 , \qquad DW = 2 \cdot 35 .$$

The figures in brackets are t-ratios.

Table 3.5. Actual and expected percentage growth of manufacturing productivity in Northern Ireland, Scotland, and Wales 1950-1976.

Years	Northern Ireland		Scotland		Wales	
	actual	'expected'	actual	'expected'	actual	'expected'
1950-1958	2·08	1·11	2·26	1·56		
1958-1970	3·84	1·22	4·15	2·81		
1963-1970					2·68	3·26
1970-1976	3·63	1·74	3·33	2·84	2·87	2·41
1950-1976	3·25	2·11	3·38	2·43		
1965-1976					2·77	2·87

Sources: *Digest of Statistics for Northern Ireland, Wales and Scotland,* various issues (HMSO, London).

Wales 1963–1976

$$\ln W_t = 0 \cdot 14 + 1 \cdot 04 \ln W_t + 0 \cdot 06 \ln \Delta V_{i/\text{UK}, t} + 0 \cdot 06 \ln \dot{y}_{i/\text{UK}, t} - 0 \cdot 1 t .$$
$$(6 \cdot 1) \quad (100 \cdot 0) \qquad (5 \cdot 7) \qquad\qquad (1 \cdot 6) \qquad\qquad (12 \cdot 7)$$

In this equation an adjustment was required for second-order serial correlation.

Northern Ireland 1962–1976

$$\ln W_t = -0 \cdot 11 + 1 \cdot 01 \ln \hat{W}_t + 0 \cdot 01 \ln \Delta V_{i/\text{UK}, t} - 0 \cdot 18 \ln \dot{y}_{i/\text{UK}, t} + 0 \cdot 01 t ;$$
$$(0 \cdot 8) \quad (31 \cdot 2) \qquad (0 \cdot 7) \qquad\qquad (1 \cdot 8) \qquad\qquad (2 \cdot 5)$$

when estimated by ordinary least squares,

$$R^2 = 0 \cdot 99 , \qquad \text{DW} = 1 \cdot 44 .$$

As anticipated, the coefficient on 'expected' earnings remains close to one in all the equations. As far as regional earnings 'shifts' are concerned, there is some evidence that changes both in the relative tightening of the local labour market and in relative productivity growth may have a small part to play. The Northern Ireland equation is very unsatisfactory, perhaps because unlike Scotland and Wales almost all the productivity growth is concentrated in one industry, textiles, and also because of the effects of the political troubles from 1969.

In all three equations the contribution of the time trend, although small, is statistically significant although not always of the same sign. This implies that at least for these regions, there are other regionally differentiated causal factors at work. Some of these other possibilities are examined below.

3.3.3 Other possible factors leading to convergence

In their examination of factors causing differential movements in earnings between industries in the United Kingdom, Ball and Skeach (1980) found that average plant size and degree of unionisation, as well as productivity had a significant influence on earnings. Insofar as these factors change differentially across regions, they could be expected to contribute to any regionally differentiated change in earnings. Some evidence is presented above to the effect that regional differences in productivity growth may have been a factor influencing relative change in earnings in some regions.

Table 3.6 shows that the average plant size as measured by employees per manufacturing establishment differs considerably across regions and has been subject to varying rates of change. The more depressed, older industrial regions of Scotland, the North, the North West, and Wales have the larger average plant sizes. The South East has by far the lowest average plant size. The correlation between average plant size and the change in regional earnings was weak, but we would hesitate at this stage, given the aggregative nature of the data, to rule out some effect.

The same applies to the effect of the degree of union militancy as measured by industrial stoppages. Table 3.7 shows average annual working days lost per 1000 employees for selected periods between 1959 and 1977. The actual figures for each period are compared with an 'expected' figure, which tells us what might have happened in the region had it had the same industrial structure as the UK as a whole.

There is a sharp distinction between the North and South of Britain. The Assisted Area regions and the West Midlands have high levels of stoppages and generally the actual exceeds the 'expected'. The reverse is the case for the Southern regions. It is clearly a possibility that, where regions have both a high level of union militancy and a good case for higher

Table 3.6. Employees per manufacturing establishment in the regions relative to the UK. (The value for the UK is set at 100.)

Region	1958	1963	1968
Scotland	108	111	118
North	155	159	162
North West	113	117	123
Wales	125	138	144
West Midlands	113	120	116
Yorkshire and Humberside	–	97	100
East Anglia	84	96	98
East Midlands	–	107	109
South West	101	98	103
South East	–	71	74

Source: *Census of Production* 1958, 1963, and 1968 (HMSO, London).

Table 3.7. Average annual working days lost per 1000 employees 1959–1977[a], actual and 'expected' (adjusted for regional variations in industrial structure).

Region	1959–1964		1965–1970		1971–1977	
	actual	'expected'	actual	'expected'	actual	'expected'
Northern Ireland	340	272	494	351	928	732
Scotland	613	369	716	489	1601	812
North	327	436	523	535	1456	959
North West	319	268	696	451	1230	862
Wales	828	320	1320	532	1129	958
West Midlands	na	na	888	666	1513	1186
Yorkshire and Humberside	na	na	281	401	661	766
East Anglia	na	na	na	na	433	826
East Midlands	na	na	198	402	413	799
South West	205	452	300	622	515	1072
South East	234	327	275	549	461	899

[a] Mining is excluded.

Source: *Department of Employment Gazette*, various issues (HMSO, London).

earnings on regional parity grounds, the convergence of earnings could have been hastened by the activity of trade unions.

A further factor promoting the convergence of regional earnings is the tendency for foreign owned firms to have located disproportionately in regions which experienced low earnings in the early post-war period. Examination of Census of Production data for 1973 shows that, after adjustment for variations in industrial structure, the average wage and salary per employee in foreign owned firms was $9 \cdot 1\%$ higher than in British owned firms. Therefore earnings can be expected to rise relatively in low-earnings regions which have attracted a high proportion of new foreign enterprises. The regions particularly attractive to foreign firms in the post-war period were Scotland, Wales, the Northern Region, and Northern Ireland, which together attracted almost 60% of the total number of foreign firms entering the UK (Howard, 1968).

Government policies, both national and regional, may also affect the convergence of regional earnings. At the national level the effects of most policies, insofar as they affect all industries similarly, are taken account of in the equations above by the inclusion of the term $\hat{W}$, 'expected' earnings. However, if it were the case that within any one industry there were, for example, concentrations of low paid workers in a region, then Government policies to help low paid workers could affect that region differentially. In most incomes-policy periods, particularly in the 1960s, there was usually some attempt to maintain wage differentials for low paid groups. Moreover, the flat rate incomes policies of 1972–1977 gave proportionately more to lower paid than to higher paid workers. Incomes policies also frequently included "exceptions" in those cases where productivity improvement could be demonstrated, for example, 1965–1969. Since it is known that some low-income regions such as Scotland have experienced high productivity growth, the incomes policy would allow this to be reflected in increased earnings.

Indirectly, regional policy will have influenced the growth of earnings by contributing to some of the effects discussed above. Regional policy undoubtedly attracted some foreign firms into the low-earnings regions. In addition, regional policy in attracting new investment into the assisted areas will have enhanced the growth of productivity in the regions.

Regional policies may also have had a direct impact on the convergence of regional earnings. The 'leakage' of subsidies, such as the Regional Employment Premium (REP) into wages is one way in which regional policy might have promoted convergence in regional earnings. A sample survey of 300 Development Area firms, which we carried out in 1972, indicated that perhaps 12% of REP had been used directly to increase wages above what they would otherwise have been, the remainder dividing fairly evenly between higher profits and lower prices. At most this is a small one-off effect adding not more than 1% to earnings, but other regional subsidies could have conceivably leaked into wages.

3.4 Conclusion

This study has shown evidence of a gradual convergence of regional earnings in the United Kingdom over the last two decades. This convergence was found to have taken place both in manufacturing and in nonmanufacturing sectors, and both for males and for females. An important part of the convergence has been the tendency for the assisted area regions, which traditionally experienced low-average earnings, to catch up with the historically high-earnings regions of the South East and West Midlands. The convergence in regional earnings persisted after adjustments had been made to take account of variations in industrial structure.

In all regions the dominant influence on the way in which earnings changed was 'expected' earnings (the change in earnings at the national level, structurally adjusted). Small, but persistent, regional differentiated movements in earnings were found to exist and it is these which we sought to explain. It was established that for seven of the eleven regions, relative changes in the demand for labour as measured by the relative change in vacancies were found to be significant. Preliminary statistical work on the importance of relative productivity growth suggested that this may also be of some importance in securing convergence.

A brief analysis of regional differences in plant size, the attraction of foreign enterprises, and the incidence of industrial stoppages suggests that these might be of minor importance in explaining convergence but this result requires confirmation from a more disaggregated analysis. Finally it was argued that regional policy may have been important, both directly and indirectly, in reinforcing the processes underlying the convergence in regional earnings.

References

Batra R, Scully G W, 1972 "Technical progress, economic growth and the North South wage differential" *Journal of Regional Science* 12 375–386

Ball J M, Skeach N K, 1980 "Interplant comparisons of productivity and earnings" *Department of Employment Gazette* October 1980 1111–1118

Bell F W, 1967 "The relation of the region, industrial mix and production function to metropolitan wage levels" *Review of Economic Statistics* 49 368–374

Bradfield M, 1976 "Necessary and sufficient conditions to explain equilibrium regional wage differentials" *Journal of Regional Science* 16 247–256

Coutts K, Godley W A H, Nordhaus W, 1977 *Industrial Pricing in the United Kingdom* monograph 26, University of Cambridge, Department of Applied Economics (Cambridge University Press, London)

Cowling R, Metcalf D, 1967 "Wage–unemployment relationships: a regional analysis for the UK, 1960–65" *Bulletin of the Oxford University Institute of Economics and Statistics* 29 31–39

DEm, 1979 *Department of Employment Gazette* April 340–348

Eatwell J, Llewellyn G E J, Tarling R J, 1974 "Money wage inflation in industrial countries" *Review of Economic Studies* 41(4) 515–523

Hart R A, MacKay D I, 1977 "Wage inflation, regional policy and the regional earnings structure" *Economica* 44 267–281

Howard R S, 1968 *The Movement of Manufacturing Industry in the U.K., 1945-1965* (HMSO, London)

Kuh E, 1967 "A productivity theory of wage levels—an alternative to the Phillips curve" *Review of Economic Studies* **34** 333-360

Malizia E, 1978 "Standardized share analysis" *Journal of Regional Science* **18** 283-291

Mayhew K, 1976 "Regional variations of manual earnings in engineering" *Bulletin of the Oxford University Institute of Economics and Statistics* **38** 11-26

Tarling R J, Wilkinson F, 1978 "Wage differentials and incomes policy: an inter-industry study" unpublished mimeo, Department of Applied Economics, University of Cambridge

Thirlwall A P, 1970 "Regional Phillips curves" *Bulletin of the Oxford University Institute of Economics and Statistics* **39** 19-32

Webb A E, 1974 "Unemployment, vacancies and the rate of change of earnings: a regional analysis" *National Institute of Economic and Social Research, Regional Papers III* (Cambridge University Press, London) pp 1-49

Regional earnings determination in the United Kingdom engineering industry, 1964–1979 [†]

R Tarling, F Wilkinson

4.1 Introduction

The largest single national wage agreement in the United Kingdom is probably that concluded between the Engineering Employers Federation and the Confederation of Shipbuilding and Engineering Unions, which, directly or indirectly, affects the vast majority of workers in the all-metals group of industries. Until 1963, the national agreements were negotiated for general wage-rate increases but, since then, a series of fixed long-term agreements have been negotiated which have concentrated wage increases on a small proportion of the lowest paid workers [1]. The long-term wage and productivity agreement of 1964 (see Marsh, 1965, pages 307–317 for details) introduced minimum earnings levels as a 'safety net' for the low paid, eliminated regional differentials in 1967 (which at the time had a range of only 2% in England; see DEm, 1967, pages 48–49 for district rates), and converted the minimum earnings levels into minimum time rates on 1 January 1968 at the end of the agreement. But while the agreement was current only two general increases were made (amounting weekly to 40p for labourers, and 50p for fitters), whereas minimum earnings levels had been increased a further six times (giving additional increases of £1.50 and £1.80, respectively). The 1968 long-term agreement continued this pattern, with two general increases and a further four increases in minimum earnings levels.

It has been argued that this changing nature of the national wage agreement in engineering has meant that these agreements bear a tenuous, if not nebulous, relationship to the movements in actual earnings. Brown and Terry (1978, page 131) concluded that "they increasingly provide no more than a 'safety net' of minimum wage. Far from pushing up earnings in their industries, increases in these nationally negotiated rates appear to

---

[†] Much of the work underlying this study was completed as part of a research project 'The economics of institutionalised wage determination' HR 4980/1, funded by the Social Science Research Council.

[1] Surveys made by the National Board of Prices and Incomes in their investigations of the 1964 agreement showed:

> "on average 3·9 per cent of the workforce had an uplift due to minimum earnings levels of not more on average than £0.47 per week. This suggests that the cost of the minimum earnings levels of the E.E.F. firms represents not more than 0·12 per cent of the total wage bill in 1967, and less in 1965 and 1966" (NBPI, 1968, page 19, footnote).

be the result of belated and increasingly unsuccessful attempts to raise the rates into a more realistic relationship with actual standard earnings. Furthermore, their coverage becomes more and more shadowy as individual employers establish their own, job evaluated and formally negotiated, company or workplace wage agreements".

The purpose of this study is to evaluate the impact that these changes may have had at regional level. In the second section, we shall describe the changes at national level in order to evaluate the claim that national agreements became increasingly irrelevant to an explanation of the movement of actual earnings for Great Britain as a whole. Since we conclude that they did, and in this agree with Brown and Terry, we shall turn our attention in section 4.3 to the movement of regional earnings relative to the national minima. We begin with the 'conventional' hypothesis of competitive pressure and bargaining power to explain differential regional change and add to this a test for the impact of minimum earnings levels in raising earnings in low-paying regions. Finally, we shall look at data on the movement of new plants to test for effects of regional policy. Because of limited data, our tests are only exploratory in nature and lead to tentative conclusions, given in section 4.4, which suggest the need for detailed case studies of earnings change at the appropriate level of wage negotiation—that is, through company settlements and bargaining in the workplace.

4.2 The national agreement

Traditionally, national bargaining in engineering has been concerned with minimum rates. The key rates for adult males in the minimum time-wage structure (termed 'consolidated time rates') are those for fitters and labourers; until 1968, minimum wage standards were also fixed for pieceworkers in the form of a minimum piecework standard (for a worker of average ability, this should give earnings equal to the piecework supplement plus $1 \cdot 45$ times the piecework basic rate)[2]. The rates agreed at national settlements since 1960 are shown in table 4.1. General increases were granted in 1960, 1962, 1963, 1966, 1967, 1968, and 1969; all other increases were in minimum earnings levels (set higher than wage rates), which gave increases only to those workers, whether on time or piece rates, with normal earnings (for a 40 hour week) below the new minimum.

The minimum earnings levels were introduced under the 1964 long-term agreement, converted into minimum time rates at the end of that agreement, and were applied equally to workers on time rates or piece rates. The general increases in time rates were accompanied by general increases in piecework rates during the 1964 agreement, but it was agreed that, after

[2] Brown (1973, page 9); but see Robertson (1960) for a detailed discussion of these wage structures in theory and in practice.

Table 4.1. National settlements in engineering—1964-1979.

Date of implementation and type of increase[a]		Fitters			Labourers		
		time rate[b,j]	piece rate[b]	MEL[c]	time rate[b,j]	piece rate[b]	MEL
16.10.58		9·33	9·87		7·86	8·22	
26.12.60	General	9·76	10·48		8·24	8·72	
9.7.62	General	10·06	10·78		8·49	9·06	
2.12.63	General	10·58	11·30		8·97	9·45	

1964 long-term agreement
Stages:

4.1.65	MEL		11·40	10·88		9·58	9·22
5.7.65	MEL		11·60	11·18		9·78	9·47
3.1.66	MEL			11·48			9·72
7.3.66	General	10·83	11·73	11·73	9·17	9·89	9·92
4.7.66	MEL			12·03			10·17
2.1.67	MEL			12·33			10·42
3.7.67[d]	General	11·08	11·98	12·58	9·37	10·14	10·62
	MEL			12·88			10·87
1.1.68	MEL converted to MTR[e]	12·88	14·81		10·87	12·50	

1968 long-term agreement
Stages:

16.12.68	General	13·18		13·18	11·12		11·12
	MEL			15·00			12·00
20.1.69	MEL converted to MTR	15·00			12·00		
1.12.69	General	15·30		15·30	12·25		12·25
	MTR	16·25		16·25	12·93		12·93
7.12.70	MTR	17·50		17·50	13·85		13·85
6.12.71	MTR	19·00		19·00	15·00		15·00

	MTR fitters[j]	MTR labourers[j]
1972 agreement		
26.8.72	22·00	17·50
25.8.73	25·00	20·00
1974 agreement[f]		
27.4.74-6.11.74	28·50	22·75
1.3.75	32·00	25·50
1975 agreement		
26.5.75	36·00	28·75
24.11.75	40·00	32·00
23.2.76	42·00	33·60
1978 agreement		
10.4.78-31.7.78[g]	57·00	43·00
9.10.78-30.1.79[h]	60·00	45·00
1979 agreement		
1.11.79	73·00	52·50

the last stage of the 1964 agreement, which fixed the minimum piecework standard at 15% over the minimum time rate, there should be *no* nationally agreed minimum piecework standard during the currency of the 1968 agreement. Thus although there were two general increases in time rates during the 1968 agreement, the determination of piecework incentive was left entirely to domestic agreement, subject only to the 'safety net' of the minimum earnings level; the nationally negotiated minimum piecework standard was not revived in subsequent agreements. Workers on time rates were left with only the 'safety net' when the 1968 agreement was replaced by the 1972 agreement.

Thus, during the 1964 agreement, the majority of workers were forced towards dependence on company or workforce agreements, time-rate and piece-rate workers both gaining only small general increases (just under 5% of the 1963 time rates) from national settlements between 1964 and 1968. From 1968 onwards, pieceworkers became wholly dependent on company or workplace agreements, whilst timeworkers obtained two small general increases (amounting to less than 5% of the 1968 time rates) from the 1968 national agreement. There were no general increases either for pieceworkers or for timeworkers after December 1969. It is interesting to note that the policy of not negotiating general increases at national level after the 1968 agreement meant that threshold agreements, allowable

Table 4.1.(continued)

---

a General increases are paid to all workers but increases in minimum earnings levels and minimum time rates are paid only to workers with normal earnings (from whatever source) for a 40 hour week less than the new nationally agreed level.

b All rates have been converted to decimal pounds.

c Minimum earnings level.

d District differentials eliminated.

e Minimum time rate.

f The implementation of the first stage of the 1974 agreement was complicated by the twelve month rule in the Pay Code; Section 11 of the 1974 agreement read

"Stage 1 available from the first full pay week containing 27th April 1974, and completed by the first full week containing 6th November 1974 as follows:

a. Where a Pay Code Stage 3 settlement has not been concluded domestically then the first increase to the national minimum rate should be implemented on the due anniversary date for that domestic settlement to the extent permissable by the Pay Code, but anyway not later than the pay week containing 6th November 1974.

b. Where a Pay Code Stage 3 settlement has been fully concluded domestically then the first increase to the national minimum rates should be implemented with effect from the pay week containing 6th November 1974.

The 1974 Agreement Stage 1 wage increase was put into the Department of Employment wage-rate index for August 1974.

g On 10th April or on domestic anniversaries when these fall between 10th April and 31st July.

h Six months after stage 1.

j Hours of work to 7.12.64, 42 hours; 7.12.64 to 5.7.65, 41 hours; from 5.7.65, 40 hours.

---

under Phase III of the 1972–1974 incomes policy, were left to local negotiations.

Earnings in Great Britain for fitters and for labourers, averaged over all engineering industries, have been taken from the half-yearly inquiries carried out by the Department of Employment, the results of which are published in the *Gazette*. For each of these occupations, hourly earnings (excluding overtime) for timeworkers and pieceworkers separately have been compared with minimum earnings levels set since their establishment through the 1964 long-term agreement. The four ratios as at June each year are plotted in figure 4.1.

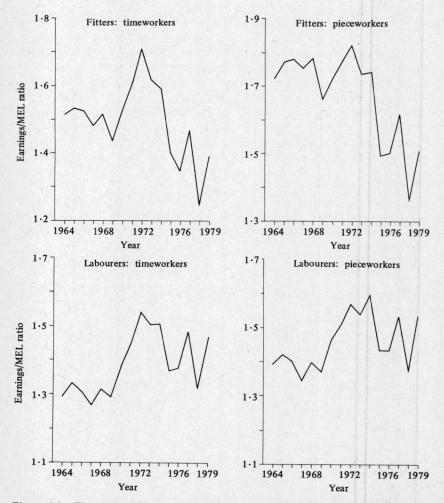

Figure 4.1. The ratio of fitters' and labourers' earnings (excluding overtime) to nationally agreed minimum earnings levels.

All four graphs, for fitters and for labourers, on timework or on piecework, show a remarkably similar pattern, with the exception that the skilled differential for fitters over labourers narrowed between 1972 and 1976 for timework and piecework. During the course of the 1964 long-term agreement, earnings remained a fairly stable markup over the minimum earnings levels. But, during the 1968 agreement, earnings increased rapidly relative to the minimum earnings level for all except fitters on piecework, the rates being around 20% higher in 1972 than they had been in 1968, before the settlements under the 1968 agreement came into effect: fitters on piecework had a small relative increase of less than 5%. The year 1972 proved to be a peak in the ratios, and the subsequent agreements which came into effect by June 1979, subject as they were to various incomes policies, have been associated with a substantial decline in earnings relative to the agreed minima for fitters (around 30%), with smaller declines for labourers (around 5% to 10%).

For the purposes of the remainder of the chapter, we shall split the period 1964 to 1979 into three subperiods: (1) 1964–1968, the term of the 1964 agreement, (2) 1968–1972, the term of the 1968 agreement, and (3) 1972–1979, the period without any general increases and subject to incomes policies with flat-rate norms or restrictions to the growth of total earnings. Under the 1964 agreement, there were eight stages; under the 1968 agreement, there were five stages; and between June 1972 and June 1979, there were four national agreements with a total of nine stages.

The relative stability of the ratios in the first period compared with the second period may be in part explained by the greater frequency of settlement in the first period. There were at least two increases in each June–June period between 1964 and 1968 and only one increase in each June–June period between 1968 and 1972. The other factor in the explanation is the faster rate of inflation in the second period; prices rose 31% between June 1968 and June 1972 compared with 17% between June 1964 and June 1968. Although the absolute and percentage increases in minimum earnings levels in the second period were larger, they were inadequate to keep up with the faster rate of inflation. A similar argument cannot be applied in the third period when the ratios were declining and then varying around a constant level. The frequency of settlement was low and price inflation rapid; this can explain wide variations around a constant level but not a decline in the ratio. To some extent, the declines can be explained in terms of incomes-policy restrictions which allowed minimum earnings levels to rise faster in percentage terms than total earnings.

The proposition that minimum earnings levels are set by reference to actual earnings, or at least that increases in the levels reflect past increases in earnings, can be considered in the light of data given in table 4.2. Over the whole period covered by agreements including settlements for minimum earnings levels, the latter were increased by 590% for fitters and by 485% for labourers. The increase in average earnings was 571% and in retail prices only 335%. Thus, over the whole period, minimum earnings levels have risen more in line with earnings than with prices, although this has not been true for the term of each individual agreement. Both the 1964 and 1968 agreement granted increases which fell between the increases in earnings and prices. Minimum earnings levels caught up during the 1972 agreement, fell behind again during the 1974 agreement (in the absence of a nationally agreed threshold agreement) and recovered again during the 1975 agreement, probably largely because of the policy of a flat rate increase of £6 per week. In the 1978 and 1979 agreements (as in the 1968 agreement), fitters gained a relative improvement in their minimum earnings levels; labourers obtained increases equal to the increase in average earnings which, in turn, was in line with the rise in prices.

Thus, the increases in the whole period are in line with the proposition but, agreement by agreement, it is only the 1972 agreement which supports the view of a backward look at earnings to fix new minimum earnings levels. The increase in retail prices appears to provide the floor to the increases in the 'safety net', and past earnings increases are eventually embodied in those increases but not in any systematic way. In this sense, we are in agreement with the view of Brown and Terry (1978) quoted in the introduction that national agreements have become increasingly irrelevant. From this point of view, it would be surprising if the introduction of minimum earnings levels had done much to improve relative earnings in low-paying regions.

Table 4.2. Increases in minimum earnings levels, average earnings, and retail prices during each agreement.

Period covered by agreement	Percentage increase		Actual earnings adjusted for overtime[a,b]	Retail prices[b]
	MEL for timeworkers			
	fitters	labourers		
1964 agreement 2.12.63–3.7.67	21·7	21·2	27·8	15·3
1968 agreement 3.7.67–6.12.71	47·5	38·0	57·4	31·2
1972 agreement 6.12.71–25.8.73	31·6	33·3	18·9	14·6
1974 agreement 25.8.73–1.3.75	28·0	27·5	43·5	29·7
1975 agreement 1.3.75–23.2.76	31·2	31·8	22·2	22·9
1978 agreement 23.2.76–9.10.78	42·9	33·9	35·6	34·2
1979 agreement 9.10.78–1.11.79	21·7	16·7	17·9	17·2
Whole period 2.12.63–1.11.79	590	485	571	335

[a] Average monthly earnings in engineering for all employees, adjusted by average hours worked in a month by operatives in engineering and metals.
[b] Where a settlement date is before the 10th of the month, the estimate of earnings or prices for the previous month is used.

4.3 Regional changes in earnings

In the analysis given in this section, we shall use the minimum earnings levels as a national standard against which to compare the movements in regional earnings. Table 4.3 shows the levels in the ratios for each region in 1964 and the percentage change during each subperiod. The movements in earnings relative to minimum levels in each of three subperiods for each region accords with the national movements discussed above. In the first period, there was a wide range of increases across regions, with fitters on piecework doing relatively well in all regions. During the second period, all groups in all regions had relative increases, again widely dispersed, and in all regions labourers faired better than fitters, whether on time rates or piece rates. The third period was characterised by decreases in the ratios for fitters in all regions: once again, there were widely dispersed changes in the regions for labourers.

The data in the table suggest that there are marked differences between periods, between fitters and labourers, and between timeworkers and pieceworkers. However, within each classification, regional rankings in earnings increases are not subject to violent change across time periods and hence it appears appropriate to set a number of hypotheses to explain the regional rankings. But it must be stressed that the hypotheses which can be tested are severely limited by the data available. In addition, it is

Table 4.3. Regional earnings relative to nationally agreed minimum earnings levels.

Region[a]	Timeworkers				Pieceworkers			
	ratio 1964	change (%)			ratio 1964	change (%)		
		1964– 1968	1968– 1972	1972– 1979		1964– 1968	1968– 1972	1972– 1979
Fitters								
NW	1·449	5·9	2·0	−9·5	1·540	8·5	1·6	−12·0
SW	1·461	1·0	12·7	−12·7	1·568	2·0	10·0	−22·3
Y/H	1·322	−3·5	17·2	−17·9	1·520	1·1	3·8	−4·2
Wales	1·393	−1·4	24·5	−21·2	1·556	4·2	12·1	−19·6
N	1·370	15·2	7·9	−13·2	1·651	5·3	7·3	−12·9
SE/EA	1·505	−2·2	16·3	−21·8	1·675	1·1	3·7	−13·3
W/EM	1·608	−0·9	16·6	−24·1	1·862	7·1	1·6	−23·2
S'land	1·330	9·0	14·0	−16·2	1·540	5·6	10·4	−19·0
Labourers								
NW	1·199	4·3	12·9	4·0	1·311	4·1	14·4	−4·9
SW	1·229	−0·7	19·3	−3·7	1·297	0·2	8·8	3·3
Y/H	1·199	−3·9	23·5	2·6	1·287	−0·2	15·5	7·1
Wales	1·316	−1·1	35·1	−14·2	1·416	−9·6	14·6	3·1
N	1·194	5·5	18·5	6·6	1·283	2·7	12·1	14·6
SE/EA	1·372	−4·5	20·7	−8·6	1·456	−2·2	13·6	−7·2
W/EM	1·292	0·2	20·5	−9·7	1·522	−3·3	9·9	−8·6
S'land	1·241	6·1	22·3	−4·4	1·339	1·1	22·7	−4·4

[a] For key to regions, see Appendix.

generally agreed (Brown, 1973, pages 22–24) that it is more appropriate
to test for hypotheses relating to the mark-up over base rates rather than
relating to total earnings: since we do not have regionally differentiated
base rates, this procedure cannot be followed, and should be considered a
defect in the analysis.

The two most frequent hypotheses encountered are (1) that differential
regional change originates from labour and/or product market pressures,
and (2) that it reflects differences in workplace bargaining. Competitive
pressures in the labour and product markets are generally proxied by
regional unemployment rates; because regional output data by industry
are not available for our sample period, it is not possible to test for the
direct effects on nonnegotiated wage-drift of payment-by-results and bonus
systems by including productivity change. Differences in workplace
bargaining are extremely difficult to measure in a simple way; we have
chosen to use the average employment size of establishment as a proxy for
workplace organisation.

The changing nature of bargaining in engineering suggests the importance
of minimum earnings level in supporting the level of earnings in low-paying
firms. Although it is not necessarily the case that a high density of low-
paying firms in a region will lead to low overall average earnings, it is
presumed that, at the standard-region level of aggregation, this will in fact
be a reasonable assumption[3]. Thus we shall hypothesise a negative
relationship between the growth of earnings over the period of an
agreement and the level of average earnings at the beginning of the period.

Over the period when the national agreement for engineering has been
changing, there has been an active regional policy favouring manufacturing
industry. Policy has taken two particular directions which might have
influenced regional relativities; first, the use of wage subsidies (the
regional employment premium), and second, investment incentives which
induce movement of firms[4] and affect location decisions of expanding
firms. The evidence on wage subsidies suggests that there was, in fact,
very little leakage into earnings (Moore and Rhodes, 1976b). But new
openings in regions may have two effects: a direct effect on the regional
average through the opening of new higher-paying plants, and an indirect
one as a 'demonstration effect' pushes up wages in competitive plants.
Using data supplied by the Department of Industry on new openings, the
total number of all manufacturing openings originating outside the region
during the period of the 1964 and 1968 agreements has been constructed;
the data are not available separately for engineering nor beyond 1976.
In order to obtain a suitable proxy for the impact on average earnings, the
number of openings in each region was divided by the number of

[3] The rank correlation between average weekly earnings and the lowest decile
earnings for full-time manual men (all industries and services) in April 1972 was 0·96
(source *New Earnings Survey* 1972, tables 54 and 69).
[4] See Moore and Rhodes (1976a, pages 28–29) for a description of these data.

manufacturing establishments in each region to normalise for regional scale differences[5].

These propositions give rise to the following specifications:

$$\dot{w}_{it}^{r} = a_t + b_{1t}\Delta U_{it} + b_{2t}S_i ,\qquad (4.1)$$

where

$\dot{w}_{it}^{r}$ is the percentage change in average earnings (excluding overtime) in region i relative to the change in minimum earnings levels in period t;

ΔU_{it} is the absolute change in the unemployment rate in region i during period t;

S_i is the average employment size of engineering establishments in region i in 1968.

$$\dot{w}_{it}^{r} = a_t + b_{it} W_{it}^{r} + b_{2t}\Delta U_{it} + b_{3t}S_i ,\qquad (4.2)$$

where

W_{it}^{r} is the ratio of actual earnings to minimum earnings levels at the beginning of period t.

$$\dot{w}_{it}^{r} = a_t + b_{1t} W_{it}^{r} + b_{2t}N_{it}^{r} + b_{3t}\Delta U_{it} + b_{4t}S_i ,\qquad (4.3)$$

where

N_{it}^{r} is the ratio of manufacturing new openings in region i during period t originating outside the region to the number of manufacturing establishments in 1968.

Specifications (4.1) and (4.2) have been estimated by maximum likelihood methods for the three periods identified as of interest in the previous section; the period of the 1964 long-term agreement (1964–1968), the period of the 1968 long-term agreement (1968–1972), and the period 1972–1979 when there were no general increases but substantial intervention through incomes policies[6]. Owing to the lack of data on moves in the third period, specification (4.3) was estimated for only the first two periods. As noted in the introduction, the analysis can only be considered as exploratory since there are consistent observations on only eight regions, thus giving only 3 degrees of freedom when estimating specification (4.3). The log-likelihoods of the three specifications and the F-statistic for specification (4.1), for each occupational category by method of payment and time period, are given in table 4.4, and the regression estimates for specification (4.3) are given in table 4.5.

Specification (4.1), with the change in unemployment and average size of establishment, fits reasonably well for timeworkers, both for fitters

[5] It is assumed that new openings are of a similar size to indigenous plants, pay higher-than-average earnings, and have an impact on earnings almost immediately. However it is known that it takes on average up to eight years for a plant to mature; but this does not indicate the length of, or even the need for, a lag.

[6] The data used in the analysis are tabulated in the appendix.

and for labourers in the first period. It is the inclusion of the ratio in the initial year [specification (4.2)] which appears to be the most relevant factor in explaining regional differential change in the final period (1972–1979); it is significant for labourers and fitters, and in both cases for timeworkers and pieceworkers. The results for the second period, when earnings rose dramatically relative to minimum earnings levels, are however disappointing, giving little support to the propositions.

The results for specification (4.1), that the change in unemployment is significant only in the first period, if then, is in agreement with the findings of Brown (1973, pages 34–35), whose analysis of firms in the Coventry area showed that the impact of changes in unemployment on pieceworker earnings after the 1950s was not significant. That is, our findings for pieceworkers and for the period 1968–1972 confirm the view that an adequate explanation of company and workplace bargaining needs a much more detailed and disaggregated analysis than can be carried out with the data available from official sources. The results for average employment size are more promising, giving significant coefficients in both the first and third periods.

Table 4.4. Log-likelihoods for the various specifications.

	Log-likelihood specification			F-statistic for specification (4.1)[a]	χ^2 for likelihood ratio test[b]	
	1	2	3		1 : 2	2 : 3
Period 1964–1968						
Fitters:						
timeworkers	22·31	22·44	23·08	39·9	0·2	1·3
pieceworkers	19·31	19·89	19·99	1·1	1·2	0·2
Labourers:						
timeworkers	23·47	24·42	24·43	20·0	1·9	0·0
pieceworkers	16·37	19·16	24·14	1·6	5·6	10·0
Period 1968–1972						
Fitters:						
timeworkers	12·29	13·76	14·13	1·1	2·9	0·7
pieceworkers	16·15	18·09	19·75	1·2	3·9	3·3
Labourers:						
timeworkers	12·11	12·26	15·63	0·6	0·3	6·7
pieceworkers	16·41	16·69	16·81	1·6	0·6	0·2
Period 1972–1979						
Fitters:						
timeworkers	13·99	17·14	na	0·7	6·3	na
pieceworkers	11·66	14·86	na	0·3	6·4	na
Labourers:						
timeworkers	11·34	19·29	na	0·9	15·9	na
pieceworkers	10·79	17·64	na	1·1	13·7	na

[a] The critical value for the F-statistic at the 5% significance level is 5·79.
[b] The critical value for the χ^2-statistic at the 5% significance level is 3·84.

The finding that the initial level of earnings in 1972 is negatively related to the growth of earnings in the period 1972–1979 could be the result of the flat-rate and earnings-related norms of the various incomes policies. However, as shown in the previous section, much of the narrowing of the differential between actual earnings and minimum earnings levels had occurred by 1976. In fact, figure 4.1 indicates that about one-third of the narrowing at national level occurred between 1972 and 1974 during the term of the 1972 agreement, when large increases in minimum earnings levels relative to actual earnings and prices were granted, and two-thirds between 1974 and 1976. Thus the 1972 agreement contributed in part to the narrowing of regional differentials, but part of the support

Table 4.5. Regression results for specification (4.3),
$$\dot{w}_{it}^r = a_t + b_{1t}W_{it}^r + b_{2t}N_{it}^r + b_{3t}\Delta U_{it} + b_{4t}S_i.$$

	Coefficient estimates [a]					Regression statistics	
	a	b_1	b_2 ($\times 10^3$)	b_3	b_4 ($\times 10^3$)	R^2	σ
Period 1964–1968							
Fitters: time	0·834	0·023	−0·8	−0·020	2·334	0·95	0·022
	(8·6)	(0·4)	(1·2)	(1·6)	(8·3)		
piece	0·916	0·062	−0·5	−0·014	0·572	0·42	0·032
	(7·9)	(0·9)	(0·5)	(0·8)	(1·4)		
Labourers: time	1·103	−0·120	0·1	−0·031	0·983	0·91	0·019
	(9·0)	(1·4)	(0·2)	(2·9)	(3·3)		
piece	1·383	−0·288	−2·7	−0·029	0·807	0·91	0·019
	(16·3)	(5·2)	(4·5)	(2·7)	(3·2)		
Period 1968–1972							
Fitters: time	1·557	−0·242	1·1	−0·019	−0·713	0·57	0·068
	(6·0)	(1·3)	(0·9)	(0·5)	(0·6)		
piece	1·208	−0·111	1·1	0·000	0·195	0·73	0·034
	(11·6)	(1·9)	(2·0)	(0·0)	(0·4)		
Labourers: time	1·050	0·152	2·8	0·033	−1·753	0·66	0·056
	(3·5)	(0·6)	(3·3)	(1·1)	(2·3)		
piece	1·182	−0·076	0·4	0·050	−0·358	0·44	0·048
	(4·1)	(0·4)	(0·5)	(1·8)	(0·5)		
Period 1972–1979 [b]							
Fitters: time	1·248	−0·315		0·021	0·882	0·64	0·040
	(7·5)	(3·1)		(1·0)	(2·4)		
piece	1·537	−0·376		−0·026	0·242	0·60	0·053
	(7·5)	(3·1)		(1·0)	(0·5)		
Labourers: time	1·687	−0·534		0·001	1·201	0·90	0·031
	(15·2)	(7·1)		(0·1)	(4·3)		
piece	2·358	−0·895		−0·053	1·322	0·88	0·038
	(9·2)	(6·0)		(2·2)	(3·8)		

[a] t-ratios are in brackets: critical values of t-ratios at 5% significance level are periods 1 and 2 (3 degrees of freedom), 3·18; period 3 (4 degrees of freedom), 2·78.
[b] Results for specification (4.2).

for the hypothesis is probably spurious in that it reflects the £6 flat-rate national agreement in 1975.

The results for specification (4.3) are disappointing. There are only two significant coefficients on the density impact of new openings, one for labourers on time rates in the second period, with the expected positive sign, and one for labourers on piecework in the first period, with the opposite sign. It may be that the number of openings is a poor proxy for the effect; for example, it may be only the policy-induced openings which pay higher earnings than indigenous plants or that the effects are not felt in indigenous plants until the new plants have matured. It is, of course, possible to try alternative measures of new openings but, with so few degrees of freedom, the results would hardly be conclusive.

4.4 Conclusions

The empirical evidence provided in the study supports the proposition that the national agreement in engineering has been of limited importance in determining the course of earnings, either at national or at regional level, during the last two decades. The 1972 agreement may have contributed a small part to the narrowing of regional differentials in the 1970s through substantial increases in minimum earnings levels.

Labour-market pressure, as reflected by the unemployment rate, has had a diminishing influence, and regional policy has not been shown to have had much effect on relative earnings. The one factor which showed up with some regularity was the average employment size of establishment.

The growth of labourers' earnings proved more susceptible to this analysis than did the growth of fitters' earnings, as also did the earnings of timeworkers relative to those of pieceworkers. This fact, combined with the relative success of the size variable, suggests that analysis of engineering earnings has to be carried out with specific reference to factors underlying company and workplace bargaining. Since these must include a distinction between the negotiated elements of increases originating from company and workplace negotiations, and the nonnegotiated elements arising from the manipulation of piecework systems and the direct effects of changes in output and productivity levels, the need is for detailed case-study material where this kind of information is available. The analysis which we have carried out with the aggregate estimates of earnings at regional level point only to the narrowing of regional differentials and the failure of conventional hypotheses to contribute significantly to an explanation.

References
Brown W, 1973 *Piecework Bargaining* (Heinemann Educational Books, London)
Brown W, Terry M, 1978 "The changing nature of national wage agreements" *Scottish Journal of Political Economy* 25 119–133
DEm, 1967 *Time Rates of Wages and Hours of Work, 1st April 1967* Department of Employment (HMSO, London)
Marsh A, 1965 *Industrial Relations in Engineering* (Pergamon Press, London)

Moore B, Rhodes J, 1976a "Regional economic policy and the movement of manufacturing firms to development areas" *Economica* **43** 17-31

Moore B, Rhodes J, 1976b "The effects of the regional employment premium and other regional policy instruments" in *Economics of Industrial Subsidies* Ed. A Whiting (HMSO, London)

NBPI, 1968 *Pay and Conditions of Service of Engineering Workers* (second report on the Engineering Industry), National Board for Prices and Incomes Report No. 104, Cmnd 3931 (HMSO, London)

New Earnings Survey, 1972 Department of Employment (HMSO, London)

Robertson D J, 1960 *Factory Wage Structures and National Agreements* Publications of the Department of Social and Economic Research, University of Glasgow, *Social and Economic Studies Volume 5* Ed. A K Cairncross (Cambridge University Press, London)

Appendix

Data used in the analysis.
Actual earnings (excluding overtime) relative to minimum earnings levels.

Year	Region							
	NW	SW	Y/H	Wales	N	SE/EA	W/EM	S'land

Fitters, timeworkers

Year	NW	SW	Y/H	Wales	N	SE/EA	W/EM	S'land
1964	1·449	1·461	1·322	1·393	1·370	1·505	1·608	1·330
1968	1·534	1·475	1·276	1·374	1·578	1·472	1·593	1·450
1972	1·565	1·662	1·495	1·711	1·702	1·712	1·857	1·653
1979	1·416	1·451	1·227	1·349	1·478	1·339	1·409	1·385

Fitters, pieceworkers

Year	NW	SW	Y/H	Wales	N	SE/EA	W/EM	S'land
1964	1·540	1·568	1·520	1·556	1·651	1·675	1·862	1·540
1968	1·671	1·599	1·537	1·621	1·739	1·693	1·994	1·627
1972	1·698	1·759	1·596	1·817	1·866	1·755	2·025	1·796
1979	1·495	1·367	1·529	1·461	1·625	1·522	1·556	1·454

Labourers, timeworkers

Year	NW	SW	Y/H	Wales	N	SE/EA	W/EM	S'land
1964	1·199	1·229	1·199	1·316	1·194	1·372	1·292	1·241
1968	1·251	1·221	1·152	1·302	1·260	1·310	1·295	1·317
1972	1·413	1·457	1·432	1·759	1·493	1·581	1·560	1·611
1979	1·470	1·403	1·460	1·509	1·591	1·445	1·409	1·540

Labourers, pieceworkers

Year	NW	SW	Y/H	Wales	N	SE/EA	W/EM	S'land
1964	1·311	1·297	1·287	1·416	1·283	1·456	1·522	1·339
1968	1·365	1·299	1·284	1·280	1·317	1·424	1·472	1·354
1972	1·561	1·413	1·483	1·467	1·477	1·617	1·617	1·661
1979	1·484	1·460	1·589	1·512	1·693	1·500	1·478	1·588

Explanatory variables.

Unemployment rate (%)

Year	NW	SW	Y/H	Wales	N	SE/EA	W/EM	S'land
1964	2·0	1·5	1·1	2·4	3·4	1·0	0·9	3·6
1968	2·4	2·5	2·5	3·9	4·5	1·6	1·9	3·7
1972	4·8	3·5	4·2	4·8	6·1	2·3	3·5	6·4
1979	6·6	5·5	5·3	7·4	7·9	3·7	4·9	7·3

New openings per thousand establishments in manufacturing

Year	NW	SW	Y/H	Wales	N	SE/EA	W/EM	S'land
1964–1967	8·0	20·8	2·5	29·3	27·5	4·6	4·1	21·9
1968–1971	7·4	29·9	2·9	70·0	46·5	6·1	6·4	16·7

Average employment size of establishment in engineering (operatives)

Year	NW	SW	Y/H	Wales	N	SE/EA	W/EM	S'land
1968	81·5	71·5	57·0	78·3	135·8	49·0	68·7	113·6

Key: NW — North West   N — North   W/EM — West and East Midlands
SW — South West   SE/EA — South East and East Anglia
Y/H — Yorkshire and Humberside   S'land — Scotland

Wage inflation in a growth region: the American Sun Belt

R Q Hanham, H Chang

5.1 Inflation trends in the national economy

One of the characteristic features of inflation within the United States of America during the late 1960s and in the 1970s is the fact that the processes which have given rise to it have been cumulative. The result has been a continuing and accelerating rate of inflation. This contrasts with the more typical form of inflation in which an isolated event or cluster of processes give rise to a singular rise in the price level. The significance of this distinction lies not only in their causal differences, but also in the fact that the anti-inflationary policies which are applicable to each, and the benefits resulting from them, may also be quite different. Between 1952 and 1967, for example, the national inflation rate averaged 2%, rising briefly to only 3·4% in 1957. The first half of the 1960s was characterized by a continuous rise in the rate of growth in the money supply, but it also saw a rise in the rate of growth of real GNP, output, and productivity, a continuous decline in the unemployment rate, and a stable, but low, inflation rate.

Since 1965 a succession of events has taken place that has transformed the process of price and wage decisionmaking in the American economy into one in which the inflationary pattern is now typified by persistently high and accelerating rates. There is great concern that the behaviour of households and firms has been so changed that the process of price and wage decisionmaking now inevitably results in a chronic inflation which stubbornly feeds on itself and speeds the wage–price spiral (Okun, 1977; 1979; Shapiro, 1977). In late 1965 the decision was made to finance the Vietnam buildup in what was an inflationary manner. Employment, production, capital spending, real incomes, and prices all rose. This was not unusual for a wartime period, but the end of it was not accompanied by the usual end to inflation. Every year since 1968 has had a higher inflation rate than any of the previous fifteen years. After a sharp rise in 1966, wage rates rose faster than productivity, raising unit labour costs and contributing to the rise in inflation. Furthermore, during the remainder of the 1960s the growth rate in the money supply exceeded that of real GNP. Although this expansion ended in 1969, the recession which followed barely affected the rate of increase in wages, and unit labour costs rose by 6·3% (Shapiro, 1977).

It appears that from this point price expectations became permanently altered, with a subsequent effect on price and wage decisionmaking. Okun argues that as people perceive that inflation is persisting, they change their behaviour in ways which make inflation more rapid and tenacious (Okun, 1979). The result is an economy that is dominated by 'cost-oriented' prices and 'equity-oriented' wages. Pricing policies are now geared to maintain a market share over the long run, and they are therefore set to exceed costs by a percentage markup. The downward rigidity of wages is encouraged by a tendency on the part of the employers to maintain long-term relationships with their workforce. Wage increases therefore tend to follow those of workers in similar situations. The fact that prices and wages no longer largely respond to excess supply and demand is due, in Okun's opinion, to the increasing importance that is attached to lasting relationships between employers and employees, particularly skilled ones. The result of these adaptations is a cumulative spiral in the inflation process.

The brief respite in 1971 and 1972 which was caused by the mandatory wage–price controls of the Nixon Administration's Economic Stabilization Program was followed by a rapid increase in inflation. A number of events about this time conspired to reinforce the changes which already were taking place with regard to price and wage decisionmaking. These include the shift from fixed to flexible foreign exchange rates in 1971, an excessive monetary and fiscal stimulus applied in 1972, and the devaluation of the dollar, the mismanagement of US grain supplies, and the sudden rise in OPEC oil prices in 1973 (Okun, 1977; Shapiro, 1977). Even the severe recession of 1973–1975 did not have a lasting effect on the ensuing inflation rate, which declined to about 6% but then began to rise steadily after 1977.

5.2 Wage inflation in a spatial setting

There can be little doubt that, as Thirlwall says, the state of the national economy is not independent of the economic performance of its constituent geographic regions (Thirlwall, 1970). It is also clear that regional economic performance can be variably influenced not only by nationally determined regional policies, but also by national economic policies which do not possess an explicit regional dimension. The regional impact of national monetary policy and of wage and price controls are two examples of the latter. The interdependence and conflict between regional and national economic policy is well known, but it frequently has not been easy to resolve in practice. The conflict between the goals of regional equity and national efficiency is an obvious case in point (Hewings, 1978; King and Clark, 1978a).

The relation between wage inflation in the national economy and the wage-adjustment process in the nation's constituent regions has attracted particular attention. Lipsey's aggregation hypothesis suggested that a more even distribution of demand for labour among regions could dampen wage inflation in the national economy as a whole (Lipsey, 1960). There followed a number of attempts either to test this assertion (for example: Archibald, 1969; Thomas and Stoney, 1971; Hewings, 1978), or to investigate the regional wage-adjustment process itself in the hope that this will eventually lead to a better understanding of the national problem. The remainder of this section is devoted to a consideration of the latter, and particularly to the role of the excess demand for labour, inflationary expectations, wage-spread effects, and national policies of wage control.

We begin with the assumption that changes in the average wage rate of the labour force within any given regional labour submarket is determined by imbalances in that submarket, as measured by the excess demand for labour. The level of unemployment in the submarket has normally been used as a surrogate for demand pressure in empirical studies of this type, although it has generally proved to be of little value in explaining changes in wage rates in practice. It is not entirely clear, however, whether these results are dictated by an incorrect assessment of the underlying process, whether they result from a misguided assumption that unemployment does indeed represent excess demand for labour, or whether the definition of regional labour submarkets is inadequate. The last two issues are not easy to resolve, but it certainly appears that the definition of submarkets is more often than not governed by the availability of data than by a rigorous application of the concept of a submarket. Furthermore, there is evidence that labour hoarding by employers seriously undermines the value of using unemployment as an indication of excess demand for labour (Taylor, 1970). An alternative view of this problem suggests that the inadequacy of unemployment as a measure of excess demand for labour may stem from the fact that the overall level of unemployment in a submarket is a composite of at least three components; structural, national, and regional (Brechling, 1967; Jeffrey, 1974). It is assumed that each component represents a distinct influence upon the overall level of submarket unemployment, resulting from local structural factors, national forces, and regional forces, respectively. The last two involve the notion that intermarket links should have some bearing upon the level of submarket unemployment and, presumably, excess demand for labour. An explicit test of the effect of these components upon submarket wage-rate changes has been outlined elsewhere (Hanham and Chang, 1979a). In this study a test of the influence of the regional component is implicitly made by investigating the role of a regional wage-spread-effect variable. This is described later in the chapter.

According to the neoclassical view, the trade-off between unemployment and wage inflation is strictly temporary and unstable. It is created by adjustment lags to inflationary expectations, and money illusion which will disappear in the long run. The effect of inflationary expectations on wage inflation in a multimarket setting has been evaluated by Brinner (1977) and Martin (1978). Both used a convergent price-expectations variable, which represents the sum of the normal rate of inflation and a fraction of the current deviation of inflation from the normal rate, and it proved to be quite influential in their models of wage inflation. In Martin's study of urban labour markets in the northeastern states of the USA, for example, the coefficients for both terms were generally positive, although for only one-half of his sample was the coefficient for the normal inflation rate term insignificantly different from one.

The effect of intermarket links upon the expectation generating process is one means of incorporating the contribution of regional submarket interdependencies to regional wage inflation. Brechling shows that the expected wage change in a given submarket can be influenced not only by its own past wage changes, but also by wage changes in other submarkets (Brechling, 1973). This dynamic market-interdependence hypothesis was examined in two ways: first, the proposition that low-unemployment regions acted as expectational leaders was found to lack empirical support; and second, the proposition that high-earning regions act as leaders was supported. Brechling assumed that this interdependent process resulted from the threatened or real migration of labour from one submarket to another where there exists a higher expected net income. Wage aspiration levels are thus shifted by wage increases in the submarket which is seen as the most attractive from the point of view of the potential migrant. Brechling actually found that western and southwestern states of the USA acted as leaders far more than other states over the period 1950–1969. This approach has been criticized for being too reliant on the assumption of a competitive free market for labour, and that more attention should be devoted to institutional factors in the wage-determination process (Clark, 1978a; 1978b; Martin, 1978). We have already noted Okun's view that the wage decisionmaking process has changed to such an extent since the 1960s that excess supply and demand factors have largely given way to institutional ones (Okun, 1979). A perfectly free market can hardly be said to exist and, as Cripps (1977) points out, the terms on which people work are now largely a matter of social convention. The role of reference groups with whom comparisons are made by employers and employees is a strong one. Even in a situation in which a high-growth sector of the economy is willing to raise wages in order to attract the type of labour it requires, the low-growth sectors are likely to follow, either to retain the investment they have made in their labour force or simply to yield to union or industry pressure. The institutional process of wage determination therefore results in a spread of wage changes through the various sectors of the economy, perhaps with little regard to productivity, market structure, demand pressure, or their geographic distribution (Clark, 1978b; Flemming, 1978). The fact that wage bargaining frequently takes place on an industry-wide basis helps to ensure the spread of a change in wages. It may be that only in those submarkets in which the excess demand for labour is particularly high is where demand will exert a direct upward pressure on wages (Martin, 1978). This, presumably, is more likely to occur in the high-growth sectors of an economy, whereupon institutional forces will effect a spread to other sectors.

The spread of wage patterns has long been observed in the US economy. Maher, for example, noted a distinct diffusion of them during the period 1946–1957 (Maher, 1961). According to him the ties that bind bargaining situations clearly imply a strong spatial dimension in the spread of wage changes. The presence of this dimension has been empirically illustrated by Brechling (1973), Cowling and Metcalf (1967), King and Forster (1973), Marcis and Reed (1974), Martin (1978), Mathur (1976), Reed and Hutchinson (1976), and Weissbrod (1976). Clearly, however, the process which has been assumed to underlie this effect differs greatly among these studies, ranging from one based on a purely competitive market criterion to one based simply on institutional principles. There can be some difficulty in assessing whether the influence of a particular term in a model, whether it be a leading submarket, relative wage, or distance-effect one, actually represents the outcome of one or other process. Moreover, regardless of the assumed process there remains the issue of defining the leaders, regions, and spatial interaction functions which are involved.

The influence of wage stabilization policies within the US economy appears to have been studied only in the context of the national economy as a whole. The regional effects of such policies are unknown, although the effects of other national policies, such as monetary and fiscal policies for example, have been investigated to a limited extent (for example, see Miller, 1978). The last major occasion on which wage and price controls were implemented in the USA was during the Nixon Administration's Economic Stabilization Program from August 1971 to April 1974. This policy was instituted after the recession of 1970–1971 had failed to reduce significantly the wage and price inflation that had been accelerating during the second half of the 1960s. The first phase of the program began with a three month freeze on wages and prices in August 1971, and it effectively halted wage inflation. The second phase lasted from November 1971 to January 1973, during which a $5 \cdot 5\%$ wage-increase standard was used and all settlements affecting more than one thousand employees had to be reported. Controls were designed to influence heavily unionized firms, and those which were either small or already paid a relatively low average wage were exempted. The effects on union negotiated wage increases were noticeably greater than on others (Darby, 1976; Vroman and Vroman, 1979). In the third phase, from January to June 1973, controls were self-administered and there was a shift from the application of a uniform standard to an individual review system. The fourth and final phase, from June 1973 to April 1974, was characterized by a steady decontrol on an industry by industry basis.

After the initial freeze, wages and prices both began to creep gradually upward until a strong acceleration took over in 1974 and 1975. Vroman and Vroman (1979) conclude that the long-run effect of the program on wage inflation was negligible and that the intention of inducing a spread in wage stabilization from unionized to nonunionized sectors of the

economy largely failed.   The regional effects of this program do not appear
to have been investigated.   It is interesting to note, however, that the graphs
of wage inflation in Martin's study of metropolitan areas from the northeast region of the USA suggest that the program was effective in most of
these places, and particularly in its early stages (Martin, 1978).   It is also
apparent that once the controls were lifted in 1974, wages rose very
rapidly.

5.3 The Sun Belt growth region
Although there is no complete agreement on what area constitutes the Sun
Belt, it is commonly suggested that it comprises those American states that
are located south of latitude 37°, namely North Carolina, South Carolina,
Georgia, Florida, Tennessee, Alabama, Mississippi, Arkansas, Louisiana,
Oklahoma, Texas, New Mexico, Arizona, and the southern portions of
Nevada and California.   By no means homogeneous in character, this
region nevertheless possesses some economic attributes which are generally
present within, but generally absent without.

     As far as population is concerned, the Sun Belt has been generally
characterized both by metropolitan and by nonmetropolitan in-migration
during the 1970s, whereas the north, with the exception of the Rocky
Mountain states and upper New England, has exhibited out-migration in
only one of either of these two categories (Morrill, 1979).   Maximum
population growth rates during this period have occurred almost entirely in
metropolitan centres and suburbs within the Sun Belt, but largely in areas
ranging from small cities to rural in the north.   During the period 1960–
1975 the growth of population in the southwest and southeast averaged
about 26%, while it was only 13% in the upper midwest and northeast.
Movement to the south accelerated after the late 1960s, and has involved
proportionally more professional or retired people with greater than
average education and income.   Perhaps the most important change from
our point of view, however, has been that of the structure of the economy
of the Sun Belt relative to that of the north.   As Rees has suggested, there
now appears to be occurring a fundamental realignment of the traditional
core–periphery relationship in the United States, involving a regional shift
in the industrial structure of the national economy (Norton and Rees,
1979; Rees, 1979).   The states within the Sun Belt averaged the highest
growth rates of manufacturing employment in the country over the period
1960–1975.   States in the upper midwest and northeast, on the other
hand, showed an absolute loss.   Overall employment growth has been
greatest in areas along the southern part of the Atlantic and Gulf coastal
belt, in Tennessee and northern Georgia, in the south-central area of
Oklahoma and Texas, and in Arizona and the Rocky Mountain states
(Beyers, 1979).

     The industrial growth of the Sun Belt has taken place because of the
relocation of industry from other parts of the country, the attraction of

branch plants, and the location there of new, growing industrial sectors (Watkins and Perry, 1977). Labour intensive, low-wage industries in particular have been induced to move to the Sun Belt, attracted by, among other things, the lower wages which have traditionally existed there. Most of these industries are characterized by low growth rates and are not regarded as the major reason for the overall industrial growth in the region. Branch plants have also been attracted to the Sun Belt, but the extent of their growth-inducing effects is questionable. It is the attraction and development of new and innovative industrial sectors which is the most significant aspect of the growth in the Sun Belt. Industries of this type are represented by electronics, computing equipment, chemicals and plastics, aerospace products and scientific instruments. The fact that these are high technology sectors has been stressed by Rees, who has argued that the economy of the north has been unable to initiate new product cycles to replace the mature or old industrial sectors of that region (Norton and Rees, 1979; Rees, 1979). The Sun Belt has been able to adapt to the changing needs of the national and international economy and is now the national leader in capital accumulation (Watkins and Perry, 1977). These shifts have resulted in a Sun Belt economy that is becoming increasingly export based, with national markets which are tied more to final demand than to intermediate producers. The reverse is the case in the north's economy, which is also having to compete increasingly with international imports (Beyers, 1979).

The original stimulus for this regional development is currently under debate. There is one train of thought, however, which strongly suggests that federal fiscal and monetary policy over the years, and particularly over the past twenty, has been one of the main stimuli. Miller, for example, has shown that, over the period 1960–1975, the regional pattern of federal monetary policy impacts and interregional net flows supported a rate of growth in nominal personal income that was less in the northeast than in the rest of the country (Miller, 1978). Federal spending has also been regionally biased over the years. The Sun Belt has been a persistent net gainer in federal per capita spending with respect to per capita taxes, and a relative leader in federal employment. Some have argued that this attention given to the Sun Belt in the past has largely been due to the strength of the southern congressional delegation and to presidential electoral politics. If this is the case, then it seems likely that the Sun Belt will continue to benefit from federal spending for similar reasons; the power of the southern congressional delegation, particularly from energy-rich states, continues to increase, and the role of the south in presidential politics remains important. Federal spending in this region has been of three main types; (1) investment in and development of urban infrastructure; (2) military; and (3) special projects such as Cape Canaveral in Florida and the Space Center in Houston. Federal involvement such as this has either directly stimulated a demand for industrial products, or indirectly so by encouraging the private sector to take advantage of the new infra-structure and invest further in the region.

There is also little doubt that the existence of a relatively low-waged and largely nonunionized labour force has made the Sun Belt attractive to many industries. The average weekly earnings of industry workers in the southeast and southwest are the lowest in the country, and the proportion of the labour force that is unionized is far lower in the Sun Belt states than it is elsewhere. Furthermore, most states in the Sun Belt, unlike those in the north, possess right-to-work laws which are designed to inhibit unionization. Many areas within the Sun Belt have also made explicit efforts to attract industry by offering tax relief and various other financial incentives (Business Week, 1976). Lastly, there is no doubt that some areas of the Sun Belt now have developed to the point where they possess self-generating agglomeration economies, for example Houston and the Dallas–Fort Worth area, which is itself an attraction to many industries (Norton and Rees, 1979).

These developments have led to a situation in which personal incomes and earnings have grown more rapidly in the Sun Belt than in the north since the beginning of the 1960s, together with a substantial growth in services and retail markets (Business Week, 1976; Beyers, 1979). Some have even suggested that the long-standing wage gap between north and south has now closed (Coelho and Ghali, 1971). The regional shift in economic development continues nonetheless.

5.4 A metropolitan wage model applied to the Sun Belt

A model of wage adjustment, involving excess demand for labour, inflationary expectations, wage-spread effects, and a national policy of wage control, was applied to thirty-three metropolitan areas from the Sun Belt (figure 5.1 and table 5.1). The areas were chosen according to their size, being the largest, and to whether an uninterrupted time series of wage

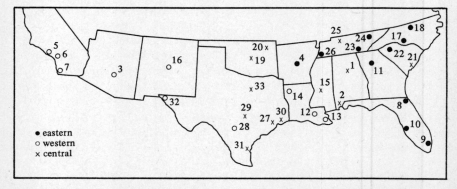

Figure 5.1. Metropolitan groups for the relative wage variable (see table 5.1 for identification of areas).

and unemployment data were available. Although they do not necessarily correspond to actual urban–regional labour submarkets, the daily urban system probably being a better approximation, these standard metropolitan statistical areas certainly constitute their core and represent a substantial majority of a submarket's labour force. The period 1965–1978 was chosen because it enclosed the change which began to occur in the character of inflation and in its relation to unemployment after the mid-1960s. It also incorporates two recessions, which took effect at the end of the 1960s and in the middle of the 1970s, and a period of national wage and price controls from 1971–1974.

The following model was used,

$$(\dot{w})_{it} = a_{i0} + a_{i1}\overline{U}_{it}^{-1} + a_{i2}(\dot{p})_{t-1}^{N} + a_{i3}(\dot{p})_{t-1}^{D} + a_{i4}(W_i/\overline{W})_{it-4} + a_{i5}Z_t + \epsilon_{it} \,,(5.1)$$

where

$$\dot{p}_{t-1}^{D} = \lambda(\dot{p}_{t-1} - \dot{p}_{t-1}^{N}) \,. \tag{5.2}$$

The wage variable, $(\dot{w})_{it}$, refers to the annual change in the average hourly earnings of manufacturing workers in a given metropolitan area, based on a four-quarter rate of change (US Department of Labor, *Employment and Earnings*). The reciprocal of the local unemployment rate, $\overline{U}_{it}^{-1}$, was used as a surrogate for excess demand for labour in the metropolitan area, the average of this measure over the four-quarter period corresponding to the wage-change variable being used in this case (US Department of Labor, *Area Trends in Employment and Unemployment*). Should wages respond to changes in the excess demand for labour in the traditional Phillips curve manner, the coefficient for the unemployment variable will be positive. A negative coefficient would indicate that wages and unemployment rise or fall together and that, assuming they are rising, stagflation exists in the metropolitan area's economy.

The price-expectations variable consists of the sum of two terms. The first is the 'normal' rate of inflation, $(\dot{p})_{t-1}^{N}$, and consists of a weighted

Table 5.1. Sun Belt metropolitan areas[a].

1	Birmingham, Al	12	Baton Rouge, La	23	Chattanooga, Tn
2	Mobile, Al	13	New Orleans, La	24	Knoxville, Tn
3	Phoenix, Az	14	Shreveport, La	25	Nashville, Tn
4	Little Rock, Ar	15	Jackson, Ms	26	Memphis, Tn
5	Los Angeles, Ca	16	Albuquerque, NM	27	Houston, Tx
6	Riverside, Ca	17	Charlotte, NC	28	San Antonio, Tx
7	San Diego, Ca	18	Greensboro, NC	29	Austin, Tx
8	Jacksonville, Fl	19	Oklahoma City, Ok	30	Beaumont, Tx
9	Miami, Fl	20	Tulsa, Ok	31	Corpus Christi, Tx
10	Tampa, Fl	21	Charleston, SC	32	El Paso, Tx
11	Atlanta, Ga	22	Greenville, SC	33	Dallas–Fort Worth, Tx

[a] See figure 5.1 for the location of these areas.

sum of six consecutive annual changes in the national consumer price index (US Department of Labor, *Consumer Price Index*). It is based on quarterly data and is computed with the linearly declining weights used in Martin's study (Martin, 1978). This was done to facilitate a comparison between the results of the two studies. The second term is a fraction of the current deviation of inflation from the normal rate, $(\dot{p})_{t-1}^{D}$, as defined in equation (5.2). A complete adjustment of wages to prices in any given area, according to the natural unemployment rate hypothesis, would be reflected in a coefficient of one for the normal term. The coefficient for the partial convergence term is expected to be positive.

The relative wage variable, $(W_i/\overline{W})_{it-4}$, expresses the earnings rate in a metropolitan area at any given time as a proportion of the average earnings rate of the metropolitan areas in the region, which is assumed to have an influence upon the wages of its labour force. A suitable regionalization of the thirty-three areas was derived in the following manner. We have assumed that the purpose of this variable is to capture the influence of a wage-spread effect upon the determination of local wages. In previous studies this has been accomplished either by identifying a leading areal submarket or by establishing a region of influence. The former probably reflects too simplistic an assumption concerning the spatial interdependencies which exist in a complex, developed economy. The latter involves the definition of a suitable region of influence for each areal submarket. In the past this has been done either by assuming that all the submarkets in the sample under investigation constitute the region of influence (Marcis and Reed, 1974; Martin, 1978), or by allocating the submarkets to administrative or census regions (Mathur, 1976). In neither case have the regions been chosen according to criteria stemming from the processes which are either known or assumed to exist. King and Forster (1973) have introduced a potential interaction term into a submarket model of inflation, but this too was conditioned by some rather arbitrary groupings of cities which they had to make and by the functional form of the term.

Although it is likely that spatial proximity does play a part in wage-spread effects, there is enough evidence of the role of national wage bargaining, widespread interregional trade relationships, extensive job control by corporations, and so on, to suggest that it may not necessarily predominate among the various influences. Ideally what is needed is a knowledge of the functional and spatial relations among the various components in the economy, something that is obviously lacking at present. One could perhaps rely on various economic–geographic theories, such as theories of industrial location, spatial interaction, central places, and diffusion, to suggest a priori what form the functional–spatial relations should take, but these theories have not been sufficiently integrated to use them in this manner.

We have resorted to the research on models of the transmission of economic impulses through an urban system to determine regions of influence for each submarket in our sample. This research assumes that the unemployment rate (excess demand for labour in our context) in any given urban submarket is determined by structural factors which are limited to that particular submarket, together with nationally originating forces, and regionally originating forces (Brechling, 1967; Jeffrey, 1974; Jeffrey and Webb, 1972; King and Clark, 1978b). By using a quadratic function of time to represent the first component, and the national unemployment rate to represent the second, the third can be derived from the residuals, $(U_{it} - \hat{U}_{it})$, of the following equation:

$$U_{it} = b_{i0} + b_{i1}t + b_{i2}t^2 + b_{i3}U_t + \epsilon_{it} \,, \tag{5.3}$$

where U_{it} and U_t are local and national unemployment rates, and t is time. The coefficients of equation (5.3), in addition to three seasonal dummy variables, were estimated by an ordinary least squares procedure for each metropolitan area in our sample, using quarterly data for the period 1964–1978. A matrix of the residuals from these equations was then factor analyzed using the principal component model, and the scores for each metropolitan area on the first two factors were extracted. These two factors, which account for 53% of the total variance in the residual data, are characterized by some very distinct regions. The first factor highlights a polarization between metropolitan areas on the western and eastern extremes of the Sun Belt on the one hand, and areas in the centre on the other. The second factor simply distinguishes between areas in the western half of the Sun Belt with those in the eastern half. The details of this analysis are recorded elsewhere (Hanham and Chang, 1979a).

The scores from these factors were then used to create a single, mutually exclusive, grouping of the metropolitan areas by means of Casetti's discriminant iterations procedure (Casetti, 1964). A three-group solution was chosen (figure 5.1) and these results used to compute the relative wage variable. The groups serve as reasonably distinct and contiguous regions: one dominates the west of the Sun Belt, another the centre, and the third the east. Furthermore, they have been derived on the assumption that areas within any given region respond to similar regional economic forces or impulses. Institutional forces in the wage-determination process, such as the effect of wage-comparability bargaining, are therefore assumed to occur in the same spatial framework as that of the regional economic interdependencies between the various labour submarkets in the economy. If this variable captures the effect of wage adjustments made on the basis of comparison and regional spread effects, then its coefficient should be negative.

The wage-control variable, Z_t, represents the period from the fourth quarter of 1971 to the first quarter of 1974, during which the Economic Stabilization Program was in operation. It is a dichotomous dummy variable in which those quarters where wage controls were in effect are given the value of one, and the remaining quarters are given the value of zero.

A negative coefficient for this variable would be indicative of the fact that a given metropolitan area's wage inflation was effectively controlled.

5.4.1 Estimation and results

The coefficients of equation (5.1) were estimated by the Cochrane–Orcutt regression technique for each of the thirty-three metropolitan areas, and the results are given in table 5.2. The Durbin–Watson statistics range from 1.55 to 2.36, and clearly exceed the upper bound of the critical value at the 5% significance level, 1.77, in most cases. Since the lowest value for any of the metropolitan equations also exceeds the lower bound of 1.34, we can conclude that in no case does positive serial correlation definitely occur. Furthermore, there is no evidence of significant negative serial correlation. The level of explained variance ranges from 0.42 to 0.91, and this is comparable with Martin's results for the northeastern metropolitan areas. There is no very clear spatial trend in this measure, except that the model appears to be less suited to explaining wage adjustments in eastern areas, particularly in Florida, North Carolina, and South Carolina.

The effect of unemployment is extremely varied. Its coefficient is positive in only fourteen cases, and significantly so in six of these. Of the nineteen cases with negative coefficients, as many as ten are significantly different from zero. The spatial pattern of places with significant

Table 5.2. Coefficient estimates for equation (5.1). Time period: 1965(3)–1978(2) representing fifty-two cases.

Area	a_{i0}	a_{i1}	a_{i2}	a_{i3}	a_{i4}	a_{i5}	R^2	DW^a	ρ^b
1	50·49*	−22·86*	0·51*	0·38*	−36·96*	−0·06	0·86	1·95	0·22
	(12·18)	(7·62)	(0·17)	(0·18)	(9·51)	(0·76)			
2	75·08*	−57·36*	0·62*	0·46*	−55·03*	0·26	0·75	1·85	0·43
	(16·87)	(16·34)	(0·17)	(0·27)	(14·24)	(0·87)			
3	86·97*	−22·07*	0·90*†	0·54*	−87·57*	1·61*	0·83	1·56	0·57
	(18·29)	(7·79)	(0·24)	(0·24)	(18·91)	(0·83)			
4	57·68*	−30·12*	−0·01	0·91*	−45·32*	−0·64	0·79	1·68	0·83
	(16·01)	(14·96)	(0·52)	(0·43)	(15·32)	(1·27)			
5	11·27	−12·51	0·32*	0·16	−4·66	−0·57	0·85	1·55	0·60
	(7·36)	(9·34)	(0·14)	(0·13)	(6·99)	(0·45)			
6	114·20*	−13·50	0·60	−0·08	−107·15*	−1·22	0·78	1·93	0·86
	(25·30)	(26·26)	(0·39)	(0·32)	(23·81)	(1·03)			
7	39·64*	14·72*	0·13	−0·67*	−34·74*	−1·72*	0·84	1·95	0·49
	(9·88)	(7·54)	(0·12)	(0·14)	(9·80)	(0·48)			
8	90·14*	−11·52	0·56	−0·57	−73·93*	2·23	0·68	1·78	0·61
	(23·52)	(11·55)	(0·51)	(0·49)	(18·15)	(1·71)			
9	45·39*	36·68*	0·55	0·35	−57·90*	1·12	0·58	2·27	0·66
	(12·82)	(16·33)	(0·48)	(0·40)	(16·12)	(1·47)			
10	51·58*	6·74*	0·62*	0·29	−48·29*	−0·58	0·58	1·95	0·23
	(15·57)	(3·42)	(0·16)	(0·24)	(15·00)	(0·70)			
11	106·75*	17·16*	0·13	−1·24*	−90·21*	0·59	0·76	1·92	0·26
	(18·33)	(6·09)	(0·26)	(0·24)	(15·11)	(0·83)			

Table 5.2 (continued)

Area	a_{i0}	a_{i1}	a_{i2}	a_{i3}	a_{i4}	a_{i5}	R^2	DW^a	ρ^b
12	149·69*	−14·77	0·82	0·16	−108·50*	5·63	0·61	2·22	0·47
	(20·19)	(48·45)	(0·87)	(0·99)	(13·79)	(3·73)			
13	98·49*	13·00	−0·08	−0·03	−84·67*	−2·35*	0·86	2·36	0·96
	(17·12)	(15·54)	(0·31)	(0·23)	(15·75)	(0·78)			
14	114·36*	−30·99*	0·74*†	0·91*	−109·70*	0·27	0·82	1·98	0·30
	(15·92)	(7·72)	(0·21)	(0·18)	(16·29)	(0·79)			
15	116·89*	−74·77*	0·13	1·29*	−111·90*	−1·32	0·91	2·06	0·49
	(8·57)	(9·59)	(0·18)	(0·26)	(8·90)	(0·82)			
16	104·68*	75·60*	0·16	−0·08	−127·50*	−0·82	0·71	1·85	0·67
	(18·20)	(36·89)	(0·58)	(0·55)	(20·61)	(1·90)			
17	69·54*	2·38	−0·34*	−0·35*	−69·54*	0·35	0·70	2·06	0·47
	(11·18)	(3·37)	(0·12)	(0·18)	(12·63)	(0·67)			
18	83·04*	−3·03	−0·06	0·22	−79·27*	0·23	0·64	2·07	0·82
	(18·02)	(7·95)	(0·43)	(0·31)	(19·65)	(1·02)			
19	44·25*	−6·79	0·94*†	0·30	−42·37*	1·84*	0·75	2·07	0·52
	(17·95)	(9·94)	(0·19)	(0·22)	(17·19)	(0·70)			
20	57·54*	1·64	0·84*†	0·38	−52·42*	−0·71	0·83	2·21	0·70
	(18·37)	(13·26)	(0·26)	(0·27)	(16·85)	(0·85)			
21	81·03*	2·17	−0·05	0·28	−77·37*	−2·36	0·61	2·01	0·63
	(17·31)	(27·52)	(0·52)	(0·53)	(18·81)	(1·74)			
22	91·49*	−1·79	0·25	0·27	−97·59*	−1·52*	0·69	1·95	0·63
	(17·32)	(6·02)	(0·23)	(0·29)	(19·32)	(0·89)			
23	40·70*	−8·24	0·02	0·11	−33·29*	0·54	0·42	1·89	0·42
	(13·64)	(10·48)	(0·23)	(0·25)	(15·59)	(0·76)			
24	130·95*	−49·53*	−0·09	1·32*	−107·40*	1·81*	0·73	2·01	0·31
	(21·80)	(9·91)	(0·22)	(0·29)	(19·84)	(0·84)			
25	55·81*	−33·29*	−0·52*	0·63*	−37·32*	−2·93*	0·78	2·11	0·58
	(13·29)	(10·42)	(0·30)	(0·29)	(13·79)	(0·90)			
26	58·79*	−20·28*	0·53*†	0·91*	−49·26*	3·01*	0·59	1·85	0·40
	(18·80)	(10·27)	(0·29)	(0·33)	(18·90)	(1·02)			
27	46·82*	−17·77*	0·48*	0·42*	−31·02*	−0·76	0·90	1·94	0·60
	(18·08)	(4·88)	(0·18)	(0·17)	(14·63)	(0·62)			
28	67·68*	11·42	0·89*†	0·41	−87·27*	−1·09	0·78	2·04	0·53
	(15·37)	(10·61)	(0·21)	(0·25)	(21·01)	(0·76)			
29	73·57*	11·25	1·62*†	−0·22	−96·57*	2·61*	0·70	2·10	0·56
	(14·43)	(8·70)	(0·39)	(0·43)	(17·81)	(1·55)			
30	35·11*	4·30	0·83*†	−0·80*	−24·13*	−0·66	0·83	2·09	0·81
	(18·29)	(21·60)	(0·37)	(0·42)	(11·76)	(1·25)			
31	80·76*	8·44	0·40*	−0·79*	−68·96*	0·34	0·85	1·85	0·40
	(18·56)	(10·70)	(0·22)	(0·22)	(16·18)	(0·84)			
32	97·37*	−32·98	1·36*†	0·22	−127·68*	−1·86	0·72	2·03	0·61
	(21·72)	(26·32)	(0·62)	(0·67)	(25·53)	(2·36)			
33	83·33*	11·66*	0·54*	0·54*	−85·48*	−0·52	0·83	1·93	0·51
	(11·71)	(4·41)	(0·16)	(0·21)	(12·72)	(0·71)			

* Significantly different from zero at the 0·10% level.
† Not significantly different from one at the 0·10% level.
^{a} DW is the Durbin–Watson statistic.
^{b} ρ is the first-order serial correlation coefficient.
Standard errors are shown in parentheses.

coefficients is reasonably distinct, with those having negative signs over-
whelmingly concentrated in an area either side of the Mississippi, and
those with positive signs widely dispersed to the west and east of it
(figure 5.2). These results suggest that very little confidence can be placed
in the traditional role of excess demand for labour in determining wages in
the Sun Belt. In fact, it is more common to find the reverse of the
traditional relationship and that stagflation has become the norm. Evidence
from the northeastern part of the country suggests that there the relationship remained either in the traditional form or that the two were independent
during the 1960s and the early 1970s (Martin, 1978). Those findings
probably stem from the fact that Martin included the first half of the
1960s in his analysis, a period during which unemployment and wage
changes were clearly inversely related. The reversal of this relationship
took place in the second half of the 1960s, which is when our time series
begins. It is not really possible to say, therefore, that there is a basic
difference between north and south with respect to this aspect of the wage-
adjustment process.

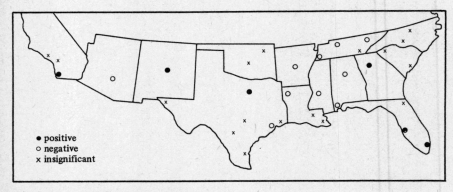

Figure 5.2. Unemployment coefficients.

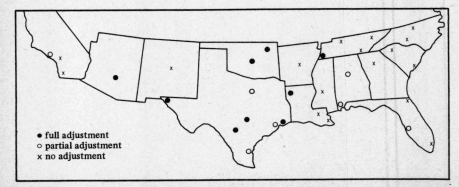

Figure 5.3. The normal rate term of inflationary expectations.

Inflationary expectations are also spatially concentrated in their effect. Twenty-six of the metropolitan areas have positive coefficients for the normal inflation term, sixteen of them being significantly different from zero. In half of the cases, therefore, wages have adjusted to price inflation in this region, but in only nine have they adjusted fully in the sense that their normal inflation term has a coefficient which is both significantly different from zero and not significantly different from one. Most of these areas are located in the centre of the Sun Belt (figure 5.3). The partial convergence term is significant and positive in only a third of the cases. But it is rather interesting to note that these metropolitan areas correspond very closely with those in which stagflation was significantly present (figure 5.4).

The wage-spread-effect variable is significant and negative in all but one case, that of Los Angeles which is negative and insignificant, and it is easily the dominant influence in our model. The extent of the influence varies a great deal throughout the Sun Belt, and spatial patterns are not easy to discern in these results (figure 5.5). The coefficients for this variable tend

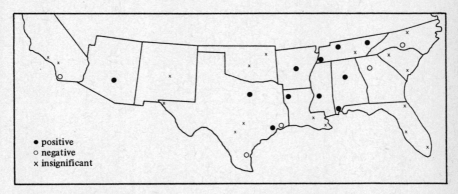

Figure 5.4. Coefficients for the convergence term of inflationary expectations.

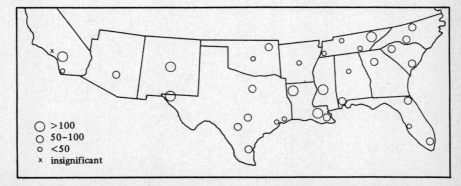

Figure 5.5. Absolute value of the coefficients for the wage-spread-effect variable.

to be greater in the western region of influence (which includes Los
Angeles; see figure 5.1). Unlike Martin's (1978) results, however, ours do
not indicate that the role of this variable is greater in those areas
characterized by partial adjustment to inflationary expectations. If
anything, it appears to be the reverse situation. The average spread-effect
coefficient for areas which have fully adjusted is significantly greater than
the average for those which have only partially adjusted, on the basis of a
t-test at the $0 \cdot 10\%$ level of significance. If one includes those areas with
insignificant coefficients in the partial adjustment group, on the other
hand, there is no significant difference. Our results therefore indicate that
those areas which benefit more strongly from wage-spread effects also tend
to be those which are more likely to adjust fully to inflationary expectations.
It could be that the latter depends on the former.

On the assumption that it is an acceptable method of representing the
effect of wage controls, the results for this variable show how inadequate
this national policy was in the Sun Belt. In only four cases is the
coefficient for this dummy variable significant and negative, whereas in
five cases it is actually significant and positive. If we ignore the issue of
statistical significance, it appears that this policy was less effective in
stabilizing wage changes in those metropolitan areas which are east of the
Mississippi than in those to the west (figure 5.6). Since wages were
already the lowest, and the labour force least unionized, in the southeast
part of the country, this is not an unreasonable finding.

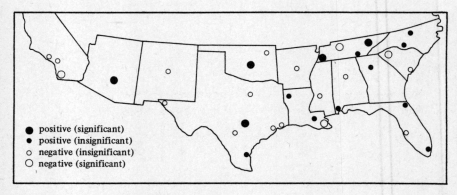

Figure 5.6. Wage-control coefficients.

5.5 Conclusions
The period 1965–1978 was characterized by persistently high and,
frequently, accelerating rates of inflation in the US economy. During this
time a number of events, both national and international in origin, occurred
which appear to have altered the decisionmaking process that underlies the
determination of wages. The traditional role of supply–demand imbalances,
in particular, appears to have diminished in importance, and may even have

become irrelevant in certain sectors of the economy. This period was also noteworthy for the distinct shift in regional economic growth and development that took place in the United States from the north to the Sun Belt. Although this shift had, to the extent of narrowing wage differentials, been happening for some time, it was not until the late 1960s and early 1970s that the striking change in industrial structure in the Sun Belt occurred. Much of the stimulus for this change came from the extensive federal spending in the region, which had reached a particularly high level at this time. It seems quite likely, therefore, that both of these major changes in the US economy, the alteration of the wage decisionmaking process and the regional shift in economic development, substantially resulted from federal (national level) actions.

When applied to thirty-three metropolitan areas within the Sun Belt, our submarket wage model generally performs well in explaining wage-rate changes during the time period 1965–1978. The explained variance is above 50% in all but one case, and above 75% in nineteen cases. Concerning the role of the excess demand for labour, our results do more than simply reinforce those of others over the past few years that have suggested that it is relatively minor, they indicate that a significant reversal of this relationship has taken place. Stagflation is apparently the norm in this region, and particularly so in the centre of it. But another striking fact about these results is their variability among submarkets. There does not appear to be a simple relation between the role played by the excess demand term and the level of excess demand for labour in a submarket, but at least in six of them demand pressure for labour does have its traditional effect on wage-rate changes. This variability could be partially due to the growth in submarket labour force. Submarkets in which demand pressure acts in the traditional Phillips curve manner are characterized by much higher than average net migration rates. Deviations from this relation might then be the result of variations in the occupational status of the expanding work force. In any case, the significant differences in the role of demand pressure between submarkets in the Sun Belt are quite striking, particularly in comparison to the relative uniformity that appears to exist in parts of the north.

Only half of the submarkets in our sample significantly adjusted to inflationary expectations, and less than a third of them did so fully. In general, then, this factor is far less important than apparently is the case in the north (for example, as in Martin, 1978). Its effect is concentrated in centrally located submarkets of the Sun Belt, and particularly in Oklahoma and Texas. What is more, full adjustment tends to take place in submarkets which are more responsive to wage-spread effects, leading to the supposition that the former may to some extent depend upon the latter process. Partial convergence is even less important a determinant of wages in the Sun Belt, but it too seems to be associated with another factor, that of demand pressure for labour. Specifically, it is a significant influence in submarkets characterized by stagflation. Whether a regional policy to control the latter could be effected through the former is open to question and further research. A further issue concerning the inflationary expectations term involves the use of a national consumer price index. Not only is it more plausible that workers try to adjust their wages to local price levels, but it presumably would be more pertinent to use the latter in any consideration of inflationary expectations as a tool of regional policy. Unfortunately, these types of data are restricted to less than thirty submarkets within the entire country, but even from these data it is clear that a great deal of spatial variation exists both in the level of prices and in their change over time.

Spread effects are the dominant influence in determining wage changes in our sample, being significant and having the correct sign in all but one submarket. The results indicate that, on the basis of the way in which the relative wage variable was derived, these spread effects can take place within discrete clusters of metropolitan areas whose economies have been shown to be similar in terms of their susceptibility to regional economic forces. Although this does not yet explicitly involve a given process of spread, the spread-effect factor that we have incorporated in the model is suggestive of the spatial context within which the particular process or processes occur. In the Sun Belt the role of union bargaining is unlikely to be very large in this process, owing to the generally very low level of unionization of the labour force throughout the area. From our own experience, however, we feel that the role of regional reference groups is probably very important, and it may be that geographical (and other) diffusion theory could make a contribution to our understanding of this process. Two problems with the spread-effect factor that we have chosen certainly need to be looked into: one concerns the use of mutually exclusive groups rather than, more realistically, overlapping ones, and the other concerns the temporal stability of the groups—an assumption that is probably quite unrealistic.

The national policy of wage controls from 1971 to 1974 had little impact in the Sun Belt, and what impact there was varied both regionally and directionally. It was marginally less effective in the southeast, and this can be attributed to the levels of unionization and average wages in the area. If it was successful at all, it was probably more so in the more heavily unionized northeast and upper midwest. Whether there resulted a form of spread effect from unionized to nonunionized sectors has already been doubted in other research (Vroman and Vroman, 1979). Although we did not specifically test for a spatial spread effect from unionized to nonunionized areas, our results do not appear to support one. On the other hand, it might be worth investigating the possibility of accomplishing the control of wages by means of a policy which operates through the wage-spread-effect process.

The economic development and growth of the Sun Belt in recent years has obviously helped to stimulate a spatial redistribution of wealth within the United States. But it may well also have helped to aggravate national inflation because of the increase in the spatial variation in demand pressure for labour that it has caused (Hanham and Chang, 1979b). What is more, the Sun Belt persists as the major net gainer in federal spending and private investment in the country at the end of the 1970s. Although there are some common elements in the wage-determination process to be found throughout the Sun Belt, a more striking characteristic is its variability among submarkets. This may contrast with a more uniform process in the generally depressed economy of the north, but that is a question currently being investigated.

One further issue with which we have not dealt concerns the structure of the wage model. Martin (1978) has already shown that the effectiveness of a model such as ours, particularly in terms of its forecasting ability, can be seriously undermined by temporal instability in the estimates of its parameters. Furthermore, there has been frequent criticism of the fact that most models of the type that we have used are expressed as single equations, and that this is too simplistic a representation of what is clearly a complex process. These are both valid grounds for being sceptical of the usefulness of the type of model presented in this paper, and certainly point out a further research need in this area.

Acknowledgement. We are grateful to the National Science Foundation for funding this research through grant number SOC 77-07076.

References

Archibald G C, 1969 "The Phillips curve and the distribution of unemployment" *American Economic Review, Papers and Proceedings* **59** 124–134

Beyers W B, 1979 "Contemporary trends in the regional economic development of the United States" *Professional Geographer* **31** 34–44

Brechling F P R, 1967 "Trends and cycles in British regional unemployment" *Oxford Economic Papers* **19** 1–21

Brechling F P R, 1973 "Wage inflation and the structure of regional unemployment" *Journal of Money, Credit, and Banking* **5** 355–379

Brinner R E, 1977 "The death of the Phillips curve reconsidered" *Quarterly Journal of Economics* **91** 389–418

Business Week, 1976 "The second war between the states" May 92–113

Casetti E, 1964 "Classificatory and regional analysis by discriminant iterations" TR-12, Computer Applications in the Earth Sciences Project, Department of Geography, Northwestern University, Evanston, Ill.

Clark G L, 1978a "Critical problems of geographical wage and unemployment models" Urban Planning, Policy Analysis, and Administration D78-33, Harvard University, Cambridge, Mass

Clark G L, 1978b "A simple model of regional stagnation" Urban Planning, Policy Analysis, and Administration D78-28, Harvard University, Cambridge, Mass

Coelho P, Ghali M, 1971 "The end of the north–south wage differential" *American Economic Review* **61** 932–938

Cowling K, Metcalf D, 1967 "Wage–unemployment relationships: a regional analysis for the U.K., 1960–1965" *Bulletin of the Oxford Institute of Economics and Statistics* **29** 31–40

Cripps F, 1977 "The money supply, wages and inflation" *Cambridge Journal of Economics* **1** 101–112

Darby M R, 1976 "The U.S. Economic Stabilization Program of 1971–1974" in *The Illusion of Wage and Price Control* Ed. M Walker, Fraser Institute, Victoria, BC, Canada pp 135–159

Flemming J S, 1978 "The economic explanation of inflation" in *The Political Economy of Inflation* Eds F Hirsch, J H Goldthorpe (Martin Robertson, London) pp 13–36

Hanham R Q, Chang H, 1979a "Metropolitan unemployment components and wage inflation in the United States Sun Belt", unpublished paper, Department of Geography, University of Oklahoma, Norman, Okla

Hanham R Q, Chang H, 1979b "Unemployment dispersion, wage controls, and national wage inflation in the U.S.", unpublished paper, Department of Geography, University of Oklahoma, Norman, Okla

Hewings G J D, 1978 "The trade-off between aggregate national efficiency and inter-regional equity: some recent empirical evidence" *Economic Geography* **54** 254–263

Jeffrey D, 1974 "Regional fluctuations in unemployment within the U.S. urban economic system: a study of the spatial impact of short term economic change" *Economic Geography* **50** 111–123

Jeffrey D, Webb D J, 1972 "Economic fluctuations in the Australian regional system" *Australian Geographical Studies* **10** 141–160

King L J, Clark G L, 1978a "Government policy and regional development" *Progress in Human Geography* **2** 1–16

King L J, Clark G L, 1978b "Regional unemployment patterns and the spatial dimensions of macro-economic policy: the Canadian experience 1966–75" *Regional Studies* **12** 283–296

King L J, Forster J, 1973 "Wage rate change in urban labour markets and inter-market linkages" *Papers, Regional Science Association* **34** 183–196

Lipsey R G, 1960 "The relation between unemployment and the rate of change of money wage rates in the United Kingdom, 1862–1957: a further analysis" *Economica* **27** 1–13

Maher J E, 1961 "The wage pattern in the United States" *Industrial and Labour Relations Review* **15** 1–20

Marcis R G, Reed J D, 1974 "Joint estimation of the determinants of wages in sub-regional labour markets in the United States: 1961–72" *Journal of Regional Science* **14** 259–267

Martin R L, 1978 "Subregional Phillips curves, inflationary expectations, and the intermarket relative wage structure: substance and methodology" in *Statistical Applications in the Spatial Sciences* Ed. N Wrigley (Pion, London) pp 65–110

Mathur V K, 1976 "The relation between rate of change of money wage rates and unemployment in local labour markets: some new evidence" *Journal of Regional Science* **16** 389–398

Miller R J, 1978 *The Regional Impact of Monetary Policy in the United States* (Lexington Books, D C Heath, Lexington, Mass)

Morrill R L, 1979 "Stages in patterns of population concentration and dispersion" *Professional Geographer* **31** 55–65

Norton R D, Rees J, 1979 "The product cycle and the spatial decentralization of American manufacturing" *Regional Studies* **13** 141–151

Okun A M, 1977 "The great stagflation swamp" *The Brookings Bulletin* **14**(3) 1–7

Okun A M, 1979 "An efficient strategy to combat inflation" *The Brookings Bulletin* **15**(3) 1–5

Reed J D, Hutchinson P M, 1976 "An empirical test of a regional Phillips curve and wage rate transmission mechanism in an urban hierarchy" *Annals of Regional Science* **10** 19–30

Rees J, 1979 "Technological change and regional shifts in American manufacturing" *Professional Geographer* **31** 45–54

Shapiro H T, 1977 "Inflation in the United States" in *Worldwide Inflation: Theory and Recent Experience* Eds L B Krause, W S Salant, The Brookings Institution, Washington, DC, pp 267–294

Taylor J, 1970 "Hidden unemployment, hoarded labour, and the Phillips curve" *Southern Economic Journal* **37** 1–16

Thirlwall A P, 1970 "Regional Phillips curves" *Bulletin of the Oxford Institute of Economics and Statistics* **32** 19–32

Thomas R L, Stoney P J M, 1971 "Unemployment dispersion as a determinant of wage inflation in the U.K., 1925–1966" *The Manchester School of Economic and Social Studies* June 83–116

US Department of Labor *Consumer Price Index* (various issues)

US Department of Labor *Employment and Earnings* (various issues)

US Department of Labor *Area Trends in Employment and Unemployment* (various issues)

Vroman S, Vroman W, 1979 "Money wage changes: before, during and after controls" *Southern Economic Journal* **45** 1172–1187

Watkins A J, Perry D C, 1977 "Regional change and the impact of uneven urban development" in *The Rise of the Sunbelt Cities* Eds D C Perry, A J Watkins (Sage Publications, London) pp 14–29

Weissbrod R, 1976 "Diffusion of relative wage inflation in southeast Pennsylvania" *Studies in Geography, 23*, Northwestern University, Evanston, Ill.

Wage-change interdependence amongst regional labour markets: conceptual issues and some empirical evidence for the United States [†]

R L Martin

6.1 Introduction

A central concept in the theoretical and empirical analysis of the labour market is that of 'wage structure', for the term refers not just to an array of intermarket (occupational, industrial, geographical) wage differentials, but also to the adjustment mechanisms presumed to determine the relative wage distribution and hence by implication the development of wages over time [1]. Copious evidence indicates that interindustry pay relativities in advanced capitalist economies exhibit a high degree of rank-order stability over periods of a decade or more, especially within the manufacturing sector (Cullen, 1956; OECD, 1965; Leiserson, 1966; UN, 1967; Papola and Bharadwaj, 1970; Godley, 1977), with this stability being more pronounced for earnings than for basic wage rates (UN, 1967, page 26). It is also a well-known fact, both within the UK and the USA for example, that the interregional (or interurban) wages hierarchy changes but slowly over time, despite persistent geographical differences in unemployment (Reynolds and Taft, 1956; Thirlwall, 1970; Brechling, 1973; MacKay and Hart, 1975; Martin, 1979). General stability of the regional earnings structure implies that whereas local wage movements may diverge in the short term, there are processes that operate to maintain the traditional configuration from one time period to the next, and which link wage changes in one market in some way with those in another [2]. Typically, empirical studies of wage interdependence have examined interactions among industrial sectors (for example, Mehra, 1976) or between the unionised and nonunionised segments of the labour force (for example, Flanagan, 1976; Johnson, 1977). Recently, however, increasing attention has been directed to wage-change interdependence among regional and subregional labour markets (for example, Thomas and Stoney, 1971;

[†] This is a revised version of a paper presented to the Twelfth Annual Conference of the British Section of the Regional Science Association held at University College, London in September, 1980.

[1] For one of the original discussions of the need to consider relative wage movements in the study of wage inflation, see Dunlop (1939).

[2] Evidence that distortions of the wage structure set in motion mechanisms that act to restore the initial pattern has been adduced in studies both of interindustry wage dynamics in the aggregate economy (for example, Packer and Park, 1973) and of intraoccupational wages within individual urban labour markets (for example, Butler and Kim, 1973).

Brechling, 1973; King and Forster, 1973; Reed and Hutchinson, 1976; Weissbrod, 1976; Hart and MacKay, 1977; Martin, 1979).

Two themes can be identified in this recent work: that dealing with the nature of the interregional wage-transfer process itself, and that concerned with the effect of regional wage interaction on macroeconomic wage adjustment. In economics, the emphasis, certainly in the earlier work, has been on the second of these themes, with questions being couched in terms of the implications of aggregating regional submodels into a national wage equation, the regional adjustment process being viewed simply as a special case of the more general multimarket framework found in the economic literature on wage inflation. Geographical studies, on the other hand, have tended to focus more on identifying the various external and internal factors which impinge on individual regional and subregional labour markets, in an attempt to elucidate the 'spatial linkages' involved. Unfortunately, this work has been somewhat restricted by its explicit or implicit appeal to rather rigid and conventional concepts of spatial economic structure and process, such as central place theory and spatial diffusion theory. Moreover, both branches of enquiry appear to have put most stress on the role of competitive pressures in regional wage determination, and have given insufficient consideration to 'noneconomic' or institutional forces, which frequently cut across the geographical boundaries by which data are organised.

The subsequent sections pursue this subject of regional wage-change interdependence. First, the principal mechanisms of wage determination that might be invoked to account for regional wage interdependence are discussed, and certain features of a simplified interregional 'wage-wage'-inflation process briefly outlined. Then, in section 6.3, we shall examine the notion that a dualism exists in the regional structure of wage determination in that one or more 'leading' regions set the pace of wage inflation in the economy. In the light of this discussion of the 'regional wage leadership' hypothesis, we proceed in sections 6.4 and 6.5 to an analysis of wage-change interaction amongst the major regions of the United States, using the patterns of regional segmentation within the US economy as the basis of a simple statistical model of regional wage-change interdependence in the country's manufacturing sector over the period 1960–1978. The chapter concludes with some brief comments on the policy implications of regional wage-change interdependence.

6.2 Mechanisms of interregional wage adjustment
Two broad sets of views have been advanced to account for the apparent interdependence of wage changes across the national labour market. One is the market theory or competitive hypothesis, the other is what has been called institutional. According to the competitive view, the transmission of inflationary impulses occurs through the medium of market forces.

Strictly, of course, neoclassical wage theory is specified in real rather than nominal terms, but it is straightforward to derive corollary proportions about the intersectoral transfer of nominal wage changes by assuming, perhaps not unrealistically, that all labour-market participants hold the same expectations about changes in the aggregate price level. The competitive theory assumes that the supply of labour to any sector of the labour market (occupation, firm, industry, or region) depends on the (real) wage offered in that sector relative to the (real) wage in other, comparable sectors, and that workers make such comparisons in arriving at their (net advantage-maximising) supply decisions. Failure on the part of any firm to meet and maintain customary wage relativities will give rise, therefore, to voluntary job-quitting by employees, who leave to move to or search for higher wage offers in other firms, sectors, and localities. If sustained, this outflow of workers will compel the low-wage firms to match wage changes elsewhere so as to restore their relative wage positions in the industry's or local labour-market's wage structure in order to maintain their desired labour forces (see Pissarides, 1976; pages 232–244). Under this approach, wherein "potential mobility is the ultimate sanction for the interrelation of wage rates" (Hicks, 1963, page 79), wages will move in like fashion across different regional labour markets as a result of intermarket supply shifts manifested by actual or threatened migration of labour in response to changes in the relative net advantages of the various markets. This interpretation fuses labour mobility and wage adjustment into a single problem: the behaviour of the intermarket wage structure is a major determinant of labour movement amongst occupations, firms, and regions, and in turn the wage structure is shaped by the actual or potential mobility of labour.

Short-run divergence of regional wage movements would, presumably, be explained in terms of incomplete information on, or lags and frictions in the adjustment of workers and employers to, what wages elsewhere are and how they are drifting. This is, after all, a central postulate of the 'island parable' model of the labour market to be found in the new microeconomic-cum-monetarist version of the competitive theory. It is also postulated by this approach, however, that in the long run, expectations are correctly adaptive, so that as uncertainty dissolves through observation of market reaction, and barriers to mobility are overcome, an equilibrium situation is postulated with wages changing at the same rate across local labour markets, a state in which wage rates on average are found—over space and over time—to be what they were expected to be (Phelps and others, 1970, page 8). A similar market-equilibrium interpretation follows from Friedman's (1975) proposition that it is the expected *real* wage rather than the expected *relative* wage that adjusts to competitive pressures. In this case, if each local labour market in the space economy faces similar price changes, and if the latter are aggregated over a similar vector of commodities, then regional and subregional wage changes may be kept in line by similar reactions to expected changes in the national cost-of-living index (see Williamson, 1975; Martin, 1979). Proponents of the competitive approach, in whichever specific form, admit that pay norms, collective bargaining, and unions and other monopolies exist in the modern labour market, but contend that such factors contribute no separate prevailing influence. To quote Hicks again:

"Demands for a rise in wages come in the first place because a rise appears to be 'fair'. And the principal motive in an employer's mind when he concedes such a rise may be a desire that his wage policy should not appear to be an 'unfair' one. But although this appears to be the motive for a very large proportion of wage changes, it is not their real reason. These rules of fairness and justice are simply rough-and-ready guides whereby the working of demand and supply is anticipated" (Hicks, 1963, page 80).

In contrast, adherents of the institutionalist model of the labour market maintain that ideas of fairness and equity concerning pay relativities constitute the most important feature of wage interdependence and contagion. It is argued that wage-inflation impulses are transmitted from one submarket to another not through the operation of market forces, but because wages perform certain social and political functions. They define relationships between groups of workers, and amongst institutional and organisational entities such as different unions, the locals in a national union, the various branch plants in a company, or the main employers in an industry or region. The thrust of money-wage transmission derives from a process of equitable comparisons and parity-bargaining between different groups of workers, all anxious about (and sometimes with inconsistent aspirations concerning) their relative rates of pay[3]. The terminology used to describe this form of wage determination has varied considerably: pattern-bargaining, wage-contour mechanism, coercive comparison, demonstration effect, spillover, key bargains, earnings spread, and wage leadership[4]. Nevertheless, all analyses of this type agree upon one central issue, that the wage change in any sector or submarket is determined to a large extent by the political comparisons that participants in that sector—workers, unions, and employers—make with wage movements

---

[3] The idea that labour does not exist separately from groups of individuals who are all trying to defend and improve their relative wage positions was first suggested by Keynes (1936, pages 14, 264). More recently, others have taken this concept further, arguing that a condition of leap-frogging wage claims generated by intergroup rivalries has resulted in a nondamped, endogenous 'wage-wage' spiral that is a major cause of the 'new' inflation of the contemporary era (for example, Tobin, 1972; Wiles, 1973; Mitchell, 1977).

[4] Seltzer (1951), Levinson (1960; 1962), Snodgrass (1963), Dunlop (1957), Ross (1957), Maher (1961), Eckstein and Wilson (1962), McGuire and Rapping (1968); Mulvey and Trevithick (1974), Mehra (1976), Burton and Addison (1977).

in some other, reference sector(s). Such 'institutional' or normative wage-setting forces serve to disjoin the wage and job markets (Kerr, 1977, pages 42–44). Workers move into, out of, and between employments largely within spatially restricted job markets, but the orbits of parity-bargaining may be spatially quite extensive: they are the spheres of influence of the policies of employer and employee organisations, of custom and convention[5]. According to this second view, then, the space economy may be pictured as a patchwork of interlocking wage contours or orbits of comparison, within which there are traditional wage relationships both among different groups within a given regional labour market and among similar groups of workers across regions. The shape of the pattern of such wage relationships may to some degree be arbitrary, the outcome of historical accident. But these relationships will also be governed by other more conventional economic demarcation lines, such as the input-output nexus of industries; their economic, organisational, and technological constitution; their geographical location; the variations across industries and regions in the degree of unionisation of the work force; and the different forms of bargaining structure—whether centralised or decentralised, connective or competitive, single employer or multiemployer, etc (Ulman, 1974).

A wage increase in a given sector, whether the result of market pressures or institutional forces, may thus trigger off a series of pattern-following wage claims that spread out across the national labour market along these orbits of comparison as workers seek to establish a new equilibrium (Rein and Marris, 1975; Piore, 1978). Individual regional submarkets will tend to respond to pressures which are largely external to their own specific supply and demand conditions, particularly during periods of slack demand. Under conditions of buoyant demand, different groups of workers in different regions may attempt with varying success to pursue autonomous wage claims. As Lerner and Marquand (1963, pages 290–291) put it:

"Increases in earnings in industrial groups which are growing fast lead to pressures for increases in groups which are growing more slowly: increases in one works of a company create pressures for increases on grounds of 'comparability' or to restore 'fair relativities' in the region where the works are, in works of the company elsewhere, and hence in other regions. A relatively low level of demand for labour is not

[5] This point was stressed by Ross (1948, page 53) when defining his concept of 'orbits of coercive comparison':
"The buyer and seller of labour do meet within some fixed geographical area, but the price at which the exchange takes place is often determined by other agencies hundreds of miles away, without necessary knowledge or concern for each of the particular markets affected by the bargain. Locality, an essential characteristic of the labour market so far as supply and demand are concerned, is of limited relevance for wage determination".

sufficient to prevent increases in earnings on grounds of comparability with earnings in other regions with a high level of demand for labour. Consequently, in most regions there is little direct connection between the level of earnings and the demand for labour. Only where excess demand for labour is particularly strong—perhaps above a certain threshold level—does it exert a direct upward pressure on earnings. Where the excess demand is less great, the effect of institutional factors upon earnings is predominant ... . Although similarity of earnings is never completely achieved, the whole inter-regional, inter-industry, and inter-works earnings structure shifts upward independently of the strength of the excess demand for labour in most parts of the market."

Institutional forces, both informal (custom and convention) and formal (codified collective bargaining) may be expected to moderate short-run market behaviour and maintain wages from year to year in closer correspondence with the long-run equilibria than would result under the competitive hypothesis taken by itself.

Assume then, for simplicity, that for any given regional labour market the proportionate rate of increase in money wages can be viewed as the sum of a 'spillover-induced' component, arising from direct equity comparisons and pattern-following, and a 'market-induced' component deriving from demand–supply pressures in the region, local productivity growth, changes in the cost-of-living, etc. The relative importance of these two components will vary over time and from one region to another. Tobin (1972) refers to spillover-induced wage change as the 'equilibrium' component, being that rate of wage increase in the absence of excess demand or excess supply. If the spillover process took place in a perfectly general way, each pay group reacting to a greater or lesser extent to the changing position of other groups, we might formalise the resultant regional wage-change interdependence as follows. Let a_{ij} denote a coefficient expressing the degree of pattern-following dependency of wage increases in region i on those of region j. If workers in region i do not refer to wage developments of workers in region j when making their own wage demands, then $a_{ij} = 0$. As pay groups in region i attempt to match any increase in wages of pay groups in region j, then a_{ij} will tend to a value of unity. If the term z_i represents the combined influence of the market forces which affect wage movements in region i, then adding this market-induced, or what Tobin (1972) calls 'disequilibrium', component, the overall proportionate growth in money wages in the ith region at time t may be expressed as

$$\dot{w}_{it} = \sum_{k=0}^{h} \sum_{j=1}^{n} a_{ij,k} \dot{w}_{jt-k} + z_{it} , \tag{6.1}$$

for all i (= 1, ..., n) regions, where $i \neq j$ for $k = 0$, and h is the time horizon of the wage-transfer mechanism.

This system can alternatively be represented in matrix form as

$$\dot{w}_t = \sum_{k=0}^{h} A_k \dot{w}_{t-k} + z_t , \tag{6.2}$$

where $\dot{w}_t$ is the n-vector of regional wage changes, z_t the n-vector of market-induced components of regional wage movements, and where the $n \times n$ array of spillover coefficients, A_k, is the 'wage-pattern matrix' of the multiregion system. Tobin (1972, page 12) describes the structure of such a matrix in the following terms:

> "Reference standards for wages differ from market to market. The equilibrium wage increase in each market will be some function of past increases in all markets and perhaps of past prices too. But the function need not be the same in every market. Wages of workers contiguous in geography, industry and skill will be heavily weighted. Imagine a wage pattern matrix of coefficients describing the dependence of the percentage equilibrium wage increase in each market on the past increases in all other markets. The coefficients in each row are non-negative and sum to one, but the distribution across markets and time lags will differ from row to row."

If the multiregional wage-inflation process can be depicted in the form shown in the expression (6.2), it is evident that the time paths and general stability of interregional wage inflation depend essentially on the structural characteristics of the wage-pattern matrix.

Assume for simplicity, but without any loss of generality, that the process has a one-period lag, that is

$$\dot{w}_t = A\dot{w}_{t-1} + z_t , \tag{6.3}$$

or equivalently

$$\dot{w}_t = A^t \dot{w}_0 + \sum_{k=1}^{t} A^{t-k} z_k , \tag{6.4}$$

where $\dot{w}_0$ is the vector of regional rates of wage change at some initial period. Consider some of the properties of this system in the absence of disequilibrium wage movements (all z's are zero). If the process is stable, regional wage-inflation rates will all converge towards a zero steady-state value. Since the matrix A is assumed to be nonnegative ($a_{ij} \geqslant 0$), a set of sufficient stability conditions can be stated directly in terms of the regional spillover coefficients themselves[6]. For the case where the structure is decomposable, that is where it is possible to group regions into two distinct sets such that spillovers occur from one set to the other, but not vice versa (no restrictions being placed on wage transfers between regions

---

[6] The properties of nonnegative matrices, from which the ensuing conditions follow as corollaries, are discussed in Gandolfo (1971, chapter 8).

within either subset), a sufficient condition for stability is that all regions have spillover coefficients that sum to less than unity. Where the structure is indecomposable, a sufficient condition is that no region has coefficients that sum to more than unity and at least one region has a row sum smaller than unity. In either case, if spillovers do not occur between pay groups within any given region, ($a_{ii} = 0$ for all i), or if interregional spillovers are asymmetric ($a_{ij} \neq a_{ji}$), then the time paths of wage inflation, though convergent towards zero, may fluctuate or oscillate in some way.

If, however, the coefficients sum to one for each regional market, then in the absence of market-induced effects and starting from irregular initial conditions, the system cannot explode but it will move towards a nonzero steady-state inflation rate. Which steady state is reached will depend upon the specifics of the wage-pattern matrix and the initial conditions. For example, where the wage-pattern structure is indecomposable, all regional markets would ultimately approach a common constant rate of wage increase, with interactive wage claims continuing indefinitely. This new steady-state inflation will be at most that of the region with the highest initial inflation rate and at least that of the region with the lowest initial rate. It might be 10%, 5%, or 15%, depending on the historical prelude. Under such conditions, however, a disequilibrium wage increase arising in any one region (say in response to increases in productivity), even if not repeated, will end up producing wage increases in all regions and will permanently raise the steady-state inflation rate. This conclusion is not just an algebraic curiosity; it is precisely what would occur in a situation of direct interactive wage determination across regions with the wage structure initially in equilibrium.

Of course, disequilibrium components of regional wage inflation assume central importance only if they persist, for then the system may not move towards a steady state. Although market induced changes over the long run are to some extent equilibrating—workers will move from excess supply regions to excess demand regions, and from low-wage to high-wage localities—new disequilibria are continually arising: new products, new technology, obsolete industries, and growing versus declining regions. These changing conditions and their differential impact across the space economy shape history and may alter the pattern of pay groups and the structure of wage interdependence. However, there is also a high degree of inertia, so that the course of wage inflation will be governed to a considerable extent by the pattern-following structure inherited from previous periods.

Not only does the concept of wage-change interdependence open up an array of interregional relationships, in which wage increases determined by bargaining or market forces in one region may influence wage movements elsewhere, but it also opens up mechanisms by which government redistribution policies may be transmitted to regions that are not directly influenced. On the other hand, it is evident that considerable latitude exists in the specification of the structure of regional wage interdependence. If future wage changes in region i depend in some way upon current or recent wage increases in region j, what regions constitute j? Do all regions exert an equal influence? If not, what variation across regions is to be expected in the domain of interdependence? Neither the market model nor the institutional hypothesis, of themselves, offer precise guidelines for the specification of the pattern of regional wage interaction (cf Addison and Burton, 1979), and further restrictions on the structure of wage-change transfer are required for the purpose of empirical analysis. The usual approach in studies of regional wage adjustment has been to postulate an asymmetric structure in which wage increases achieved by workers in one or more 'leading' regions effectively determine the rate of wage change in the remaining sectors of the labour market. It is to an examination of this 'regional wage-leadership' hypothesis that we now turn.

6.3 The regional wage-leadership hypothesis

A critical presumption underlying the 'regional wage-leadership' (RWL) hypothesis is that there exists a two-fold division of regional labour markets into a 'leading' set, say S_L, and a 'nonleading' set, S_{NL}, implying a corresponding partition of the regional wage-pattern matrix of the form,

$$\mathbf{A} = \begin{bmatrix} \mathbf{A}_{L,L} & \vdots & \mathbf{A}_{L,NL} \\ \cdots\cdots\vdots\cdots\cdots \\ \mathbf{A}_{NL,L} & \vdots & \mathbf{A}_{NL,NL} \end{bmatrix} , \tag{6.5}$$

where $\mathbf{A}_{L,L}$ and $\mathbf{A}_{NL,NL}$ are square submatrices of coefficients, and not necessarily of equal dimension. It is also usually assumed that the structure is decomposable in that wage transfers are unidirectional from the leading to the nonleading regions, in which case

$$\mathbf{A} = \begin{bmatrix} \mathbf{A}_{L,L} & \vdots & \mathbf{O} \\ \cdots\cdots\vdots\cdots\cdots \\ \mathbf{A}_{NL,L} & \vdots & \mathbf{A}_{NL,NL} \end{bmatrix} . \tag{6.6}$$

In empirical work this pattern is often simplified further by ignoring wage interactions within the leading and nonleading regional groups, wage changes in the former being solely market-induced and those in the latter group being predominantly spillover-induced. In the notation of the previous section,

$$\left. \begin{aligned} \dot{w}_{jt} &= z_{jt} , &&\text{in all leading regions } (j \in S_L) , \\ \dot{w}_{it} &= a_{iL}\dot{w}_{L,t-h} + z_{it} , &&\text{in all nonleading regions } (i \in S_{NL}) , \\ & &&0 < a_{iL} \leqslant 1 , \qquad z_{it} \geqslant 0 , \end{aligned} \right\} \tag{6.7}$$

where $\dot{w}_L$ is representative in some sense of the proportionate rate of increase of money wages in the leading regions, and h is the time lag in the wage-transfer mechanism. Specifications of this sort assume that once wage settlements are made in the leading regions, settlements in the remaining regions follow relatively passively, and in any case do not feed back into wage changes in the leading regions.

At a more general level, several interrelated questions are clearly involved in the RWL hypothesis, concerning, for example:

(a) the identity of the leading regions, and thus whether there is mono' or multiregional leadership;

(b) the stability of the assumed leading region(s) over time, that is whether regional wage leadership is taken to be potentially variable or not;

(c) the determinants of wage changes in the leading regions;

(d) the structure of wage interaction; for example, are wage transfers simply unidirectional or are there multidirectional influences?

Table 6.1 summarises a number of recent empirical studies of the RWL hypothesis, from the United Kingdom and the USA, according to certain of these characteristics. It is immediately evident that most previous work has employed two criteria to identify leading regional markets: relative unemployment and/or relative wages (or wage changes). Thus for the United Kingdom, the typical approach has been to divide regions into low-unemployment and high-unemployment markets, and to assume that wage-change transfers operate from the former to the latter. In practice this has meant that the South East and Midlands regions have been cast in the role of the dominant wage leaders (Lerner and Marquand, 1963; Cowling and Metcalf, 1967; Thomas and Stoney, 1971; Webb, 1974; MacKay and Hart, 1975; Hart and MacKay, 1977). For example, in their study of wage inflation in the United Kingdom over the period 1950–1966, Thomas and Stoney define the leading regions as those which at some time or other have the lowest unemployment rates (*assumed* to be synonymous with the regions with the highest rates of wage change). Although there is no single geographical region which can be identified as a minimum unemployment region, there are three areas (London and South East, Midlands, Yorkshire and Lincolnshire) which at sometime during the study period qualify for this distinction. Thomas and Stoney then estimate two regional wage-transfer models, one with a single leading region, the identity of which varies over time, and another in which the three regions are regarded as comprising a leading group (within which no transfer mechanism operates). They then postulate a wage-change transmission process whereby the pressure of demand for labour in the leading region(s) causes large wage increases which then spillover to regions where the demand for labour is not as high, as a result of comparability bargaining on the part of unions located in these nonleading submarkets. Thomas and Stoney find some empirical support for these unidirectional specifications of RWL, although in the form of an aggregated, economy-wide wage equation.

A somewhat similar criterion is used by MacKay and Hart in their analyses of regional wage determination in the UK engineering industry, in

Table 6.1. Recent empirical studies involving the regional wage-leadership hypothesis.

Author(s)	Regional system analysed	Mono- or multi-regional leadership	Stable or variable leadership	Identification of leading regions	Determinants of wage change in leading regions
Lerner and Marquand (1963)	UK. British engineering industry. Ministry of Labour regions and Engineering Employers' Federation districts, 1962	Multi	Stable	Areas with the 'greatest demand pressure' (lowest unemployment)	Demand pressure (unemployment) and union push-fulness in leading regions
Cowling and Metcalf (1967)	UK. Ministry of Labour regions, 1960–1965, biannual	Multi	Stable	Regions with the highest employment (lowest unemployment)	Unemployment and rate of change of unemployment in the leading regions
Thirlwall (1970)	UK. Ministry of Labour regions, 1962–1968, biannual	Mono	Stable	Region with the highest pressure of demand for labour (lowest unemployment)	Unemployment rate in the leading region
Thomas and Stoney (1971)	UK. Ministry of Labour regions, 1925–1938 and 1950–1966, annual	Mono and multi	Stable and variable	Regions with the lowest unemployment (assumed to be those regions with highest rate of wage change)	Average rate of unemployment in leading regions, and national price inflation

Study	Data	Structure	Type	Leading area	Explanatory variables
Brechling (1973)	USA. Selected states, 1950–1969 quarterly	Multi	Stable	Regions with the highest 'expected' wages (calculated as the wage rate multiplied by one minus the unemployment rate for the region)	Regional unemployment rate, and national price inflation
Webb (1974)	UK. Standard regions, 1960–1969, biannual	Mono	Stable	Region with the lowest unemployment rate	Unemployment rate in the leading region, and national price inflation
Ehrenberg and Goldstein (1975)	USA. Municipal Public sector, cross-section of metropolitan areas, 1967	Multi	Variable	Suburban municipalities	Degree of union coverage
MacKay and Hart (1975); Hart and MacKay (1977)	UK. British engineering industry. Engineering Employers' Federation districts, 1925–1939, 1951–1969, annual	Multi	Stable	Areas with the lowest unemployment and highest wage rates, plus certain other subregional leaders	Expected price inflation, unemployment in the region and rate of wage change in other leading regions
Reed and Hutchinson (1976)	USA. Mid-western metropolitan areas 1961–1972, quarterly	Mono	Stable	Metropolitan area with the highest wage rate (highest order urban centre)	Unemployment rate and price changes in leading metropolitan market
Weissbrod (1976)	USA. Metropolitan labour markets in SE Pennsylvania, 1962–1973, monthly	Mono	Stable	Metropolitan area with the highest wage rates (highest order urban centre)	Unemployment rate in leading metropolitan area

that a region is defined as a national leader if in each and every year it is both in the top third of the interregional earnings hierarchy and in the bottom third of the regional unemployment distribution, a specification which again yields London and the Midlands as the key group. However, in contrast to Thomas and Stoney, they test for multidirectional transfers, and find evidence of interactions between the national leading regions and other, second-order subnational leading regions (Hart and MacKay, 1977).

In studies of the USA, leading regions have usually been defined as those at the top of the wage hierarchy rather than in terms of the lowest unemployment criterion[7]. In a variant of this approach, Brechling (1973) defined leading regions by ranking US states according to their relative 'expected' earnings, which for any state i were calculated as the product of the wage rate and one minus the unemployment rate in that area, that is $W_i(1 - U_i)$, where $(1 - U_i)$ was assumed to be a surrogate measure of the probability that a worker will receive the wage W_i in that state. Then, Brechling argued, RWL may be attributed to 'dynamic market inter-dependence' whereby wage aspiration levels are shifted upward not by general wage increases but by wage increases in the regions which are most attractive to potential migrants, namely the highest-expected-earnings regions. The reason for interdependence, then, is the actual or threatened migration of workers to the leading regions. Evidently this mechanism does not operate when the employee already resides in one of the high-expected-earnings regions, so that for these areas wage movements are determined solely by market forces. In the low-expected-earnings regions, local labour-market conditions play only a minor role, the major impact on wages being brought about by changes in the mean wage of the leading regions which influence the expected and hence actual wage among the followers. A test of this unidirectional version of the RWL hypothesis, in the form of an aggregated wage equation, with twelve Southern and South–Western states as expected-earnings leaders, appears to give a better explanation of US regional wage developments than a model based upon the Thomas–Stoney lowest-unemployment criterion. More recent work in the USA context has investigated the transmission of wage inflation at the level of the urban system, under the assumption of a unidirectional transfer mechanism in which excess-demand-initiated wage increases in the highest-order urban centres (defined as the high-wage, high skill-mix cities) are propagated downwards to successively lower order urban places. Weissbrod (1976) argues that it is the migration of workers from the low-wage, lower order urban centres to the high-wage, higher order urban centres that generates the diffusion of wage changes downward through the urban hierarchy. A similar rationale underpins the model by Reed and Hutchinson (1976), although they do qualify their argument by suggesting

[7] A notable exception is the study by Ehrenberg and Goldstein (1975), in which leading regions (here suburban municipalities) were defined on the basis of density of union coverage.

that migration flows are likely to have greatest impact over the long run, and then primarily through their effect on unemployment levels, and that, in the short term, interurban wage-change transmission is primarily attributable to union bargaining forces.

Now a number of issues are raised by these and other studies of the RWL hypothesis. In the first place, most specifications are predicated on the assumption that the 'key' or 'leading' wage changes originate in those regions which experience the greatest and/or earliest labour-demand pressures and in which the responsiveness of wages to increases in the demand for labour is most pronounced. In British empirical work these regions have been defined according to the low-unemployment criterion, but in American studies on the basis of high relative wages. However, in neither country is there a close statistical connection between low unemployment and high wages, nor between low unemployment and the rate of wage change: some regions with high unemployment have high relative earnings, other regions which are wages leaders have high unemployment in certain periods, and wage-leading regions sometimes differ as between industries. This lack of a consistent relationship rests uncomfortably with the competitive model of wage-change transmission, for the latter implies that the crucial regions in propagating wage inflation are the high-wage–high-demand pressure regions, since it is only wage increases in these markets which cause a widening of wage differentials that in turn will stimulate actual and threatened migration. In fact, there is plentiful evidence to suggest that the interregional wage structure within advanced economies has as much to do with the regional distribution of industries having a high degree of product market power and high levels of unionisation as with geographical variations in unemployment. This is not to argue that the differential rate of economic expansion and decline between regions is unimportant. To the contrary, rapidly expanding industries have been found to experience faster rates of relative wage growth, at least in the short run (OECD, 1965; UN, 1967), and market pressures of this sort will interact or conflict in important ways with normative forces to establish fair relativities. Not only, that is, are the effects of institutional and normative forces modified in various directions by market pressures, but these market pressures may themselves be shaped by normative forces. The influence of demand and related market-induced adjustments is an integral and internally generated part of the 'wage-wage' spiral, since such market pressures may determine whether or not the wage settlements of pay-groups in a particular region lead those elsewhere. For important influences on the settlements of workers in a leading region may stem from the normative settlements in certain other regions which, but for market-demand pressures, would have been nonleading sectors. Thus, high-wage levels or low-unemployment rates taken in isolation may not be the most appropriate criteria for identifying 'key' demand regions.

Second, the specification of one-way wage transfers from leading to nonleading regions may be questioned on several grounds. Thus it seems to assume little feedback from the extra demand created in 'leading' regions to the products of, and hence the wages in, the 'nonleading' regions. It also appears to assume that the pressure of demand for labour in nonleading regions has no affect in these areas until it is at least as great as that in the leading regions. Yet there is no reason a priori to suppose that workers in a given market will not attempt to maintain their earnings differentials as workers in other regions seek to maintain theirs: relative wages must be acceptable to all parties, otherwise they become a force making for further wage demands[8]. Even if the pattern of inter-regional differentials were acceptable it may be that economic forces, for example productivity improvements, produce higher wage increases in low-wage regions, thus distorting the wage structure and giving rise to spillovers from these markets to high-wage regions as workers in the latter pursue parity wage claims.

Of relevance here are the apparent differences in wage determination between the higher-unionised and less-unionised sectors of the economy. Recent work suggests that wage movements in highly unionised industries show below-average direct sensitivity to unemployment and above-average direct sensitivity to price inflation, whereas the converse appears to hold for the less-unionised sector (Mitchell, 1980, chapter 4). These differences in average characteristics not only are themselves interrelated but also can be related to the dualistic nature of the industrial structure of advanced economies (see Averitt, 1968; Bluestone et al, 1973). The highly unionised industries tend to be the oligopolistic, capital-intensive, high-wage industries (typified by heavy durable-goods manufacture), whereas the less-unionised sector is characterised by low-wage, labour-intensive, more competitive industries (for example, much of nondurable-goods production). Using a similar sectoral division, Wachter (1970) and Ross and Wachter (1973) hypothesise and find evidence that relative wage movements are dominated by the high-wage, highly unionised sector during periods of slack aggregate demand (high unemployment) and/or rapid price inflation, but by the low-wage, less-unionised sectors in periods of aggregate demand expansion (low unemployment), as these industries react more quickly to changing market conditions. This 'industrial structure' idea effectively reverses the direction of causation implied by the usual formulation of the institutional model in which the high-wage, highly unionised, concentrated sectors act as the

[8] Of course, the relative wage aspirations of different groups of workers may be inconsistent (excessive), leading to a potentially unstable situation. The following example by Hicks (1955, page 396) illustrates the point:
"In the simplest possible terms, if A-workers think that their wages should be 10% higher than B-workers, while B-workers think that their wages should be equal to those of A-workers, the satisfaction of the claims of one party must necessarily give rise to claims by the other."

'key group' in wage-setting (cf Eckstein and Wilson, 1962; Maher, 1961; Mehra, 1976); now it is the low-wage, less-unionised sectors that 'lead' in the wage-inflation process and the high-wage, highly unionised industries react sluggishly to changes in the wage structure. Additional empirical support for this view is to be found in the studies of post-war American data by Flanagan (1976) and Johnson (1977), whose results indicate that the unionised sector emulates, via its attempt to maintain a desired union differential, the wage developments in the nonunionised sector, but not vice versa. Given regional variations in industrial structure and degree of unionisation, this body of work would imply that low-wage regions may well be wage leaders, particularly if they are also the most rapidly expanding areas. At the very least, it suggests multidirectional spillovers as different pay groups in different regions attempt to catch up on relative wage losses incurred in previous periods, in a manner dependent in part on the economic cycle and in part upon the timing, incidence, and nature of wage negotiations (cf OECD, 1978, page 26).

Third, and related to these points, there is the question of the type of transfer mechanism involved. Whilst British work has recognised the importance of normative forces, American work has given preeminence to the effects of potential migration: the potential migrant is assumed to maximise his own (expected) wage income and thus to search amongst regions and to focus on the one for which the net gain in (expected) wages is greatest. Such models are simply interregional versions of the voluntary job-search theory of wage dynamics (Phelps and others, 1970). Yet both survey and census data show that job changes take place mainly within rather than between local labour markets, and that job opportunities in general rather than just wage differentials constitute the major stimulus to migration. Further, wage effects attributed to migration can be easily over-stated. Migration frequently involves a change of occupation; thus to attribute changes in regional wages to migration itself may be unreasonable. Also, migration often follows an investment in human capital—most migrants are relatively young and better educated—so that the measured wage differences may be related more to recent human investments than to the migration process per se. However, the issue is not really whether individual job-quitting–job-search activity and migration are ultimately sufficient to influence interregional wage adjustment, but that normative pressures and custom have a far greater 'spatial reach' and require no mobility for their effectiveness. Since unions and other labour groups are often organised on an industry-wide basis or are represented in several member industries or firms, and hence are multilocational, they are able to monitor and influence wage conditions across large segments of the space economy.

There is no rigorous theory to guide the specification of the structure and dynamics of regional wage leadership. Some (neoclassical) writers have argued that this absence undermines the usefulness of the hypothesis, and that inductive attempts to delimit spillover patterns are an inadequate substitute for rigorous a priori theory (for example, Burton and Addison, 1977). On the other hand, Wood (1978) has shown that it is possible to erect a plausible (and rigorous) theory of wage bargaining under conditions of leadership and interacting normative and market pressures, but that the identification of actual leaders and reference sets is very much a matter of empirical analysis of specific situations.

6.4 Identifying leading regions in the US labour market

Against the background of the previous discussion, we now turn to the problem of specifying a plausible RWL structure which may form the basis of a simple empirical test for regional wage interdependence in the United States. The US Bureau of the Census divides the country, for statistical purposes, into four primary regions, and these in turn into nine geographical divisions; these and their constituent states are shown in figure 6.1. The analysis in this and the subsequent section will focus on the nine geographic regions. Since consistent wage data for individual industries are not available for these regions or for states, the empirical work in section 6.5 will be confined to the manufacturing sector as a whole. Of course, major subnational regions may conceal significant

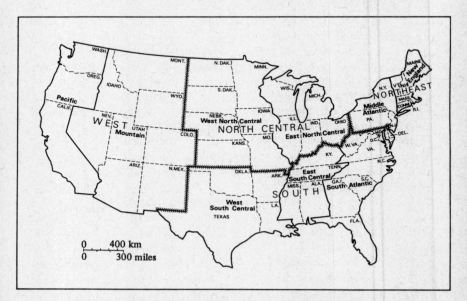

Figure 6.1. Census regions and geographic divisions of the United States. Note: For census purposes the Pacific region includes Alaska and Hawaii, but throughout the remainder of this chapter these two states have been excluded. Source: *Annual Survey of Manufacturers, 1975*, Bureau of the Census, US Department of Commerce (1977, page iii).

internal variations; on the other hand, certain regional structures may only appear in these seemingly gross characteristics.

The previous section suggested a number of 'conjunctural' factors that should be considered in formulating any RWL hypothesis. These factors included relative employment growth and economic expansion, relative wages and unemployment, industrial structure, degree of unionisation, and associated institutional pressures.

6.4.1 Regional employment growth

Several writers have recently drawn attention to the marked regional dualism in employment growth in the USA over the past two decades, involving a dramatic interregional job-shift to the Southern and Western states and a new configuration of core–periphery relationships (Sternlieb and Hughes, 1975; Weinstein and Firestine, 1978; Norton and Rees, 1979; Clark, 1980). The magnitude of this dualism is substantial. From 1960 to 1977 total national nonagricultural employment increased by 55%, but this growth was not shared equally among the regions. Both the South and West experienced employment gains of around 80% or more, while the North Central region realised a gain of 47% and the North East only 23%. A more pronounced pattern is observed by focusing on employment changes in manufacturing industry. Manufacturing has displayed a slow employment growth since the mid-1960s, the total number of jobs having expanded by only 7% since 1965. Thus the growth of manufacturing in one region has usually entailed a decline in another region. Table 6.2 highlights this development. Since 1965, the New England, Middle Atlantic, and East North Central regions have suffered

Table 6.2. Employment growth in the USA, by region, 1960–1977.

Region	Change in total nonagricultural employment, 1960–1977		Change in manufacturing employment, 1965–1977	
	absolute (000's)	%	absolute (000's)	%
New England	1309·3	35·8	−87·5	−6·0
Middle Atlantic	2318·5	19·4	−643·0	−15·4
East North Central	4854·8	42·3	−66·1	−1·7
West North Central	2082·5	64·0	193·1	17·8
South Atlantic	5893·3	82·8	438·9	18·7
East South Central	2214·1	82·4	306·9	30·0
West South Central	3693·0	87·2	461·0	47·5
Mountain	1902·9	100·8	128·4	44·1
Pacific[a]	4589·5	72·1	314·9	17·2
USA[a]	28862·9	54·8	1046·6	6·9

[a] Figures exclude Alaska and Hawaii.
Source: *Employment and Earnings*, Bureau of Labor Statistics, US Department of Labor (various issues).

contractions in manufacturing employment of 6%, 15%, and 2% respectively (see table 6.2). At the same time that these areas have been losing jobs, all other parts of the country have been gaining, with the East South Central, West South Central, and Mountain states showing the fastest rates of growth in the number of industrial jobs (30%, 47%, and 44%). Thus while manufacturing employment increased in the South and West by more than 1·2 million and 400000, respectively, it declined in the three 'traditional manufacturing belt' regions of the north-east by almost 800000.

One of the correlates of this division into high-growth and low-growth regions is the migration response of workers. During the 1965–1970 period, in-migration accounted for 12% of the population growth in the South, and during 1970–1975 this proportion increased to 55%. Except for certain years during 1965–1970, net migration to the West has consistently accounted for about half of the population growth in that region for the past twenty-five years. Since 1970, the South Atlantic and Mountain regions have experienced the greatest in-migration (see table 6.3). By contrast to the South and West, net out-migration has been primarily responsible for the slow population growth of the North-Eastern and North Central states. As early as 1955, the North Central region experienced net out-migration, a process that has continued ever since, with the exception of the period 1965–1970. Between 1970–1975, the North East became an out-migration region. Since 1970 the Middle Atlantic and East North Central divisions have shown the most pronounced out-migration rates, having lost 2·3% and 2·6%, respectively, of their 1970 populations. Some sixteen states have experienced net out-migration and all but one are in the North.

This pattern of migration-flows to the economically expanding regions signifies a degree of equilibration in the regional structure of the US

Table 6.3. Net migration of population in the USA, by region, 1970–1976.

Region	Number of migrants (000's)	Percentage of 1970 population
New England	5	0·5
Middle Atlantic	−2	−2·3
East North Central	−1060	−2·6
West North Central	−178	−0·5
South Atlantic	1970	6·4
East South Central	235	1·8
West South Central	734	3·8
Mountain	913	11·0
Pacific[a]	846	3·3

[a] Excluding Alaska and Hawaii.
Source: Weinstein and Firestine (1978).

labour market.   However, the extent to which this response of workers
has derived from, and in turn influenced, wage differentials is debatable.
Long and Hansen (1979), using survey data for 1974-1976, found that
59% of all interregional migrants cited job-related factors as the major
reasons for moving.   Among these job-related factors, 'job transfers' (27%)
and 'new jobs or looking for work' (23%) were the most important.
Although these results emphasise the importance of job opportunities (as
against simply relative wages) in migration decisions, they also demonstrate
that economic reasons fail to account for the movement of a sizeable
proportion of the migrating work force.   Moreover, DaVanzo (1977) found
that individuals respond less to the relative average income between states
and regions than to differences in specific job opportunities.   Families with
heads who are looking for work are more likely to move than other
families; of those looking for work, the unemployed are more likely to
move than those who are employed.   In fact, unemployment status was
found to be the most important economic determinant of interregional
migration, and the unemployment rate at the place of origin relative to
possible destinations is a decisive influence on the occurrence and direction
of a move.   Results such as these raise doubts on Brechling's explanation
of regional wage interdependence in the USA in terms of a theory of
regional migration.   It appears that almost half of the workers who migrate
do so for noneconomic reasons [9].   Furthermore, to the extent that a large
proportion of actual or potential migrants are unemployed, the impact on
wages of actual or 'threatened' job-quitting and migration is thereby
lessened.   Also, if relative unemployment is a major determinant of
migration then the aggregate rate of wage change may be shifted upwards
not because of wage increases in Brechling's leading, high-earnings regions,
but by a relative rise in unemployment in the lagging, low-earnings regions.
This 'wrong' behaviour is contrary to the predictions of Brechling's model.

   In terms of the *job market*, then, tables 6.2 and 6.3 indicate that the
southern and western states are the 'leading', employment-expanding
regions, whereas the East North Central and northeastern states are the
'lagging' areas.

6.4.2 Relative wages and unemployment

Table 6.4 gives the annual average gross hourly wage of production and
nonsupervisory workers in manufacturing, together with the annual average
total unemployment rate by region for selected years during the period
1957-1977.   Both for wages and unemployment the regions have also
been ranked in descending order from high to low values.   A number of
facts emerge from an examination of these data.   With few exceptions, the

---

[9] Long and Hansen (1979) show that the most important noneconomic factors
affecting migration decisions are the desire to be nearer relatives and other family-
related reasons, and the search for a better living environment (of which climate is
only a part).

rankings óf regions by average hourly wages are very similar throughout the period: the regional wage structure has a high degree of rank-order stability and changes only over time. There are some regions which show changes in relative position but, given the time span over which the comparisons are made and given that the comparisons are based on gross hourly earnings which, in the short run, are likely to be more volatile than any other wage index (such as wage rates), the degree of rank-order stability is quite striking. The relative dispersion of regional wages within this structure is best seen with the aid of figure 6.2. The distribution is dominated by the two high-wage regions of East North Central and Pacific, which have average manufacturing wages between 15% and 20% above the national average. A second group comprises the Mountain, Middle Atlantic, and West North Central regions, all with wages much closer to the national figure. The remaining four regions of South Atlantic, East South Central, West South Central, and New England make up a third group of low-wage areas typically having wage levels around 84% to 90% of the national average. Notwithstanding the general rank-order stability of the regional

Table 6.4. Average hourly earnings in manufacturing, and average unemployment rate in the USA, by region, for selected years.

Region	1957	1962	1967	1972	1977
Average hourly earnings $ (rank)					
New England	1·76(7)	2·06(7)	2·48(7)	3·30(7)	4·70(9)
Middle Atlantic	2·11(4)	2·46(4)	2·88(4)	3·95(3)	5·75(3)
East North Central	2·26(2)	2·68(2)	3·17(2)	4·42(1)	6·73(1)
West North Central	1·95(5)	2·35(5)	2·78(5)	3·70(5)	5·55(5)
South Atlantic	1·67(9)	2·00(8)	2·43(8)	3·25(8)	5·00(7)
East South Central	1·70(8)	1·95(9)	2·34(9)	3·17(9)	4·83(8)
West South Central	1·88(6)	2·11(6)	2·51(6)	3·36(6)	5·17(6)
Mountain	2·20(3)	2·57(3)	2·99(3)	3·80(4)	5·62(4)
Pacific	2·33(1)	2·74(1)	3·27(1)	4·34(2)	6·46(2)
Total unemployment rate % (rank)					
New England	4·0(7)	4·4(8)	2·9(8)	6·9(2)	5·5(7)
Middle Atlantic	4·6(3)	6·4(1)	3·6(6)	6·1(3)	7·2(1)
East North Central	4·2(5)	5·8(3)	3·5(7)	5·5(4)	5·8(5)
West North Central	3·0(9)	3·6(9)	2·6(9)	3·9(9)	4·0(9)
South Atlantic	4·5(4)	5·6(5)	3·8(4)	4·6(8)	5·9(4)
East South Central	4·7(2)	5·7(4)	4·2(3)	4·7(7)	6·1(3)
West North Central	4·1(6)	5·3(6)	3·7(5)	5·1(6)	5·6(6)
Mountain	3·8(8)	5·0(7)	4·9(2)	5·3(5)	5·0(8)
Pacific	5·1(1)	6·3(2)	5·7(1)	7·7(1)	6·6(2)

Sources: *Statistical Abstract of the United States*, Bureau of the Census, US Department of Commerce (various issues); *Geographic Profile of Employment and Unemployment*, Bureau of Labor Statistics, US Department of Labor (various issues).

wage structure, figure 6.2 shows that there have been some notable shifts in relative wages. On the one hand, the East North Central and South Atlantic regions have progressively improved their relative wages (the former especially after 1970), while on the other, relative wages in the Mountain region, and to a much smaller extent in Middle Atlantic and New England, have declined.

These manufacturing wage differentials are of course closely linked to the nature of employment in the regions. In 1978, some 51% of manufacturing employees nationwide were in industries with average hourly wages above $6.50, but only 32% of those in the South were so employed. The South has the smallest proportion of manufacturing employment in those durable-goods industries which have the highest average hourly wage (primary metals, transportation equipment, machinery, fabricated metals). Those durable-goods industries with high-employment concentration in the Southern regions are relatively low paying industries. More than 40% of

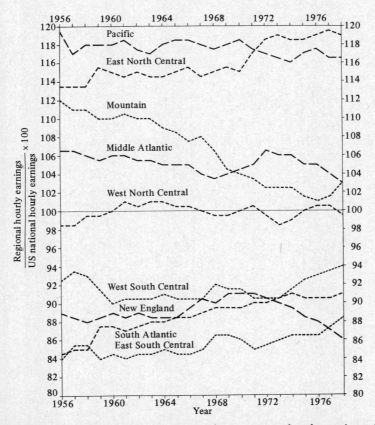

Figure 6.2. Ratio of regional to national gross average hourly earnings of production and nonsupervisory workers in manufacturing in the USA, 1956–1978.

all nondurable-goods manufacturing employment in the South is in two sectors—textile and apparel—compared with only 12% in these industries in the rest of the country. These sectors are traditionally low paying industries: their combined average hourly wage in 1978 was only just over $4.00, compared with $5.70 for all other nondurables. Although these regional wage relativities can be partly attributed to differences in industry mix, recent studies suggest that other important sources of the North–South differential evident in figure 6.2 lie in 'human capital differences' and wage discrimination against nonwhite workers in the South, with the net effect of capital/labour ratios exerting a wage-differential influence more favourable to the North, and similarly with differences in degree of unionisation. The general conclusion is that the low relative wages of Southern states arise from important 'noneconomic' or institutional factors which cannot be eliminated by labour-market adjustments.

If we now turn to unemployment, table 6.4 shows that the regional (total) unemployment structure is much less stable than that for earnings, and in every year there are significant changes in the rank-order positions of certain regions. [The figures in table 6.4 thus seem to refute Brechling's (1973) claim that the relative ranking of regions by unemployment remains 'remarkably constant'.] These shifts in large part relate to the economic cycle as it impinges differentially upon regions according to their industrial structures (Gellner, 1974). In the East North Central and Middle Atlantic regions many jobs are concentrated in durable-goods industries, the sectors most sensitive to fluctuations in aggregate demand, whereas in Southern states many jobs are concentrated in nondurable-goods sectors which tend to be less cyclically sensitive. Generalising, high average unemployment rates characterise the Pacific region (at the top of the distribution in almost every year), whereas low average unemployment rates occur mainly in the New England and the West North Central region, the latter being the lowest-unemployment market throughout the period. A more detailed analysis of these data indicates that the degree of dispersion in the regional unemployment distribution has varied inversely with the overall national unemployment rate, but has also tended to increase since the late 1960s (Sum and Rush, 1975).

The usual specification of leading regions in RWL studies, it will be recalled, has been in terms of low relative unemployment and high relative wages. For the major geographic divisions of the USA there is no region which can be said to fulfil these criteria. Comparison of the regional unemployment and wage distributions indicates that there is no correlation between high wages and low unemployment: some high-wage regions have the highest average unemployment rates (Pacific, Middle Atlantic), certain low-wage regions also have low average unemployment (West South Central, New England), and the consistently lowest unemployment region (West North Central) has only median wage levels. In fact, in every period, the rank-order correlation between wage levels and unemployment rates across regions is positive (though not statistically significant). Thomas and Stoney suggest that leading regions should also have the highest rates of wage change. The annual average rates of change of manufacturing wages by region for selected subperiods between 1959–1978 are shown in table 6.5. Every region has been in the upper half of the wage-inflation hierarchy on some occasion. Some five areas (East North Central, West North Central, South Atlantic, East South Central, and West South Central) have at one time or another had the highest rate of wage increase, but there is no single region which has invariably been the wage-change leader. However, even though regional differences in average wage inflation are small, taking all subperiods two features of interest are discernible. First, two areas have had wage-inflation rates above the national average in every subperiod, namely East North Central and South Atlantic. Second, taken as a group, the three southern regions (East South Central, West South Central, and South Atlantic) have consistently had rates of wage increase above the national average since the mid-1960s. These latter, as we have seen, are the areas of pronounced employment expansion. The above-average wage growth of the East North Central region, however, has been against a background of declining employment, thereby suggesting the impress of other factors.

Table 6.5. Rate of change of manufacturing wages in the USA, by region, for selected periods, 1959-1978.

Region	Annual average change (%)[a]					Average differential between regional and national rates of wage change, 1959–1978
	1959–1962	1963–1966	1967–1970	1971–1974	1975–1978	
New England	**3·40**	**3·48**	5·45	6·57	7·64	−0·17
Middle Atlantic	3·17	3·07	5·23	**7·38**	8·05	−0·20
East North Central	**3·52**	**3·36**	**5·98**	**7·62**	**8·95**	0·21
West North Central	**3·57**	3·10	5·40	6·72	8·78	−0·06
South Atlantic	**3·44**	**3·56**	**5·88**	**7·36**	**8·98**	0·26
East South Central	2·95	3·17	**6·04**	**7·14**	**9·41**	0·17
West South Central	2·65	3·22	**5·83**	**7·01**	**9·59**	0·10
Mountain	3·13	2·61	4·44	6·75	8·94	−0·40
Pacific[b]	3·18	**3·52**	5·40	6·38	8·81	−0·12
USA	3·28	3·24	5·53	6·98	8·89	

[a] Regional rates of wage change greater than the national average are shown in bold type.
[b] Excluding Alaska and Hawaii.
Source: Compiled from *Employment and Earnings*, Bureau of Labor Statistics, US Department of Labor (various issues).

6.4.3 Unionisation and institutional pressures

It is frequently contended that the marked diversity of the US wage structure reflects the 'turbulence of a market economy' only partially subject to collective bargaining and institutional pressures. Although the overall degree of unionisation is lower in the USA than in the United Kingdom, for certain sectors the coverage levels are not that different. Also, beneath the *formal* collective bargaining surface the USA may not in principle be too dissimilar from European market forms: the USA may be just as institutionalised, but in a different way and perhaps with different effects. In the major oligopolistic sectors of manufacturing, wage determination typically takes place between the single company and one or more industry-wide unions[10], the latter 'connecting' the different company-wide settlements within and between particular industries via a

Table 6.6. Unionisation and industrial disputes in the USA, by region.

Region	Degree of unionisation				Degree of industrial conflict. Annual average number of working days lost per 1000 employees (all stoppages)[c]		
	Percentage of total non-agricultural employment[a]		Percentage of workers covered by labour-management agreements, 1960–1976[b]				
	1964	1974	all industries	manufacturing	1960–1965	1966–1971	1972–1977
New England	23	21 }	72	78	**320**	544	373
M Atlantic	36	33 }			**369**	**679**	**539**
E N Central	40	36 }	77	86	**414**	**1067**	**603**
W N Central	19	16 }			277	**723**	**588**
S Atlantic	19	17 }			186	360	256
E S Central	20	19 }	45	57	310	**697**	**545**
W S Central	16	15 }			197	344	295
Mountain	24	23 }	67	72	**377**	578	270
Pacific[d]	39	36 }			309	419	412
USA[d]					318	640	440

[a] Percentage of workers belonging to national and local unions.
[b] Percentage of workers employed in establishments in which a contract covered the majority of the workers.
[c] Regions with stoppages greater than the national average are shown in bold type.
[d] Excluding Alaska and Hawaii.
Sources: *Statistical Abstract of the United States*, Bureau of the Census, US Department of Commerce (various issues); *Handbook of Labor Statistics*, Bureau of Labor Statistics, US Department of Labor, 1979.

---

[10] For example, over 90% of the unionised workers in the primary metals, electrical machinery, nonelectrical machinery, and fabricated metals industries are covered by single-employer, company-wide agreements (US Bureau of Labor Statistics, 1974).

process of pattern-bargaining. As a result wages may be set throughout wide geographical areas, connecting pay groups in quite distinct regions. When centralised (multiemployer) bargaining structures are found, they most frequently involve locally or regionally competitive markets (as in certain nondurable-goods manufacturing industries). In this sense they often represent the institutionalisation of wage similarity that would have existed under competitive forces.

The regional pattern of union-coverage is shown in table 6.6. There is a clear distinction between the North and West, and the three southern regions. The high-wage areas of East North Central and Pacific have the highest degree of unionisation, whereas the lowest levels of union membership are found in the low-wage regions of the South. The table also gives an indication of the different levels of industrial unrest amongst the regions, as measured by the annual number of working days lost through industrial stoppages, for three subperiods between 1960–1977. The East North Central region has had the highest incidence of industrial conflict, but perhaps the most revealing feature of the table is the distinctly higher degree of strike activity amongst the three major north-eastern regions (Middle Atlantic, East North Central, and West North Central) as compared with the three southern regions.

There is some evidence that industries whose earnings move ahead (fall behind) in relation either to the rate of price inflation or the average rate of wage inflation experience less (more) industrial conflict. That is, a tendency has been observed for workers' involvement in work stoppages to increase when 'catch-up' pressure either of the absolute or the relative type develops. Thus two interpretations may be placed on the high levels of industrial unrest in the Northeast. Either it represents catch-up pressure to protect absolute real wages, in which case these regions might be regarded (bearing in mind their industrial structures and degrees of unionisation) as being key or leading sectors; or it may represent catch-up pressure to achieve parity with wage increases occurring elsewhere, particularly in the employment-expanding regions of the South.

It is clear from these various observations that a diversity of labour-market conditions exists amongst the regions of the USA. However, it does seem possible, as a first approximation, to hypothesise two broad

Table 6.7. Alternative specifications of 'leading' regions.

Model I Areas of high relative wages and high unionisation	Model II Areas of employment growth and labour- market expansion
East North Central Middle Atlantic Pacific West North Central	South Atlantic East South Central West South Central Mountain

alternative specifications of 'leading' regions, or at least partitions of the regional 'wage-pattern matrix'. The first (model I) specifies leading regions to be those that have high wages and high levels of unionisation or industrial conflict. Four regions can be identified as 'leading' in this way: East North Central, Pacific, Middle Atlantic, and West North Central (table 6.7). The hypothesis is that the pace of wage inflation stems from these regions not because of the pressure of demand for labour (since these are areas of declining manufacturing employment or, in the case of the Pacific area, high unemployment), but because of union 'pushfulness' with regard to productivity bargaining and real wage claims (the latter particularly through the mechanism of cost-of-living escalator clauses). Wage increases in these 'leading' sectors might then be assumed to spillover to the remaining regions through the actions of unions and the effects of custom, convention, and worker morale. In a sense, model I is the geographical counterpart of the 'key group' of high-wage, capital-intensive, oligopolistic, highly unionised, heavy durable-goods manufacturing industries identified as the leading sector by Eckstein and Wilson (1962), Maher (1961), and others in earlier interindustry studies of US wage determination, since these industries are spatially concentrated in the central north-eastern and western states of the country.

In the second specification (model II), leading regions are assumed to be the areas of high employment growth, labour-market expansion, and net in-migration. The four regions selected under this specification are South Atlantic, East South Central, West South Central, and Mountain, embracing almost all of the so-called sunbelt. As a group these areas have low wages, low levels of unionisation, and less industrial conflict than the nation as a whole. As the regions of much of the country's new industrial growth and expanding job markets, these areas may well be the source of considerable upward pressure on wages in the economy. The transmission of wage growth from these markets to the remaining parts of the country need not be attributable to the migration of workers, considerable though this has been, but mainly to relative wage 'catch-up' pressures in the more unionised 'lagging' regions. To a very limited extent, therefore, this second model bears some affinity with the 'industrial structure' hypothesis of Ross and Wachter (1973).

6.5 Some empirical estimates of regional wage interdependence
The regional wage-change series to be used in the regression analysis presented below are shown in figure 6.3. The series, which are quarterly from 1960 to 1978, measure the annual (four-quarter) percentage change in the gross hourly earnings of production and nonsupervisory workers in manufacturing industry. All regions display a similar overall pattern of fluctuating but generally untrended wage change up to the mid- or late 1960s, and thereafter a steadily rising inflation rate characterised by distinct cyclical movements. Three main peaks in the rate of wage increase

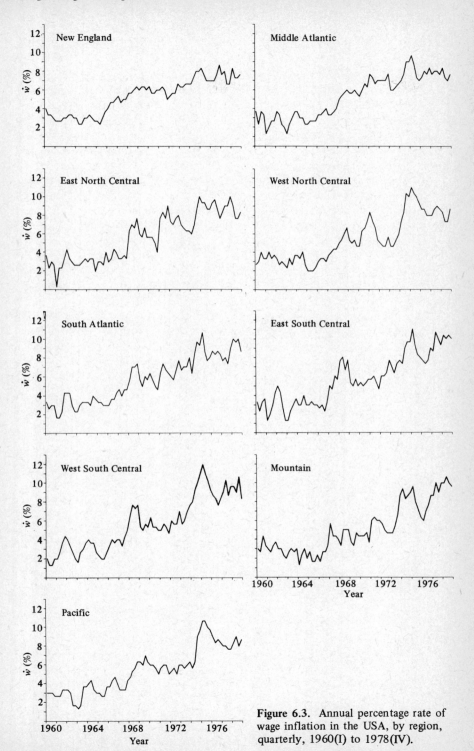

Figure 6.3. Annual percentage rate of wage inflation in the USA, by region, quarterly, 1960(I) to 1978(IV).

are evident, in 1968–1969, 1970–1971, and 1974–1975, although their intensity and precise timing vary from region to region. These peaks are especially marked in the East North Central and West North Central regions, and may well reflect the 2–3 year periodicity of major wage contracts that are common in many unionised sectors of manufacturing in the USA. The 1968–1969 and 1974–1975 peaks in wage inflation also occur in the three southern regions and in the Pacific area, but the 1970–1971 peak appears to be missing in these regions. Casual inspection of the graphs suggests that the wage controls imposed to a varying degree during the Nixon Economic Stabilisation Program (mainly 1972–1973) may have had some measure of success in holding down the rate of wage inflation in the high-wage, highly unionised markets in northeastern and Pacific states, though not in the South.

Turning first to the role of market factors and real demand pressures in regional wage determination, we give in table 6.8 regression estimates for the relationship

$$\dot{w}_{it} = \beta_{i0} + \beta_{i1}(L)U_{it} + \beta_{i2}(L)\dot{p}_t + \epsilon_{it}, \qquad i = 1, ..., n, \tag{6.8}$$

Table 6.8. US regional wage-change regressions with unemployment and price inflation variables.

Region	Constant	Almon distributed lag variables (lag = 8 quarters)		$\overline{R}^2$	Standard error of estimate	Durbin–Watson
		U_{it}	$\dot{p}_t$			
New England	4·946* (3·76)	−0·399* (−3·35)	0·664* (8·74)	0·548	0·785	1·68
Middle Atlantic	3·922* (5·65)	−0·262 (−1·791)	0·739* (6·86)	0·623	0·976	1·79
East North Central	3·903* (4·76)	−0·232 (−1·30)	0·782* (6·99)	0·412	1·144	1·48
West North Central	2·629* (4·45)	0·081 (0·070)	0·733* (9·16)	0·554	1·120	1·60
South Atlantic	4·718* (4·20)	−0·395* (−2·238)	0·635* (6·70)	0·607	1·128	1·86
East South Central	4·066* (5·89)	−0·487* (−3·813)	0·569* (5·05)	0·480	1·551	1·30
West South Central	3·708* (3·53)	−0·289* (−2·864)	0·830* (5·72)	0·466	1·478	1·88
Mountain	2·843* (2·62)	0·054 (0·239)	0·472* (4·33)	0·387	1·499	1·65
Pacific	2·630 (1·44)	−0·241* (−2·946)	0·650* (4·41)	0·210	1·689	1·57

Notes: Quarterly data (period of fit: 1960–1978). The coefficient shown for each variable is the sum of the coefficients for all the lags of the variable. t-values are in parentheses. * Significant at 95% level.

where $\beta_{i1}(L)$ and $\beta_{i2}(L)$ are polynomial lag operators such that

$$\beta(L)x_t = \sum_{k=0}^{m} \beta_k L^k x_t , \qquad \text{and} \quad L^k x_t = x_{t-k} ,$$

m being the length of the lag distribution. The variable U_i is the total civilian unemployment rate in the region, assumed to be a proxy for the local pressure of demand for labour, and $\dot{p}$ is the annual rate of change in the national 'consumer price index for urban wage earners'[11]. In addition to being an indicator of product market pressures and competitive real-wage determination, the price inflation variable also affects wages through escalator clauses. A large proportion of formal wage contracts in the USA incorporate cost-of-living clauses that automatically change basic wage rates according to recent changes in the consumer price index. With the exception of about 100 000 workers linked directly to individual city cost-of-living indices, all workers under clauses are tied to the national consumer price index.

To allow for lags in the adjustment of wages to these market factors, the relationship was estimated according to the Almon distributed lag method, using a third degree polynomial. Departure from the normal version of this technique is effected in that the constraint that the weights for the endpoints of the distributed lags must be zero is not imposed. Such a constraint, if not true, leads to biased and inconsistent estimates and to invalid tests. The results given in table 6.8 are those for a uniform lag of eight quarters for each of the independent variables and each region. A number of lag structures were tried, from a minimum of two quarters to a maximum of twelve (including variable lags for the two independent variables). As would be expected, the optimum lag structure (the one yielding the lowest standard error of regression) varies between regions. A lag of eight or nine quarters, however, typically yields either the lowest standard error or one which differs very little from the lowest. Accordingly, in table 6.8 the same lag (eight quarters) is shown for each region.

The regression results do not give overwhelming support for a Phillips type of relationship throughout the set of regions. Seven of the nine areas have the correct, negative sign for the coefficient on the unemployment variable[12], but the rate of wage change is significantly sensitive to this index of labour-market conditions in only five cases. However, these do include all four of the below-average wage regions (New England, South

[11] Unemployment data were compiled from *Geographic Profile of Employment and Unemployment, Employment and Earnings*, and *Area Trends in Employment and Unemployment*, various issues, Bureau of Labor Statistics, US Bureau of Labor. The national consumer price index is published in the *Monthly Labor Review*, Bureau of Labor Statistics, US Bureau of Labor, and is derived from a cross-section of metropolitan areas from all of the major regions.

[12] The model was also estimated using the reciprocal of the regional unemployment rate, U_{it}^{-1}, but for the majority of regions the linear form in equation (6.8) yielded smaller residual sums of squares for almost all of the different lag distributions tried.

Atlantic, East South Central, West South Central) together with the Pacific region, the area with the highest wages but also the highest average unemployment rate. Each region has a statistically significant coefficient of positive sign on the price inflation variable, although in only two cases (East North Central and West South Central) is the coefficient insignificantly different from unity, which is the value postulated by the 'natural rate' (accelerationist) version of the Phillips curve. With the exception of the West South Central region the price sensitivity of wages tends to be slightly higher in the high-wage, more heavily unionised sectors.

The empirical detection of wage interdependencies is far from straight-forward. One approach would be to use time-series cross-correlation methods to determine the interregional covariance structure of wage inflation. The difficulty with this type of analysis is that the presence of substantial serial correlation within each regional series is likely to render the interpretation of cross-region correlation functions somewhat difficult. On the other hand, prewhitening procedures recommended by time-series analysts (for example, Box and Jenkins, 1970; Bennett, 1979) may in fact bias the results towards the null hypothesis of no cross-region inter-dependencies. Mehra (1976) has suggested a technique whereby, as a first step, regression analysis is used to filter out from industry wages the influence of external factors such as labour-market conditions and serial correlation. The resultant residuals should be uncorrelated across industries unless some sort of spillover mechanism is operative. The second step thus consists of using these residuals in regression models to test for alternative spillover structures. However, this method is also questionable. If too much 'data cleaning' is done there is nothing left to explain and the residuals are simply random variables. To exclude wage-spillover influences from the initial regression specification is to precondition the relative importance ultimately assigned to market and exogenous factors. The fact that large firms and bargaining units often operate in more than one industry classification should surely lead to some spillover as Mehra himself defines it. His failure to detect significant interdependence casts doubt on his technique.

The approach adopted here, therefore, was to incorporate wage-change interdependence variables directly into the distributed lag regression in equation (6.8). For each region i, two spillover variables were defined as $(\dot{w}_\mathrm{I} - \dot{w}_i)$ and $(\dot{w}_\mathrm{II} - \dot{w}_i)$, where $\dot{w}_\mathrm{I}$ and $\dot{w}_\mathrm{II}$ denote the weighted average rates of wage increase in the two 'leading' groups of regions as specified by models I and II in the previous section, that is

$$\dot{w}_K = \sum_{j \in S_K} \alpha_j \dot{w}_j \,, \qquad K = \mathrm{I} \text{ or } \mathrm{II} \,,$$

where α_j $(= E_j/E_K)$ is the employed manufacturing labour-force share accounted for by region j. The use of these labour-force-share weights to calculate $\dot{w}_I$ and $\dot{w}_{II}$ is intended to reflect the idea that the larger a region j is in terms of the geographical concentration of manufacturing workers, the greater the probability that it will be used as a reference sector for any given wage claims by workers in region i. The 'spillover' regressions therefore took the form,

$$\dot{w}_{it} = \beta_{i0} + \beta_{i1}(L)U_{it} + \beta_{i2}(L)\dot{p}_t + \beta_{i3}(L)[\dot{w}_{I,t} - \dot{w}_{it}]$$
$$+ \beta_{i4}(L)[\dot{w}_{II,t} - \dot{w}_{it}] + \epsilon_{it}, \qquad i = 1, ..., n, \qquad (6.9)$$

where as before $\beta_{i3}(L)$ and $\beta_{i4}(L)$ are distributed lag functions set at a length of eight quarters. The assumption underlying this model is that wage movements in any given region i adjust, in part at least, to eliminate discrepancies between the average rate of wage increase in one or other of the hypothesised reference sectors and the rate of change of wages in the region itself. Because wage negotiations take place infrequently, this adjustment is expected to be distributed over time. If no such catch-up wage adjustment occurs in a region, then $\beta_{i3}(L) = \beta_{i4}(L) = 0$. Conversely, positive and statistically significant coefficient sums for certain regions would be consistent with the existence of wage-interaction effects. Thus the pattern of nonzero coefficients, $\beta_{i3}(L)$ and $\beta_{i4}(L)$, across regions should give some idea as to which, if any, of the two hypothesised leadership structures is dominant, as well as to whether more general multidirectional interdependencies are present.

Table 6.9 gives the results for the set of regressions in equation (6.9). All of the estimated equations are superior to the Phillips-type relationships in table 6.8, as judged by the improvement in the R^2 values and Durbin–Watson statistics, and the fall in the standard errors of the regressions. For most regions, the addition of relative wage-growth catch-up variables is associated with a decline in the magnitude of response of wages to price inflation, although the coefficients remain statistically significant throughout. Of particular interest is the distinctly higher price sensitivity of the four high-wage, more highly unionised regions (Middle Atlantic, East North Central, West North Central, and Pacific) as compared with the southern regions. On the other hand, the four low-wage areas (South Atlantic, East South Central, West South Central, and New England) appear to be much more sensitive to labour-market conditions than the high-wage markets; in the latter the coefficient on the unemployment variable is either insignificantly different from zero or, in the case of Middle Atlantic and West North Central, positive and significant, indicating the existence of stagflationary conditions.

If we now consider the impact of wage-change spillovers, the results confirm the existence of regional wage interactions within the US manufacturing sector. All statistically significant spillover coefficients have the expected positive sign, and every region appears to exhibit some degree of adjustment to relative wage movements elsewhere in the economy.

Furthermore, comparison of the coefficient sets $\beta_{i3}(L)$ and $\beta_{i4}(L)$ across regions suggests that the data provide more empirical support for the regional leadership structure of model II than that of model I, for whereas in some eight of the nine regions wage changes seem to be related to general wage developments in the group of low-wage, employment expanding areas, only four regions display any interaction with the average rate of wage change in the group of high-wage, more unionised markets when this influence is summed over several quarters. This pattern is emphasised by the regional elasticities of response to the two differential wage-growth variables, shown in table 6.10. These elasticities, which are calculated at the means, seem reasonable. The large (individual or combined) elasticities for East North Central, South Atlantic, East South Central, and West South Central are consistent with the above-average wage growth in these regions noted in table 6.5. Tables 6.9 and 6.10 also indicate the presence of interdependencies among the low-wage regions, and within the group of high-wage markets. There is in addition evidence of multidirectional interactions: thus wages in the Pacific, South Atlantic, West North Central, and New England divisions appear to be related to wage movements both within the high-wage and the low-wage groups.

Table 6.9. US regional wage-change regressions with spillover variables.

Region	Constant	Almon distributed lag variables (lag = 8 quarters)				$\bar{R}^2$	SEE[a]	DW[b]
		U_{it}	$\dot{p}_t$	$(\dot{w}_I - \dot{w}_i)_t$	$(\dot{w}_{II} - \dot{w}_i)_t$			
New England	2·880* (4·02)	−0·315* (−5·35)	0·602* (5·17)	0·184* (2·05)	0·526* (4·70)	0·702	0·714	1·96
M Atlantic	1·099* (3·08)	0·252* (2·39)	0·519* 2·76	−0·104 (0·68)	0·764* (3·63)	0·840	0·692	1·98
E N Central	0·343 (0·78)	−0·098 (−1·08)	0·820* (4·25)	1·088* (7·31)	0·057 (0·43)	0·901	0·759	1·81
W N Central	−0·098 (−0·32)	0·209* (2·67)	0·614* (7·27)	0·132 (1·43)	0·375* (2·84)	0·753	0·913	1·94
S Atlantic	1·040* (4·01)	−0·195* (−2·69)	0·404* (3·21)	0·315* (3·28)	0·622* (5·79)	0·503	0·902	2·02
E S Central	0·689 (1·54)	−0·293* (−3·06)	0·492* (3·76)	−0·216 (−1·23)	1·164* (6·72)	0·867	0·880	2·14
W S Central	−0·051 (−0·13)	−0·370* (−2·84)	0·263* (3·65)	−0·064 (−0·47)	0·850* (4·84)	0·718	0·897	2·25
Mountain	−0·542 (−1·07)	0·125 (1·68)	0·286* (2·99)	−0·109 (−1·67)	0·645* (6·20)	0·609	0·782	1·97
Pacific	0·392 (1·33)	0·035 (0·56)	0·543* (4·08)	0·628* (6·15)	0·308* (3·13)	0·618	0·834	2·08

Notes: Quarterly data (period of fit: 1960–1978). The coefficients shown for each explanatory variable is the sum of the coefficients for all the lags of the variable. *t*-values in parentheses. * Significant at 95% level.
[a] SEE—standard error of estimate; [b] DW—Durbin–Watson.

Of course, these equations cannot be regarded as estimates of structural relations like those in the model of section 6.2. They are more plausibly regarded as descriptive equations of relationships between the variables over the period covered. In general, the sectoral coefficients on a wage-spillover index will tend to cluster around unity because, on average, wages increase at the average rate. Nevertheless, the fact that for most regions the rate of wage increase clusters around the average rate for the expanding southern regions, allowing for lags in the process of adjustment, does suggest that it has been the labour markets of these areas that have acted as the main reference sector for the diffusion of relative wage inflation within manufacturing industry in the United States. (Subject, of course, to the qualification that we have ignored interactions from the nonmanufacturing sectors of the economy.) In view of the discussion of section 6.4, one plausible interpretation of this pattern would be that the rapid employment growth and associated pressure of demand for labour, together with favourable shifts in industrial structure in recent years, have generated above-average rates of wage increase in the South, which increases have spilled over into labour markets in the northeast and west coast areas, mainly through the bargaining activities of unions in these latter regions. Given their lower sensitivity to labour-market conditions and the higher sensitivity to price inflation, the adjustment of wages in northern and western states to general wage movements in the South might be expected to be greatest during periods of labour-market slack and/or rapidly rising prices. On the other hand, the longer the period of labour-market slack, then the larger the widening of the wages dispersion through wage increases in the high-wage, more unionised regions of the northeast, and the greater the catch-up inflation potential in the low-wage markets of the South once labour-market conditions tighten again. To the extent that levels of

Table 6.10. Elasticities of US regional wage change with respect to the two differential wage-growth variables (lag = 8 quarters).

Region	Elasticities[a] with respect to	
	$(\dot{w}_{\mathrm{I}} - \dot{w}_i)$	$(\dot{w}_{\mathrm{II}} - \dot{w}_i)$
New England	0·273	0·542
Middle Atlantic	[b]	0·680
East North Central	1·099	[b]
West North Central	0·141	0·427
South Atlantic	0·430	0·783
East South Central	[b]	1·116
West South Central	[b]	1·021
Mountain	[b]	0·700
Pacific	0·602	0·397

[a] The elasticities are evaluated at the means.
[b] Not calculated because the relationship is not statistically significant.

unionisation are generally lower in the South, this interpretation is supported by Flanagan's (1976) finding that wage spillovers in US manufacturing have been far more pronounced from the nonunion sector to the union sector than in the opposite direction. The results given here, however, run contrary to the Eckstein–Wilson/Maher type of hypothesis that it is the high-wage, heavily unionised durable-goods industries situated primarily in northeastern and north central states that represent the dominant leading sector.

6.6 Implications

This chapter has been concerned with the question of regional wage-change interdependence. The discussion has centred more specifically on certain conceptual issues surrounding the so-called regional wage-leadership hypothesis, and on an exploratory analysis of regional wage interactions in the US economy. Although this analysis was largely descriptive and the results cannot be regarded as wholly unambiguous, the data do suggest a general north–south wage pattern structure with wage-transmission effects apparently more dominant from the south to the north than vice versa. The existence of such regional wage interdependence is of interest for several reasons, not perhaps so much for the insight it throws upon the wage-determination process per se, as for the implications for regional unemployment, regional policy, and the control of inflation.

If wage contagion is pervasive across regions, the allocative role of wages in the space economy may be substantially reduced. Spillovers and transfers may operate to hold the regional wage structure together more rigidly than might otherwise occur under more competitive conditions, and hence may distort the reallocation of labour from one area to another. The basic point is that, because of institutional wage-setting forces and wage-change interdependence, systematic and persistent differences in unemployment across regions will have little impact on the relative wage structure. This is, of course, consistent with the observed obstinacy of the 'regional problem'. In fact regional wage transmission may be one of the key dimensions of the problem, because if money wages do not respond to differences in local labour-market conditions then persistent differences in efficiency wages can arise. A further difficulty stems from the adjustment which may be required over the medium term to bring the relative wage structure in line with the changing regional pattern of demand and supply conditions for different types of labour. If money-wage increases are unresponsive to slack labour demand in regions of slowly growing or declining employment, then the only way in which the relative wage change which may be required on resource-allocation grounds can come about is with a rise in the relative rate of wage inflation in the regions where there is a growing demand for labour. Not only will this tend to give an inflationary bias to the economy, but to the extent that wage increases in the expanding regions spillover to the declining and stagnating areas, the unemployment problems in these latter regions may be intensified, and it is in such regions that stagflation is likely to be more pronounced.

The operation of wage spillovers amongst regions thus has significant implications for the design of general economic measures to reduce the national rate of unemployment. Macroeconomic policymakers should prefer a situation in which regions occupy a similar position on the unemployment scale. If all regions were facing an unemployment rate of, say, 5%, planners would not have to be as concerned with potential sectoral shortages when expansionary fiscal and monetary policies were implemented nationally. The slack in labour markets could quite likely be reduced proportionately among regions. If, however, the distribution of unemployment rates across regions has a high dispersion, then those regions with low unemployment rates may encounter severe inflationary pressures before the levels of unemployment in the more depressed regions have been reduced to desirable levels. Thus it has been frequently contended that policies that aim to achieve a more equal distribution of unemployment across regions should enable the economy to be run at a lower aggregate level of unemployment without generating inflationary pressures (for example, Higgins, 1973; Hewings, 1978). Now this policy conclusion rests on a number of assumptions, two of which are: (a) that wage-inflation–unemployment-tradeoff curves are steeper, at prevailing local unemployment rates, in low unemployment regions than in areas where unemployment is high, and (b) regional labour markets are independent of one another. In the case of the United States, the limited results presented suggest that Phillips-curve relationships do tend to be steeper in the regions of expanding labour demand. However, there are exceptions to this pattern as well as a lack of stability in the regional unemployment structure as compared to that for wages. The presence of regional wage-change interdependence clearly runs counter to the second of the above assumptions. Nevertheless, the argument regarding reduction in unemployment dispersion still holds when markets are not independent of one another provided a further condition is met, namely that such interdependence is asymmetric, with wage transfers occurring from low-unemployment (high-labour demand) to high-unemployment (low-labour demand) regions. The presumption here is that wage increases in the latter imitate those in the former, which must be the regions that are the most wage-responsive to increases in unemployment. In broad terms, there is evidence of such a pattern in the USA, at least in the context of the manufacturing sector, although there are important feedback effects from the depressed areas to the high-growth regions. Thus, although the evidence is by no means conclusive, there may be some scope for reducing the national rate of unemployment without additional adverse inflationary effects by means of economic policies which focus more heavily upon specific tax and expenditure policies to expand employment in the depressed, slack labour-demand regions at the outset of the expansionary process.

Finally, there is the question of the regional impact of and response to direct intervention in the wage-determination mechanism. An important issue for public policy is whether wage spillovers have a leader–follower structure or whether wage-inflation transmission is a more complex system of mutual interactions. If controls are based on a leader–follower hypothesis, government attention naturally turns to a few key sectors, to the separation of 'inflationary' from 'noninflationary' markets. In practice this has often meant that it is the high-wage, highly unionised sectors that are identified with inflationary pressures by policymakers (for example, as in the incomes policy of the Nixon Administration in 1972–1973). However, the present analysis suggests that, at the regional scale, low relative wage, expanding sectors may be just as important in the inflationary process. Although wage guidelines and norms may temporarily restrain (union) wages that might otherwise have been higher, they can also provide a target for workers whose wage increases would have been lower given their sensitivity to market conditions. Under these circumstances, therefore, wage norms could lead to a slower rate of inflation in some regions than in others, and if imposed for more than temporary periods are likely to frustrate the relative wage positions of workers in certain sectors and areas and thus lead to a sharp acceleration in wage change following the relaxation of controls. In fact, the very forces of wage interdependence which make for long-run relative wage stability in the face of labour-market reallocation signals, which stability provides one of the bases of imposing wage controls, may then actually act as destabilising forces once the controls are lifted. The general implication is that the strength and structure of regional wage interdependence has undoubted significance for the formulation of national economic policy, regional and labour-market measures, and even inflation controls, not only because real phenomena can be identified with regional segments of the labour market but also because wage interdependence can influence the degree and direction of impact of such policies.

References
Addison J T, Burton J, 1979 "The identification of market and spillover forces in wage inflation: a cautionary note" *Applied Economics* **79** 95–104
Averitt R, 1968 *The Dual Economy* (Horton, New York)
Bennett R J, 1979 *Spatial Time Series* (Pion, London)
Bluestone B, Murphy W M, Stevenson M, 1973 *Low Wages and the Working Poor* Institute of Labor and Industrial Relations, University of Michigan, Ann Arbor
Box G E P, Jenkins G M, 1970 *Time Series Analysis, Forecasting and Control* (Holden-Day, San Francisco)
Brechling F P R, 1973 "Wage inflation and the structure of regional unemployment" *Journal of Money Credit and Banking* **5** 355–379
Burton J, Addison J T, 1977 "The institutionalist analysis of wage inflation: a critical appraisal" *Research in Labour Economics* **1** 333–376

Butler A, Kim K, 1973 "The dynamics of wage structures" *Southern Economic Journal* **39** 588–600

Clark T A, 1980 "Regional and structural shifts in the American economy" in *The American Metropolitan System: Present and Future* Eds S D Brunn, J O Wheeler (Edward Arnold, London) pp 111–125

Cowling K, Metcalf D, 1967 "Wage–unemployment relations: a regional analysis for the U.K., 1960–1965" *Bulletin of the Oxford University Institute of Economics and Statistics* **29** 31–39

Cullen D E, 1956 "The inter-industry wage structure" *American Economic Review* **46** 353–369

DaVanzo J, 1977 *Why Families Move* Monograph 48, Employment and Training Administration, US Department of Labor, Washington, DC

Dunlop J T, 1939 "Cyclical variations in wage structure" *Review of Economic Studies* **22** 30–39

Dunlop J T (Ed.), 1957 "The task of contemporary wage theory" in *The Theory of Wage Determination* (Macmillan, London) pp 3–27

Eckstein O, Wilson T A, 1962 "The determination of money wages in American industry" *Quarterly Journal of Economics* **76** 379–414

Ehrenberg R G, Goldstein G S, 1975 "A model of public sector wage determination" *Journal of Urban Economics* **3** 223–245

Flanagan R J, 1976 "Wage interdependence in unionized labour markets" *Brookings Papers on Economic Activity* **3** 635–681

Friedman M, 1975 *Unemployment versus Inflation?* (Institute of Economic Affairs, London)

Gandolfo G, 1971 *Mathematical Methods and Models in Economic Dynamics* (North-Holland, Amsterdam)

Gellner C G, 1974 "Regional differences in employment and unemployment, 1957–72" *Monthly Labour Review* March 15–24

Godley W A H, 1977 "Inflation in the United Kingdom" in *Worldwide Inflation* Eds L B Krause, W B Salant (The Brookings Institution, Washington, DC) pp 449–474

Hart R A, MacKay D I, 1977 "Wage inflation, regional policy and the regional earnings structure" *Economica* **44** 267–281

Hewings G J D, 1978 "The trade-off between aggregate national efficiency and inter-regional equity: some empirical evidence" *Economic Geography* **54** 254–263

Hicks J R, 1955 "The economic foundation of wage policy" *Economic Journal* **65** 389–404

Hicks J R, 1963 *The Theory of Wages* second edition (Macmillan, London)

Higgins B, 1973 "Trade-off curves and regional gaps" in *Development and Planning* Eds J N Bhagwati, R S Eckaus (MIT Press, Cambridge, Mass) pp 152–177

Johnson G E, 1977 "The determination of wages in the union and non-union sectors" *British Journal of Industrial Relations* **15** 211–225

Kerr C, 1977 *Labor Markets and Wage Determination* (University of California Press, Berkeley)

Keynes J M, 1936 *The General Theory of Employment, Interest and Money* (Macmillan, London)

King L J, Forster J, 1973 "Wage rate change in urban labour markets and inter-market linkages" *Papers of the Regional Science Association* **34** 183–196

Leiserson M W, 1966 "Wage decisions and wage structures in the United States" in *Wage Structure in Theory and Practice* Ed. E M Hugh-Jones (North-Holland, Amsterdam) pp 3–69

Lerner S W, Marquand J, 1963 "Regional variations in earnings, demand for labour and shop stewards' combine committees in the British engineering industry" *The Manchester School* **31** 261–296

Levinson H M, 1960 "Pattern bargaining: a case study of the automobile workers" *Quarterly Journal of Economics* **74**(2) 296-317

Levinson H M, 1962 *Collective Bargaining in the Steel Industry: Pattern Setter or Pattern Follower?* Institute of Industrial Relations, University of Michigan, Ann Arbor

Long L H, Hansen K A, 1979 "Reasons for interstate migration" *Current Population Reports, Special Studies, Series P-23, number 81* (US Bureau of the Census, Washington, DC)

McGuire T W, Rapping L A, 1968 "The role of market variables and key bargains in the manufacturing wage determination process" *Journal of Political Economics* **76** 1015-1036

MacKay D I, Hart R A, 1975 "Wage inflation and the regional wage structure" in *Contemporary Issues in Economics* Eds M Parkin, A R Nobay (Manchester University Press, Manchester) pp 88-119

Maher J E, 1961 "The wage pattern in the United States" *Industrial and Labour Relations Review* **15** 1-20

Martin R L, 1979 "Subregional Phillips curves, inflationary expectations, and the intermarket relative wage structure: substance and methodology" in *Statistical Applications in the Spatial Sciences* Ed. N Wrigley (Pion, London) pp 64-110

Mehra Y P, 1976 "Spillovers in wage determination in manufacturing industries" *Review of Economics and Statistics* **48** 300-312

Mitchell D J B, 1977 "Wage determination" *Labor Law Journal* **28** 483-488

Mitchell D J B, 1980 *Unions, Wages, and Inflation* (The Brookings Institution, Washington, DC)

Mulvey C, Trevithick J A, 1974 "Some evidence on the wage leadership hypothesis" *Scottish Journal of Political Economy* **21** 1-11

Norton R D, Rees J, 1979 "The product cycle and the spatial decentralization of American manufacturing" *Regional Studies* **13**(2) 141-152

OECD, 1965 *Wages and Labour Mobility* (OECD, Paris)

OECD, 1978 *Economic Surveys: United States* (OECD, Paris)

Packer A H, Park S H, 1973 "Distortions in relative wages and shifts in the Phillips curve" *Review of Economics and Statistics* **55** 16-22

Papola T S, Bharadwaj V P, 1970 "The dynamics of industrial wage structure: an inter-country analysis" *Economic Journal* **80** 72-90

Phelps E S, and others, 1970 *The Microeconomic Foundations of Employment and Inflation Theory* (W W Norton, New York)

Piore M J, 1978 "Unemployment and inflation: an alternative view" *Challenge* May 24-32

Pissarides C A, 1976 *Labour Market Adjustment: Microeconomic Foundations of Short-run Neoclassical and Keynesian Dynamics* (Cambridge University Press, Cambridge)

Reed J D, Hutchinson P M, 1976 "An empirical test of a regional Phillips curve and wage rate transmission mechanism in an urban hierarchy" *Annals of Regional Science* **10** 19-30

Rein M, Marris P, 1975 "Equality, inflation and wage controls" *Challenge* March 42-50

Reynolds L G, Taft C H, 1956 *The Evolution of Wage Structure* (Yale University Press, New Haven, Conn.)

Ross A M, 1948 *Trade Union Wage Policy* (University of California Press, Berkeley)

Ross S A, 1957 "The external wage structure" in *New Concepts in Wage Determination* Eds G W Taylor, F C Pierson (McGraw-Hill, New York) pp 173-205

Ross S A, Wachter M L, 1973 "Wage determination, inflation and the industrial structure" *American Economic Review* **63** 675-692

Seltzer T, 1951 "Pattern bargaining and the United Steelworkers" *Journal of Political Economics* **59** 319-331

Sternlieb G, Hughes J W, 1975 *Post-Industrial America: Metropolitan Decline and Inter-Regional Job Shifts* Centre for Urban Policy Research, Rutgers University, New Brunswick, NJ

Snodgrass D R, 1963 "Wage changes in 24 manufacturing industries, 1948-1959: a comparative analysis" *Yale Economics Essays* **3**(1) 177-221

Sum A M, Rush T P, 1975 "The geographic structure of unemployment rates" *Monthly Labor Review* March 3-9

Thirlwall A P, 1970 "Regional Phillips curves" *Bulletin of the Oxford University Institute of Economics and Statistics* **32** 19-32

Thomas R L, Stoney P J M, 1971 "Unemployment dispersion as a determinant of wage inflation in the United Kingdom, 1925-66" *The Manchester School* **39**(2) 83-116

Tobin J, 1972 "Inflation and unemployment" *American Economic Review* **62**(1) 1-18

Ulman L, 1974 "Connective and competitive bargaining" *Scottish Journal of Political Economy* **31** 97-109

UN, 1967 *Incomes in Post-War Europe* (United Nations, Geneva)

US Bureau of Labor Statistics, 1974 *Characteristics of Agreements Covering 1,000 Workers or More, July 1, 1973* Bulletin 1822, US Department of Labor (US Government Printing Office, Washington, DC)

Wachter M L, 1970 "Relative wage equations for U.S. manufacturing industries" *Review of Economics and Statistics* **52** 405-410

Webb A E, 1974 "Unemployment, vacancies and the rate of change of earnings: a regional analysis" *National Institute of Economic and Social Research, Regional Papers III* (Cambridge University Press, Cambridge)

Weinstein B L, Firestine R E, 1978 *Regional Growth and Decline in the United States* (Praeger, New York)

Weissbrod R S P, 1976 "Diffusion of relative wage inflation in Southeast Pennsylvania" *Studies in Geography 23* Northwestern University, Evanston, Ill.

Wiles P, 1973 "Cost inflation and the state of economic theory" *Economic Journal* **83** 337-398

Williamson J, 1975 "The implications of European monetary integration for the peripheral areas" in *Economic Sovereignty and Regional Policy* Ed. J Vaizey (Gill and Macmillan, Dublin) pp 105-121

Wood A, 1978 *A Theory of Pay* (Cambridge University Press, Cambridge)

The regional impact of stagflation: a conceptual model and empirical evidence for Canada

G L Clark

7.1 Introduction

Academics have become increasingly interested in the performance of local labour markets, both from the policy and from the theoretical perspective. In particular, estimating and accounting for the differential regional impacts of national fluctuations has been seen as an important goal of enquiry (Clark, 1980). A characteristic of this research program has been the many attempts to relate local industry structure to regional performance and thus to develop hypotheses that could explain regional variations in cyclical unemployment (see Brechling, 1967; and Thirlwall, 1966; for early contributions to this field). With the recent recession these issues have gained increased importance as academics and policymakers have become concerned with more disaggregative policies (ECC, 1976b). This study is concerned with analyzing two possible mechanisms that may account for the differential regional impacts of national stagflation upon regional unemployment.

The combination of high unemployment and inflation in recent times has moved many economists to argue that the aggregate Phillips curve (the so-called trade-off between unemployment and inflation) has become more 'perverse' and unstable. The crisis in economic conditions has called into question both orthodox theory and policy practices (Robinson and Wilkinson, 1977). However, the spatial pattern of unemployment and the impact of recent economic conditions has also been virtually ignored by geographers. There are many related issues that could be considered. For example, it could be questioned whether traditional regional policies are adequate given the rapid increases and consistently high levels of national and regional unemployment. As Chisholm (1976) has noted in the British case, the assumptions behind a given regional policy developed in the 1960s may be invalid in the face of prevailing stagflation conditions. Moreover, as macropolicy has attempted to come to grips with stagflation, these policies themselves may have had important implications for the effectiveness of regional policy and may have led to regional stagflation itself. In this contribution it is argued that restrictive demand policies pursued by the Canadian Federal Government, coupled with rapid increases in money wage rates, may have reinforced and concentrated a particular pattern of regional stagnation. Patterns of regional response and the links between the national economic environment and the regional system are analyzed. A model of regional response is developed and general propositions (related to local industrial structure) concerning why regional responses may be differentiated are derived and empirically considered.

The model of regional adjustment I shall present has the following general characteristics. First, it deals exclusively with national fluctuations in demand and money-wage-rate conditions over the short-run time span where labour and capital are relatively fixed locationally and sectorally. Second, the model focuses upon the recent problems of stagflation and disequilibrium; and third, the role of expectations and uncertainty are basic to the functioning of the model. The central issue is not the determination of the path or conditions for labour-market equilibrium but rather how and why a firm will adjust to short-run fluctuations, regardless of equilibrium (Pissarides, 1976). The analytical unit is a 'representative' firm which has a location in space and time.

In the first section a model of regional adjustment is presented. This model is primarily conceptual and is used to illustrate the possible causes of differential regional impacts of national stagflation. This leads in the subsequent section to the specification of an empirical model which is designed to evaluate the impact of stagflation upon Canadian regional unemployment. The results of analysis are then presented and discussed, with reference to their descriptive content and relevance for the theoretical adjustment model. In the final section conclusions are drawn with respect to the model and the possible options for macro and regional economic policies.

7.2 The determinants of regional adjustment

7.2.1 Overview

First, firms are assumed to operate under conditions of pure competition with labour, subject to diminishing marginal product, the only variable input. Second, it is assumed that the supply of labour is fixed with downwardly rigid money wages in a labour market at less than full employment. The competitive assumption implies marginal cost pricing on the part of any given firm, so that

$$P_i^{e\,l} = \frac{W}{M} \,, \tag{7.1}$$

where

$$M = f(L) \,, \qquad \frac{dM}{dL} < 0 \,,$$

and

P^e is the expected market price for producing a given quantity of output Q,

W is the money wage rate,

M is the marginal product of labour,

W/M is the marginal cost,

L is the effective labour services used.

Rearranging expression (7.1) produces the usual implicit labour-demand function, $W = P^eM$; that is, labour is paid the expected value of its marginal product, and this result is represented in figure 7.1(a). Given a fixed money wage rate the labour supply curve is L_s [see figure 7.1(c)]. Hence this general format represents in very general terms the conventional Keynesian labour market. Given that the money wage is above its market clearing value, employment (unemployment) can be demand derived.

An important element of the model is uncertainty and its effects upon economic activity. Interpretations of uncertainty in space have traditionally dealt with it as a problem of risk to which a probability distribution can be linked (see Webber, 1972, for example). In this tradition, Curry's (1976) description of a stochastic world in which random shocks are

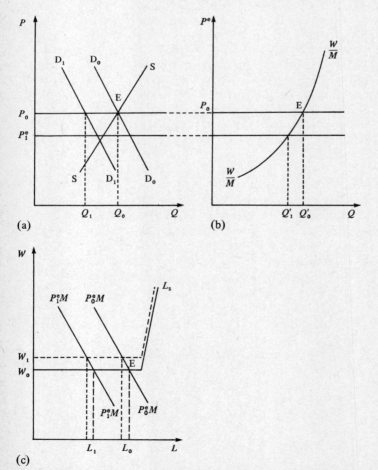

Figure 7.1. Expectations, output, and employment in a Keynesian system. (a) The industry (or region); (b) the firm; (c) the aggregate labour market.

integrated with process is suggestive of a world in which there is not complete knowledge of the future. In contrast, the model developed here follows the work of Keynes (1936) and Shackle (1974), where uncertainty has a different meaning.

Essentially, Keynes developed a model in a world where individual short-run expectations may be falsified by the passage of subsequent events, although they may have little to do with the state of long-run expectations. Basically, not only may expectations be falsified but the future remains unknown beyond the simple imposition of risk and probability. The process of adapting to unrealized expectations links immediate expectations with past performance and is inherently a disequilibrium dynamic formulation. Keynes (1936, pages 50–51) noted:

"The process of revision of short-term expectations is a gradual and continuous one carried on largely in the light of realized results; so that expected and realized results run into and overlap one another in their influence. For although output and employment are determined by the producers short-term expectations and not by past results, the most recent results usually play a predominant part in determining what these expectations are."

The relationship between expectations, output, and employment can be illustrated with reference to the following example and figures 7.1(a), (b), and (c). Suppose that the goods market is in equilibrium at a point such as E in figure 7.1(a) where the market price is P_0. Further, assume the typical firm A fully anticipates this price so that $P^e = P_0$. Thus firm A produces the quantity of goods, Q_0', by employing a certain quantity of labour, L_0, (the exact relationship being determined by A's production function). To produce Q_0' firm A must, however, lay out a wage bill, $W = WL_0$, on the expectation of being able to sell that quantity of goods produced. In time, t, this expectation is in fact realized, since $P^e = P_0$. Imagine, however, that in time $(t+1)$ market demand for firm A's product falls [a shift of D_0 to D_1 in figure 7.1(a)]—a number of outcomes are likely.

First assume expectations are unchanged. The typical firm will continue to produce Q_0', where $P^e = P_0 = W/M$. By implication the market supply will be Q_0. The typical firm will find itself unable to sell all of its output, given aggregate excess supply. In the face of excess supply we may assume that the firm will adjust its expected price downwards to, say, P_1^e, in which case the typical firm cuts output from Q_0' to Q_1' [see figure 7.1(b)], reducing its use of labour. In the aggregate, this can be represented in figure 7.1(c) by a leftward shift of the labour-demand curve. Unemployment will rise as labour input falls from L_0 to $L_1^{(1)}$.

(1)
$$W = P^e M(L), \qquad \text{implying} \qquad \frac{\mathrm{d}L}{\mathrm{d}P^e} = -M' > 0.$$

Although we are concerned here primarily with impact multipliers, it can be seen that this will not be the end of the story. With the fall in output, employment, and prices, incomes of consumers will fall which might be expected to lead to further reduction in demand for goods. This will produce the usual Keynesian multiplier effects as demand continues to shift inwards. Given stability, a new short-run equilibrium will be reestablished at lower output, income, and employment, where expectations have caught up with the market clearing price and demand has ceased to fall.

A similar conceptualization, although derived from different theoretical roots (basically cost-minimizing behavior), has been proposed by Barro and Grossman (1976). They suggested that if trade and exchange were allowed to take place at prices that did not represent equilibrium prices (that is, in the absence of the Walrasian auctioneer and the principle of recontracting), then two important qualifications to the orthodox macroeconomics of exchange and production would occur. First, given such prices, there would no longer be an automatic equivalence between the quantity of goods transacted and the quantity of goods supplied or demanded. Second, consumers and producers could no longer expect with absolute certainty to buy and sell all they wanted at the prevailing prices. Instead, in situations where there is excess demand or supply, the short-side (or short-run time period) of the market would prevail.

7.2.2 Formal approach

To illustrate the implications of this analysis for regional unemployment, consider the following case:

Case 1, Two regions i and j

Assume:

(a) Initial competitive assumptions.

(b) Two regions i and j, where region i is specialized in the production of consumer durables and where region j specialized in agricultural products.

(c) Suppose in time, t, the government engineers (cf Tufte, 1978) a fall in consumer demand through, for example, an income-tax increase.

Implications

(1) In time $(t + 1)$, as demand falls, the impact, in terms of lower employment, is likely to be concentrated in region i as its goods are more income and price elastic.

(2) By the above analysis, employment will initially fall in both regions, but one may expect a greater increase in unemployment in region i than in region j.

(3) The more rapid increase in unemployment in region i suggests a greater fall in incomes. This will lead to the above multiplier effects, which could be expected to spill over into region j. Nonetheless, given the income

elasticity of demand for durables, these multiplier effects could still be expected to have the greatest effect on region i's unemployment [2].

These implications then imply two propositions:

(1) Restriction on aggregate demand will create more unemployment in regions specializing in durable manufacturing-goods production than in regions specializing in agricultural goods production.

(2) The impact of national fluctuations in demand, in the short run, is likely to be reflected in changes in all regions' unemployment rates.

Recently debate in the economics literature has proliferated with respect to the process of wage determination, inflation, and economic policy (see Wiles, 1973; for example). The view taken here was expressed best by Hicks (1974), who argued for the inclusion of a sociopolitical mechanism of wage-rate determination as a fundamental element in the functioning of the economy. Hicks (1974) emphasized the issue of fairness with respect to wage and price increases. This concept embodies the principle that wages are not simply pushed by a dominant trade-union but that employers as well tend to pay money wages in comparison to other reference groups in the community. Thus wage-rate increases may not be related to the level of unemployment or even to productivity but rather to the influence of class bargaining and the social context. Robinson (1972) has also argued that this process is superimposed on the economy which is dichotomized into high-growth versus low-growth industries, where the former may pay progressively higher wages to attract both a quality and a quantity of labour, and the latter, to maintain fairness as well as yielding to union and industry pressure, has to follow the general trend in money-wage-rate increases. This assumption is then more than 'Keynesian' wage rigidity and Phillips curve demand inflation; in this context, wages are institutionally determined (see Burton and Addison, 1977, for a critical review of this position) and flow (drift) to all sectors of the economy without regard to productivity, market structure, demand elasticity, the demand for labour, or the spatial configuration of economic activity (see Kaldor, 1970; on this point). This is what Hicks (1974) characterized as Stage II, the stagflation of the 1970s.

To trace the implications of such wage behavior on output and employment, a typical firm could be envisaged as operating in the following manner. With an expected price P^e for firm A's product and a money wage rate, W, determined exogenously, any change in W would necessitate an adjustment by the typical firm through M in the short run. An increase in W [from W_0 to W_1 as in figure 7.1(c) for example] under conditions of constant prices P_0^e, would increase the average cost of producing a given

[2] The disturbance to aggregate demand might arise initially as a result of a fall in export demand for agricultural products. The impact of this will be initially to reduce employment the most in region j. However, given income inelastic demand for agricultural products, it is conceivable that most of the subsequent multiplier effects will fall on region i so that, in the end, region i is still the hardest hit.

unit of output. This would result in a decrease in firm A's output and a cut back on its level of employment [in figure 7.1(c) this implies a shift up the P_0^eM curve]. Such adjustment behavior is the product of our initial assumptions of profit maximization and the limiting assumptions that labour is subject to diminishing marginal product and is the only variable input factor in the short run.

If such an adjustment were general for the total industry, aggregate output would be cut back so that the market price will increase as supply decreases. Thus price inflation is only possible if the product is not subject to exogenous market-pricing forces. The consequence of money-wage-rate changes in one market (sectoral or spatial) is that they become inputs to the behaviour of other markets, with no guarantee that the structures of other markets will be able to absorb an exogenously determined wage-rate increase without increasing unemployment. The following case can be used to illustrate this point.

Case 2, Two regions i and j
Assume:
(a) As in *Case 1*.
(b) Two regions where $dM_i/dt > dM_j/dt$.
(c) Assume on the basis of such an increase in M_i, the money wage rate is also bargained upwards in time, t, W_0 to W_1 in figure 7.1(c), in region i so as just to match the increase in M_i. However, also assume that the wage-rate increase is passed on in total to region j.
Implications
(1) In time $(t+1)$ the effect of an increase in W for region i will be to maintain the level of employment and to generate additional demand in the local economy.
(2) Region i could also then be characterized as a growth economy, as output itself would also rise through increased labour productivity.
(3) The effect on region j, however, will be to reduce the level of employment and increase region j's unemployment rate[3].
    These implications then imply a further proposition:
(4) Money-wage-rate inflation may have either a positive or a negative effect on local unemployment. The exact effect will depend on the spatial concentration of industries and their differential growth patterns of labour productivity.
    A number of authors have also argued that the structure of capitalism itself makes simultaneous inflation and unemployment a necessary outcome. Robinson and Wilkinson (1977), for example, argued that without institutional (such as trade-union) pressures for increases in money wages,

---

[3] It should also be noted, however, that expansion in region i also implies an expansion in demand for secondary input materials. For example, heavy steel construction demands iron ore, which could come from region j. Thus there may also be positive spillover effects in the scenario outlined above.

high-productivity and growth industries would stagnate as mass consumption could not match productive capacity. Yet such wage-rate increases become extra costs for marginal and less productive industries. The characteristics of this dualism has been argued by Bluestone (1971) to be:

Primary sector or high-growth industries	Secondary sector or low-growth industries
High growth	Low growth
High productivity	Low productivity
Income elastic demand	Income inelastic demand
High market concentration	Low market concentration

Duality may also be an important factor in stagflation. Means (1975) claimed that much of current price inflation can be related to highly concentrated (primary) sectors administrating price increases. The planned sector is considered to have market characteristics such that wage increases are not absorbed in the form of lower profits but rather are passed on to the secondary sector in the form of higher prices. This latter sector may not be able (owing to low productivity and competition) to increase prices and thus may have to absorb wage-rate increases internally. This then leads to the possibility that wage price increases in the primary sector create the conditions for higher unemployment in other sectors. Because of size and growth characteristics, Galbraith (1975) has claimed that the secondary sector must depend on the market for investment funds, whereas the planned sector develops such funds internally. This implies that a government policy designed for deflation (high corporate taxation, budget surplus, and high interest rates) is likely to affect the secondary sector before the primary sector.

7.3 An empirical model of regional response
7.3.1 A time-series format
The empirical model draws its rationale for the inclusion of certain variables from the preceding discussion, although it is emphasized that subsequent analysis is designed primarily to describe the regional impact of national fluctuations.

Let

U_{it} the unemployment in region i, time t, be the dependent variable or the measure of regional response over time;

$U_{i(t-1)}$ the unemployment in region i, time $(t-1)$, be independent such that it reflects conditions in the local market in time $(t-1)$. U_{it} is assumed to vary directly with $U_{i(t-1)}$;

U_{Nt} be unemployment at the national scale, time t, an independent variable where U_{it} varies directly with U_{Nt} and is assumed to represent national cyclical or demand changes attributable, at least in part, to government macropolicy; and let

W_{Nt} be the money wage rate per hour worked in Canadian manufacturing
          industries, time t; an independent variable designed to capture the
          response of regions to money-wage-rate inflation. The parameter
          sign could be positive or negative [4].

In general terms, the empirical model is stated as follows:

$$U_{it} = \beta_0 + \beta_1 U_{i(t-1)} + \beta_2 U_{Nt} + \beta_3 W_{Nt} + \epsilon_t , \qquad \text{where} \quad \beta_2, \beta_3 \lesseqgtr 0. \quad (7.2)$$

To accommodate the recent criticisms of Pierce (1977) concerning the
estimation of economic relationships over time, the model can be respecified
such that

$$[U_{it} - \rho U_{i(t-1)}] = \beta_0[1 - \rho] + \beta_1[U_{i(t-1)} - \rho U_{i(t-2)}] + \beta_2[U_{Nt} - \rho U_{N(t-1)}]$$
$$+ \beta_3[W_{Nt} - \rho W_{N(t-1)}] + \epsilon_t , \qquad (7.3)$$

where $\beta_2, \beta_3 \lesseqgtr 0$.

This then becomes a dynamic model of adjustment, emphasizing not the
actual levels at any given time but rather the adjustment to changes in
the independent variables over time and the relative significance of these
independent variables in explaining adjustment. The ρ coefficient is derived
from the Cochrane–Orcutt (1949) method of ordinary least squares (OLS)
regression and is defined as the first-order autoregressive (AR) parameter
derived from the regression error structure [5]. The procedure involves first
estimating the OLS regression model in the form of equation (7.2), then,
after inspection of the error terms and using a preliminary estimate of ρ,
the equation is reestimated in the form of equation (7.3). This process is
repeated until the parameter is stable and the final model can be evaluated.

A number of writers have argued that in similar circumstances such a
system of equations and the estimation of their parameters should be
subject to an aggregation constraint. Denton (1977) argued that this would
remove the possibilities of parameter bias or inconsistency if each variable
was weighted by the actual work force of the given region. However, in
the case under discussion this is not appropriate, as a condition for such
an estimation procedure is not met; namely, identical sets of regressors.

---

[4] In the context of the model discussed above, which is primarily a price-fixed model,
the appropriate variable should more realistically be W_{Nt}/P_{it}. However, since real-wage
data are not available at the regional level and price data are also very limited, the
money-wage-rate variable was included. Clearly, if prices were to rise in a given region
so as to match an increase in W_N, then there may be no discernable impact of W_{Nt} on
U_{it}. However, it is that effect which is unknown in the Canadian regional context.
[5] Note that the first-order AR parameter may not be totally adequate in capturing
the effects of serial autocorrelation (Clark, 1979); for example, a moving-average
component may also be present. Feedback (interregional) effects are not considered
nor the possibility that national impacts may have lags beyond one month. King and
Clark (1978) provide evidence, albeit in a regression format, that regional lags may in
fact be quite small in the Canadian case.

Both the parameter ρ, and the use of the lagged regional-unemployment rate $U_{i(t-1)}$ as an independent variable mean that each regression equation is unique to each particular region and that, in fact,

$$\sum_{i=1}^{42} U_{it} \neq U_{Nt} .$$

It was judged that the problems of serial autocorrelation may be more significant than the suggested problems of aggregation bias, and consequently the Cochrane–Orcutt (1949) method was utilized.

7.3.2 Data sources

King and Clark (1978) have described the *Statistics Canada* Labour Force Survey regions used in this study. All provinces are represented and the population distribution has been used as the criterion for boundary selection. These regions are constructed from the Camu et al's (1964) definition of functional economic regions for Canada and consist of thirty-three nonmetropolitan and nine metropolitan regions. The Labour Force Survey is conducted each month by *Statistics Canada* and is based on a sample of, on the average, 3000 households over all Canadian regions. The unemployed are defined as those persons during the interview week who are either without work and seeking work, or who are laid-off temporarily. This definition presumes to include only those people involuntarily unemployed, and not those unemployed owing to illness or for other voluntary reasons. The labour-force participation rate is defined as all those in the labour force (employed plus unemployed) divided by all those people over 14 years of age eligible to work [6].

Money-wage data were derived from the monthly survey of wages and salaries conducted by *Statistics Canada*. These relate to the aggregate hourly rate of pay for all Canadian manufacturing industries at the national level. The data were not price deflated and were aggregate over all regions and sectors. Structural data on local regional characteristics were derived from the 1970 Geographic Survey of Employment (*Statistics Canada*), which is based upon the Camu et al (1964) regional economic system. More recent data were deemed inappropriate since they would simply serve to reflect the impact of the current recession rather than the structure of industry and employment before the recent economic crisis. The industrial structure of regional employment was used to imply economic structure not variations in employment itself.

---

[6] Note that those people who are unemployed but not seeking work are defined neither as employed nor as unemployed. The data were made available by Statistics Canada in published and unpublished forms for all regions at monthly intervals over the period, 1969–1976. Unfortunately, after January 1976 the boundaries of the regions were so altered that further consistent time-series analysis was rendered impossible.

7.4 Canadian regional adjustment to stagflation

7.4.1 Preliminary analysis

Consideration was also given to incorporating the supply response of labour
to changing economic conditions by weighting regional unemployment by
local participation rates. In doing so it was hoped to account for biases in
the estimation of regional adjustment that could occur simply on the basis
of people leaving the labour market rather than becoming involuntarily
unemployed. However, preliminary testing of the relationship between
regional labour-force participation rates and national unemployment
fluctuations disclosed that very little relationship existed. This is consistent
with many time-series macroeconomic studies of participation-rate
behaviour (see Hartley and Revanker, 1974), and consequently the labour-
supply response was not incorporated in the analysis (see Clark, 1978; for
further details).

   The model [equation (7.3)] was estimated using the OLS–Cochrane and
Orcutt (1949) regression method with a number of preliminary steps.
First, all variables were deseasonalized and transformed to natural logarithms
(ln) prior to estimating the model. The standardized beta coefficients can
be then interpreted as beta-elasticities measuring the response of the
dependent variable to unit changes over time in the independent variables
(Brechling, 1967). Second, the model was estimated over the period July
1969 to December 1975: The initial point was chosen because a number
of earlier commentators (see Donner et al, 1973), backed-up by recent
studies on Canadian business fluctuations (Chung, 1976), considered July
1969 to be the start of the 1970s recessionary period. December 1975,
was chosen as the terminal date since no comparable date is available
beyond that date.

7.4.2 Calibration and results

Table 7.1 summarizes the values obtained from estimating equation (7.3).
The results are recorded according to the region and are presented in a
summary form. Each variable is dealt with separately and attention drawn
to its parameter value, sign, and significance with respect to each region
and also with respect to the Canadian regional system.

   An immediate observation that can be made with reference to the national
money-wage variable and its significance for regional unemployment is the
general east–west dichotomy. Table 7.2(a) shows that the eastern regions
(including Québec and the Maritime regions) generally have positive
parameters whereas the western regions (the Prairies) have negative parameters. Two of the three eastern regions with negative signs are the
metropolitan regions of Montreal and Toronto. Of the western regions
with positive signs, both are in British Columbia. Of the eight nonmetropolitan regions with significant and positive parameters in the east,
five are in the Maritime regions, one is in Québec, and the two others are

in central and southwestern Ontario. The one metropolitan region with a significant and positive b_3 parameter in the east is Québec–Levis. In understanding the beta-elasticities, it should be remembered that the differenced and lagged form of the variable implies change and adjustment over time. For example, in region 10, Northeast New Brunswick, a $1 \cdot 0\%$ increase in W_{Nt} over one time period, t, to the next $(t+1)$, would cause a $1 \cdot 23\%$ increase in regional unemployment. In contrast, in the western region of Medicine-Hat/Lethbridge, a 1% increase in W_{Nt} would stimulate a $1 \cdot 54\%$ decrease in local unemployment. The impact of W_{Nt} in the east varies from a maximum b_3 parameter value of $1 \cdot 23$ to a minimum of $0 \cdot 354$. In most Ontario regions, the parameters are positive but not significant whereas in Québec the majority of regions do not have a significant b_3 parameter value. The parameter values of W_{Nt} in the Prairie regions are generally larger than the parameter values of the eastern regions.

There are a number of implications to be drawn from these results. First, stagflation—simultaneously high money-wage inflation and unemployment—creates problems particularly for the Maritime regions. In essence, increasing money-wage rates add to the problem of regional unemployment, which may already be under considerable pressure from macropolicies directed to deflating the national economy. Thus, there is evidence for what could be termed a 'reverse' Phillips curve. Second, although there is also evidence of a positive association between U_{it} and W_{Nt} in Ontario, most parameter values are not statistically significant. This implies that stagflation may not be a problem for the spatioeconomic core of Canada. It could be contended that the source of W_{Nt} determination is often Ontario, and creating disturbances with a 'spillover' of such determinations into the Maritimes may cause increases in Maritime unemployment but not significantly affect the Ontario economy. There are two exceptions to this general statement in Ontario: southwest Ontario (region 20) which is dominated by the automobile industry, and Kitchener (region 19), also with a strong transportation-equipment industry. These regions have positive and significant W_{Nt} terms, which implies that if money-wage-rate increases in Canada are greater than those in the United States (which they have been over the 1970–1976 period), this could lead automobile companies to decrease production in Canadian branch plants and switch to United States production facilities.

Evidence from a variety of sources (see ECC, 1976a; 1976b) has been noted that suggests strong economic expansion in the western regions under conditions of national stagnation over the 1969–1976 period. This prompts the conclusions that either the Prairie regions themselves were the source of rapid money-wage expansion based primarily on the tightness of local labour markets, or that money-wage contracts concluded elsewhere in the country generated further economic growth in the western regions simply because the cost-structure of prairie economics were able to absorb wage-rate increases. The exceptions to the generally positive W_{Nt} parameter

Table 7.1. Results for regional stagflation adjustment model, equation (7.3). OLS estimates (adjusted for serial autocorrelation using the Cochrane–Orcutt, 1949, method) 1969(7)–1975(12).

Region	Model parameters[a]				F value	R^2	DW[b]	Final ρ
	b_0	b_1	b_2	b_3				
Maritime Regions								
1 Avalon	1·200	−0·082 (0·180)[c]	+0·026 (0·264)	+0·940* (0·221)	76·349	0·758	1·952	0·651
2 Newfoundland/Labrador	0·775	+0·274 (0·191)	+0·177 (0·200)	+0·980* (0·157)	101·218	0·806	2·324	0·500
3 Prince Edward Island	0·232	−0·194 (0·189)	+0·896 (0·566)	+0·169 (0·436)	14·045	0·366	2·070	0·596
4 Cape Breton	0·364	−0·060 (0·205)	+0·889* (0·257)	+0·394* (0·187)	38·280	0·611	1·916	0·525
5 Annapolis, South Shore	0·689	+1·281* (0·137)	+0·193 (0·134)	+0·048 (0·090)	26·674	0·523	1·903	−0·231
6 Halifax, North Shore	0·189	+0·758* (0·147)	+0·541* (0·129)	+0·082 (0·066)	45·515	0·651	2·106	−0·093
7 Moncton	0·089	+0·718* (0·193)	+0·394 (0·252)	+0·527* (0·183)	27·167	0·526	1·913	0·170
8 St John Valley	1·586	−0·113 (0·175)	+0·499 (0·364)	−0·546* (0·264)	8·334	0·255	2·017	0·468
9 Upper St John Valley	−0·146	−0·006 (0·174)	+0·877* (0·305)	−0·289 (0·224)	20·886	0·462	2·024	0·533
10 Northeast New Brunswick	1·103	+0·083 (0·215)	−0·061 (0·298)	+1·233* (0·228)	61·020	0·715	2·059	0·498
11 Gaspé-North Québec	0·965	+0·312* (0·120)	+0·603* (0·215)	+0·253 (0·205)	61·294	0·715	1·594	0·743

Canada Central							
12 Laurentians	0·860	−0·042 (0·185)	+0·394* (0·156)	+0·345* (0·112)	31·210	0·562	2·048	0·466
13 Montreal region	0·801	+0·062 (0·139)	+0·893* (0·080)	−0·399* (0·050)	146·705	0·857	2·065	0·268
14 Eastern Townships	0·258	+0·217 (0·194)	+0·785* (0·237)	−0·181 (0·182)	66·765	0·732	2·115	0·638
15 Western Québec	−0·101	+1·103* (0·202)	+0·712* (0·220)	+0·116 (0·128)	67·242	0·734	2·102	0·259
16 Eastern Ontario	−0·025	+0·848* (0·106)	+0·617* (0·148)	+0·074 (0·671)	97·581	0·800	1·901	−0·139
17 Toronto region	−0·303	+0·633* (0·101)	+0·903* (0·144)	−0·064 (0·052)	178·498	0·880	1·961	0·011
18 Niagara	−0·445	−0·099 (0·167)	+1·055* (0·226)	+0·215 (0·153)	32·683	0·573	2·036	0·427
19 Central Ontario	−1·804	−0·062 (0·139)	+1·436* (0·356)	+0·511* (0·249)	32·828	0·574	1·978	0·436
20 Southwest Ontario	−0·205	+0·066 (0·169)	+0·382 (0·456)	+0·824* (0·374)	37·74	0·608	1·940	0·648
21 Kitchener	−4·320	−0·093 (0·519)	+2·830* (0·519)	+0·230 (0·379)	44·253	0·645	1·662	0·557
22 Northern Ontario	−0·446	+0·172 (0·172)	+1·016* (0·197)	+0·160 (0·121)	48·750	0·667	2·063	0·349

Table 1 (continued).

Region	Model parameters[a]				F value	R^2	DW[b]	Final ρ
	b_0	b_1	b_2	b_3				
Canada Prairies								
23 Winnipeg	−0·799	+0·091 (0·321)	+1·713* (0·321)	−0·673* (0·209)	55·303	0·694	1·700	0·477
24 South Manitoba	−0·454	−0·167 (0·102)	+1·664* (0·458)	−0·939* (0·377)	28·911	0·543	1·889	0·660
25 Regina	2·953	−0·287* (0·092)	+0·211 (0·524)	−1·515* (0·499)	34·273	0·584	1·947	0·729
26 Saskatoon	0·794	−0·602* (0·123)	+1·280* (0·626)	−1·041 (0·581)	14·453	0·372	1·927	0·728
27 Parklands	1·259	+0·312* (0·084)	+0·448 (0·239)	−0·774* (0·198)	30·349	0·555	2·040	0·084
28 Medicine-Hat/Lethbridge	0·153	−0·033 (0·085)	+1·650* (0·361)	−1·544* (0·266)	45·563	0·651	2·049	0·407
29 Calgary region	0·933	+0·949* (0·092)	+0·311 (0·170)	−0·297* (0·097)	41·676	0·631	1·871	−0·355
30 Edmonton region	0·175	+0·596* (0·099)	+0·872* (0·180)	−0·413* (0·108)	40·210	0·623	1·917	−0·219
Canada West and Northwest								
31 British Columbia Interior	−0·013	+0·192 (0·195)	+0·978* (0·178)	+0·082 (0·108)	47·506	0·661	2·103	0·337
32 Vancouver region	0·256	−0·368* (0·177)	+1·394* (0·193)	−0·426* (0·144)	92·092	0·791	2·034	0·613
33 Vancouver Island	−0·078	+0·342 (0·208)	+0·741* (0·263)	+0·317 (0·171)	43·690	0·642	1·877	0·387

Metropolitan Regions

34 Calgary	0·773	+0·877* (0·104)	+0·450* (0·191)	−0·324* (0·110)	28·683	0·541	1·845	−0·349
35 Edmonton	0·222	+0·624* (0·111)	+0·846* (0·198)	−0·380* (0·117)	24·427	0·501	1·981	−0·273
36 Halifax	0·474	+0·798* (0·125)	+0·336 (0·253)	+0·061 (0·093)	18·297	0·429	2·032	−0·205
37 Hamilton	0·310	+0·809* (0·138)	+0·494* (0·188)	+0·008 (0·106)	19·470	0·444	2·073	−0·157
38 Montreal	0·740	+0·171 (0·144)	+0·886* (0·091)	−0·431* (0·060)	106·657	0·814	2·073	0·243
39 Ottawa–Hull	−2·695	−0·130 (0·114)	+2·024* (0·384)	+0·410 (0·249)	58·587	0·706	1·911	0·498
40 Québec–Levis	1·109	−0·080 (0·175)	−0·205 (0·301)	+0·598* (0·223)	16·841	0·409	2·108	0·526
41 Toronto	−0·308	+0·649* (0·093)	+0·852* (0·141)	−0·002 (0·053)	158·578	0·867	2·011	−0·093
42 Vancouver	0·426	−0·437* (0·169)	+1·473* (0·207)	−0·649* (0·166)	91·448	0·789	2·088	0·640

a Summary form of equation (7.2).
b DW—Durbin–Watson statistic.
c Standard errors.

* Significant at the 95% level.

values of the west are the Interior BC and Vancouver Island regions which offer indirect evidence of the latter conclusion.   Both regions are dominated by wood-processing industries with cost structures which are less competitive than or equal to those of United States competitors.   The positive signs suggest that recent industry claims that money wages are reducing international competitiveness may be well founded.

The results with respect to the sign, significance, and value of the b_3 parameter, national money-wage rate, suggest strong links between national aggregate-wage-rate conditions and the performance of local economies. Regional abilities to cope with or adjust to increasing money-wage rates vary greatly; further, the strongly regionalized impact of national stagflation conditions also have some tendency to affect adversely those regions already designated high-unemployment development areas by the Department of Regional Economic Expansion (for example, Cape Breton Island).

Consideration of the signs of the b_2 parameters leads to rather different results than those discussed above concerning the W_{Nt} parameter.   If tables 7.1 and 7.2(b) are consulted, it is clear that of all the Canadian regions only the regions of Northeast New Brunswick and Québec–Levis have negative signs and these are not significant.   In fact, in direct contrast to the results with respect to money-wage rates, thirty of the forty-two regions have positive and significant beta elasticities for the U_{Nt} variable.

Table 7.2. The sign and significance of (a) the national money-wage parameter; (b) the national unemployment parameter; (c) the lagged regional unemployment parameter.

Regional group	Nonmetropolitan regions[a]		Regional group	Metropolitan regions[b]	
	+ve	−ve		+ve	−ve
(a) The national money-wage parameter					
East[c]	8	2	East	1	1
West[d]	−[e]	8	West	−	3
(b) The national unemployment parameter					
East	14	−	East	5	−
West	8	−	West	3	−
(c) The lagged regional unemployment parameter					
East	6	−	East	3	−
West	3	3	West	2	1

[a] Regions including Avalon to Vancouver Island.
[b] Regions including Calgary to Vancouver.
[c] Those regions in the provinces of Newfoundland, Nova Scotia, Prince Edward Island, Québec, New Brunswick, and Ontario.
[d] Those regions in the provinces of Manitoba, Saskatchewan, Alberta, and British Columbia.
[e] No regions in that group.

Although in the above discussion the regions with significant parameter estimates in the east were in the Maritime Regions, now, in the case of the national unemployment variable, most are in Ontario and Québec. Regions in the west with significant b_2 parameter estimates include Winnipeg, South Manitoba, Saskatoon, Medicine-Hat, Edmonton, and all of the regions in British Columbia.

The interpretation of elasticities in this context is open to a number of criticisms. It cannot be assumed that the 'business cycle' is symmetrical both for increases and for decreases in unemployment. Clearly the elasticities are average responses and moreover they are particular to a given period. But since the concern here is with parameter significance and not so much with estimating the month-to-month impact of macro-policy, a number of comments can be made. First, Ontario regions generally have quite high beta elasticities. For example, for Kitchener, region 21, a 1% increase in national unemployment on the average would induce a $2 \cdot 83\%$ increase in regional unemployment. The lowest, significant, regional b_2 coefficient for Ontario was $0 \cdot 617$ in Eastern Ontario, region 16, although the average was $1 \cdot 177$. Western regions similarly have quite high significant beta-elasticities. In South Manitoba, region 24 for example, a 1% increase in U_{Nt} would induce on average a $1 \cdot 665\%$ increase in unemployment in that region. The lowest beta coefficient is $0 \cdot 741$, Vancouver Island, and the average b_2 coefficient for western regions was $1 \cdot 186$. Metropolitan regions had in general lower beta coefficients, with the exception of the value for Québec–Levis, with by far the greatest value in Ottawa–Hull ($2 \cdot 024$). On average, however, the metropolitan regions beta-coefficient value was $0 \cdot 795$.

The greater sensitivity of Ontario regions to national unemployment (and hence to demand conditions) is in direct contrast to their relative lack of sensitivity to changes in money-wage rates. These regions are more demand and consumer-good orientated, with most regions having at least 10% of their total manufacturing employment (in 1970) devoted to electrical products, and a further 30% made up of textiles, automobile manufacturing, chemicals and machine industries. On average, few Ontario regions have a food-and-beverage component greater than 10%. Within Québec, however, each region is not dominated to such an extent by consumer-demand industries and this may be reflected in their lower b_2 coefficients. In contrast to the Ontario regions, those Prairie regions with significant b_2 terms have manufacturing structures which include very few consumer-demand industries, and their quite low values could also be thought to reflect their economic structure. Interior BC and Vancouver Island, which have a strong wood-industry component and are consequently tied directly to housing construction, also show large b_2 terms and this is reflected in the b_2 values of Maritime regions such as Halifax North Shore, Upper St John Valley and Gaspé-North Québec which have significant b_2 parameter estimates.

Macroeconomic policies of demand restriction at the national level instituted by the federal government may have significant impacts for the central spatioeconomic core of the economy, particularly for the Ontario regions, but less so for the Prairie regions owing in part to compensatory money-wage forces. This is not an unusual result since the orthodox macroeconomic policy of reducing expenditure and lowering demand should be expected to have its greatest impact on regions specializing in demand industries. This would imply a wide variation in the ability of Canadian regions to adjust to national money-wage and demand fluctuations. At the same time, however, the Prairie regions, over the period 1969– 1976, have been able to cope with restrictive demand policies and yet at the same time expand employment and money wages. The implications for the Maritime regions of the variations in national unemployment and demand fluctuations may not be as important as in Ontario for example. Nevertheless, there is evidence that national unemployment is often a significant variable that could help explain differential regional adjustments. Coupled with the importance of the W_{Nt} variable, many of the Maritime regions could be seen to be intimately linked to the functioning of the national economy.

Very few eastern regions have significant b_1 terms [see tables 7.1 and 7.2(c)] and all that are significant are positive and concentrated in Nova Scotia and northern New Brunswick. There are two exceptions, Western Québec and Eastern Ontario, which have significant b_1 parameter estimates. The b_1 parameter estimates for the western regions are more difficult to generalize, and are equally likely to have either a positive or a negative sign and to be associated with negative b_3 coefficients. Both Calgary and Edmonton have positive and significant b_1 terms, whereas Vancouver is significant but negative. The largest beta elasticity is to be found in region 5 (Annapolis South Shore), and it suggests that a 1% increase or decrease in national unemployment would induce a $1 \cdot 281\%$ increase or decrease in regional unemployment.

In testing the relationship hypothesized in equation (7.3), it was found that many regions had R^2 values greater than $0 \cdot 6$, and F ratios significant at the 99% level. At the same time, the Durbin–Watson test for serial autocorrelation confirmed that there was no significant autocorrelation for almost all regions. Only Prince Edward Island, St John Valley, and Regina had R^2 values that could be described as very low, and only in Gaspé- North Québec was an ambiguous result obtained for the presence or absence of serial autocorrelation. In almost all cases, the ρ value (the first-order AR coefficient) was at least $0 \cdot 4$, signifying an important weighting to previous observations for all variables in time (the exceptions being in the Toronto region, Parklands, and the Toronto metropolitan region). In essence, the relationship performed quite well although in a number of cases only one independent variable was significant.

7.4.2 The results and adjustment model

In the context of seeking to establish reasons why the impact of money-wage inflation and policy may be regionally differentiated, the model emphasized those attributes of a given region that might influence regional adjustment. The results noted in this section provide some measure of acceptance for the propositions derived above [7].

In section 7.2.2 it was argued that demand-restriction policies in the form of, for example, increased income tax could generate differential regional adjustments. It was proposed that:

(1) Restriction on aggregate demand will create more unemployment in regions specializing in the production of durable manufacturing goods than in regions specializing in the production of agricultural goods.

and that

(2) The impact of national fluctuations in demand, in the short run, is likely to be reflected in changes in all regions' unemployment rates.

The implication of our results [tables 7.1 and 7.2(b)] is that propositions (1) and (2) should be provisionally accepted. In particular, it was noted that Ontario regions on the average are affected most through changes in macroeconomic policy and trends and cycles in national unemployment. However, apart from noting that stagflation is very much spatially polarized and that effects of W_{Nt} and U_{Nt} in combination create wide variations in regional adjustment, it is difficult to discriminate between marginal variations in consumer demand and the impacts upon consumer-demand industries. This is particularly true in the case of the Québec regions versus the Ontario regions.

There remains a problem of interpretation of the results for Ottawa–Hull. Although it could be argued intuitively that the Ottawa–Hull economy should be very stable owing to the government-service-sector components, this is not the case. One explanation is to be found in the rather dualistic structure of the city region. Western Québec and the city of Hull are dominated by wood, and by printing and publishing industries, which were noted above as being associated significantly with strong demand and wage fluctuations over the 1969–1976 period. On the other hand, Ottawa and the Eastern Ontario region have rather more diverse economies and they reflect the pattern for most Ontario regions. For instance, over 40% of total manufacturing employment in 1970 in Eastern Ontario was accounted for by high-growth and technological industries such

[7] There is a problem in relating time-series results to cross-sectional regional characteristics. The correlations between structural attributes and parameter signs and values may only establish association not causality, and although the traditional means of resolving this problem is a pooled econometric model, in this paper such an approach was considered inappropriate since 'pooling' implies that the estimated parameters come from the same population, regardless of region. Consequently a pooled model would tend to reduce the interregional parameter variations, which are central to this study.

as electrical and machinery products. Although these were subject also to demand pressures, the impact on them and hence on regional unemployment of wage fluctuations and demand policies has not been as great.

In general, metropolitan regions were less sensitive to demand pressures. Hamilton and Halifax with their steel and fabricating industries did not appear on average to be as affected as surrounding regions. Also, Montreal and Toronto had below-average U_{Nt} parameter terms, particularly compared with Vancouver. These two cities are also the most diversified in Canada and have quite similar industrial structures, except that Montreal has a higher component in clothing industries.

In section 7.2.2 it was also argued that variations in national money-wage rates could have the following impacts:

(4) Money-wage-rate inflation may have either a positive or a negative effect on local unemployment. The exact effect will depend on the spatial concentration of industries and their differential growth patterns of labour productivity.

It was considered also that for regions dominated by low-growth industries the appropriate sign for the b_3 parameter would be positive, whereas for regions with a more balanced industrial structure the sign could be negative. The results, at first sight, would seem to validate the proposition (4). The Maritime regions, which have a large component of low-growth industries and industrial stagnation, have positive and significant b_3 coefficients. Central Canadian regions generally have statistically insignificant parameter estimates and the Western regions have negative parameter signs. There is a problem in interpretation here, however; the Prairie regions have a higher proportion of defined low-growth industries that the Maritime regions and yet the signs are reversed.

The problem is simply that of adequately defining low-growth industries. It was argued above that a low-growth industry could be defined in terms of low labour productivity, low industry concentration, and low employment growth; in accordance with this general characterization a group of such industries was defined for Canada. The problem of interpretation derives from the relatively broad SIC classifications used by the Department of Industry, Trade and Commerce—the source of our data used in making the classification. Thus, although the Food and Beverage Industry group, for example, is defined as a low-growth industry, there are clear differences of labour and capital productivity between Prairie range agriculture and the smaller, labour intensive agriculture of the Maritimes. If the low-growth-industry proportion of the Maritime regions is compared directly with other regions and account is taken of recent trends in Prairie economic development, proposition (4) could be tentatively accepted. That the Prairie regions have negative b_3 parameter signs reflects the productivity of labour in agriculture as well as the growth since 1970 of the capital intensive oil, gas, and chemical industries; industries which could be defined as high-growth, highly concentrated, and with high labour productivity.

Both Calgary and Edmonton, even in 1970 (the start of the oil boom and exploration), showed signs of growth in chemical based products. At the same time, with higher energy prices since 1974, the Prairies in particular may have benefitted from price inflation, in contrast to the experience of the Maritime regions.

7.5 Conclusions

The model of regional adjustment developed in this chapter emphasized the problems of short-run expectations, uncertainty, and price–quantity adjustments at the level of the individual firm with a location in time and space. It was argued that regional adjustment is conditioned by the immediate past performance of national aggregates and local conditions. Thus expected or anticipated wage-rate increases may cause overadjustment in local firms, as local conditions themselves may affect employers' perception of likely market conditions. In most Canadian regions, the coefficient for U_{Nt} or for W_{Nt} is significant and, owing to the different structure of these variables, the coefficients relate change or adjustment in one variable to change over time in the independent variable. In this respect, both aggregate variables imply a significant degree of local adjustment to national fluctuations, which has generally gone unrecognized in the literature.

Alonso (1975) claimed that a basic characteristic of many peripheral regions is their relative isolation from broad national economic forces. Yet on the basis of the results given here, it could be argued that peripheral regions are too well integrated with national forces and that changes in national money-wage rates and macroeconomic policy-induced demand conditions have a direct and perverse response in changes in regional unemployment. Thus, the island 'parable' attributed to Phelps and others (1970) may be rather irrelevant, as national conditions of wage determination flow over time and space according to institutional constraints. Lagged regional unemployment and its change over time has relatively little significance for many regions, as in only three Maritime regions is this parameter significant, and in only one of those cases is that parameter alone significant. In the western regional system, those regions with significant, lagged regional unemployment terms also have significant U_{Nt} or W_{Nt} terms.

The clear evidence of national and regional interdependencies established in this paper for the Canadian context raises a number of issues with respect to the design and impact of public policy. First, it can no longer be assumed that national macroeconomic policy and regional development policies operate in isolation of one another (Clark, 1979). While this is particularly the case for the demand side of macropolicy planning, it should also be recognized that how governments approach wage determination issues is clearly of relevance for the pattern and future of regional unemployment disparities. Any policy that is designed to slow or halt wage-rate increases will clearly benefit depressed regions as well as the national inflation rate. It should be noted, however, that such a policy could slow growth rates in other regions. Thus there are clear political choices to be made that may have marked regional impacts.

Second, our results imply a reconsideration of existing regional development policies. Any policy that does not address the wage-structure issue may be doomed to failure. That is, even if firms are encouraged to develop, through capital grants, in depressed regions, policymakers may be simply encouraging further concentration of 'secondary-sector' industries. This would lead to even greater regional vulnerability to money-wage-rate changes and thus, perhaps, to higher regional unemployment. One option may be to create wage subsidies for firms so as to maintain their competability and flow of liquidity.

Acknowledgements. This paper is a revised version of DP 78-33, Department of City and Regional Planning, Harvard University, which was presented at a special meeting of the IGU Commission on Industrial Systems, University of Illinois, Urbana, November 1978. Thanks are due to Les King, Geoff Hewings, and Jon Harkness for comments and advice. Research for this paper was supported in part by the Canada Council (Grant S74-0276) and the W F Milton Fund of Harvard University. The author remains solely responsible for any errors that remain.

References
Alonso W, 1975 "Industrial location and regional policy in economic development" in *Regional Policy: Readings in Theory and Applications* Eds J Friedmann, W Alonso (MIT Press, Cambridge, Mass) pp 64-96
Barro R J, Grossman H I, 1976 *Money, Employment and Inflation* (Cambridge University Press, Cambridge)
Bluestone B, 1971 "The characteristics of marginal industries" in *Problems in Urban Political Economy* Ed. D M Gordon (D C Heath, Toronto) pp 102-107
Brechling F B, 1967 "Trends and cycles in British regional unemployment" *Oxford Economic Papers* **19** 1-21
Burton J, Addison J, 1977 "The institutionalist analysis of wage inflation: a critical appraisal" *Research in Labor Economics* **1** 333-376
Camu P, Weeks E P, Sametz Z N, 1964 *Economic Geography of Canada* (Macmillan, Toronto)
Chisholm M, 1976 "Regional policies in an era of slow population growth and higher unemployment" *Regional Studies* **10** 201-213
Chung J H, 1976 *Cyclical Instability in Residential Construction in Canada* Economic Council of Canada (Queens Printer, Ottawa)
Clark G L, 1978 "Regional labour supply and national fluctuations: Canadian evidence for 1969-1975" *Environment and Planning A* **10** 621-632
Clark G L, 1979 "Predicting the regional impact of a full employment policy in Canada: A Box-Jenkins approach" *Economic Geography* **55** 213-226
Clark G L, 1980 "Critical problems of geographical unemployment models" *Progress in Human Geography* **4** 157-180
Cochrane D, Orcutt G H, 1949 "Application of least squares regression to relationships containing autocorrelated error terms" *Journal of the American Statistical Association* **44** 32-61
Curry L, 1976 "Fluctuation in the random spatial economy and the control of inflation" *Geographical Analysis* **8** 339-353

Denton F T, 1977 "On the aggregation properties of single-equation estimates for equations with identical sets of regressors" WP 77-01, Department of Economics, McMaster University, Hamilton, Ontario

Donner A, Kilman M, Lazer F, 1973 *Issues in Canadian Economic Policy* (Butterworths, Toronto)

ECC, 1976a *Thirteenth Annual Review: The Inflation Dilemma* Economic Council of Canada (Queens Printer, Ottawa)

ECC, 1976b *People and Jobs: A Study of the Canadian Labor Market* Economic Council of Canada (Queens Printer, Ottawa)

Galbraith J K, 1975 *Economics and the Public Purpose* (Signet Books, Scarborough)

Hartley M J, Revanker N S, 1974 "Labor supply under uncertainty and the rate of unemployment" *American Economic Review* 64 170-175

Hicks J R, 1974 *The Crisis in Keynesian Economics* (Basic Books, New York)

Kaldor N, 1970 "The case for regional policies" *Scottish Journal of Political Economy* 17 337-348

Keynes J M, 1936 *The General Theory of Employment, Interest and Money* (Macmillan, London)

King L J, Clark G L, 1978 "Regional unemployment patterns and the spatial dimensions of macro-economic policy: the Canadian experience 1966-1975" *Regional Studies* 12 283-296

Means G C, 1975 "Simultaneous inflation and unemployment: a challenge to theory and policy" *Challenge* 18 6-21

Phelps E S, and others (Eds), 1970 *Microeconomic Foundations of Employment and Inflation Theory* (W W Norton, New York)

Pierce D A, 1977 "Relationships—and the lack thereof—between economic time series, with special reference to money and interest rates" *Journal of the American Statistical Association* 72 11-22

Pissarides C A 1976 *Labour Market Adjustment: Microeconomic Foundations of Short-Run Neoclassical and Keynesian Dynamics* (Cambridge University Press, Cambridge)

Robinson J, 1972 "The second crisis of economic theory" *American Economic Association Papers and Proceedings* 62 1-10

Robinson J, Wilkinson F, 1977 "What has become of employment policy?" *Cambridge Journal of Economics* 1 5-14

Rowley J V R, Walton D A, 1977 *The Determination of Wage-Change Relationships* Economic Council of Canada (Queens Printer, Ottawa)

Shackle G L S, 1974 *Epistemics and Economics* (Cambridge University Press, Cambridge)

Statistics Canada, 1970 *Geographic Survey of Employment* (Queen's Printer, Ottawa)

Thirlwall A P, 1966 "Regional unemployment as a cyclical phenomenon" *Scottish Journal of Political Economy* 13 205-219

Tufte E R, 1978 *Political Control of the Economy* (Princeton University Press, Princeton)

Webber M J, 1972 *The Impact of Uncertainty Upon Location* (MIT Press, Cambridge, Mass)

Wiles P, 1973 "Cost inflation and the state of economic theory" *Economic Journal* 83 377-398

The labour-market behaviour of employers: a framework for analysis and a case study of a local labour market

C L Carmichael

8.1 Introduction

Regional economists and geographers have traditionally focused much of their attention on describing and explaining differences in the economic health of areas. In Britain this interest has increased following the steep rise in unemployment in recent years. This study is one contribution to the debate, emphasising the demand side of the labour market. The local labour market (LLM) and the individual employer[1] are introduced as appropriate scales of analysis. This is followed in section 8.3 by the presentation of a framework for studying the two together. Sections 8.4 and 8.5 draw on data collected in a single LLM. First, employment change at the establishment level is looked at, and second, employer responses to manpower imbalance are examined.

8.2 The problem of scale in labour-market analysis

The analysis of economic change has been carried out from a number of viewpoints, emphasising the problem of scale inherent in such studies. By scale is meant the level of disaggregation, particularly in the dimensions of time, space, and economic organisation. No perfect level of scale exists for an analysis of labour-market change. The choice depends on the particular problem at hand, and on the data available. All the possible levels should be regarded as complementary.

The spatial scale has generated studies at a variety of levels, including the region and subregion (for example, Chisholm and Oeppen, 1973), the Metropolitan Economic Labour Area (for example, Hall et al, 1973), the Travel to Work Area (for example, Salt, 1976), the conurbation (for example, DEm, 1977), and the inner city (for example, Lambeth IAS, 1977). However, where employment and unemployment change are being considered, the LLM is the most appropriate level. This is because it relates most closely to the area in which individuals and organisations generally operate. Kerr (1954) defined an LLM as "an area of indistinct geographical and occupational limits within which certain workers customarily seek to offer their services and certain employers to hire them" (page 93). Several similar general definitions exist (such as Goodman, 1970). However, problems arise in operationalising the basic

[1] Throughout this chapter the words 'employer', 'firm', 'organisation', and 'company' are used synonymously. 'Employers' are recognised as groups of individuals with possibly conflicting interests.

definitions which relate to the availability of data, and to the reconciliation of the factors influencing worker mobility (for example, age, sex, occupation). Carmichael (1978; 1980) briefly discusses these problems and several alternative working definitions. The system of labour-market areas defined by Smart (1974) is preferred, in the British context, because (a) it most faithfully represents 'on the ground' commuting behaviour, (b) it gives national areal coverage, (c) Department of Employment Travel to Work Areas have been based on this definition since 1968, (d) it most faithfully defines 'local' areas, and (e) it features a consistent minimum self-containment level. However, this definition is still a compromise and retains several problems (see Ball, 1980). The second major scale problem is that of time. Typically studies are comparative static, using data for two particular dates (such as April 1961 and April 1971 in the case of the Census of Population), and ignore potentially important changes that have occurred in between. Alternatively, studies use time series of data (monthly or quarterly unemployment returns or annual employment returns). Techniques used to examine the sensitivity and timing of these series provide very good descriptions of changes but ignore the underlying dynamics (for example, Brechling, 1967; Frost and Spence, 1979). This is a serious omission, particularly in the context of the design of policies to modify employer and employee behaviour.

If the processes of change in the labour market are to be better understood, more research needs to be conducted at finer levels of spatial and temporal disaggregation, emphasising the interrelationship of decisions about work made by individuals inside and outside employing organisations in the short run. This would involve the third area of the scale problem, that of economic organisation. By this is meant whether research looks at industry groupings, thereby assuming near homogeneous behaviour within the group, or whether research should also look at the level of the individual employing organisation. Steps have been taken in the latter direction by researchers constructing 'microdata' banks (for example, Dennis, 1978; Lloyd and Mason, 1978; Gudgin, 1978). This work has mainly been concerned with recording changes in populations of firms, and with breaking down net employment change in an area into its components (namely growth due to firms starting up or moving in, decline due to firms dying or moving out, growth/decline at firms remaining in situ). This work has been supported by more qualitative research into reasons for closures, migration, etc (CDP, 1977; Massey and Meegan, 1979). The rest of this chapter follows such a disaggregated approach.

8.3 A framework for studying the labour-market behaviour of employers
8.3.1 Manpower imbalance and adjustment
The area of interest is the behaviour of employing organisations in the labour market, which leads to employment changes at a particular factory or office location. This is equivalent to studying the ways in which

organisation managers respond to changes in product demand, and to changes in labour supply, to maintain a reasonably efficient balance between desired and actual employment.

Figure 8.1 shows the various stocks and flows in the local labour market. On this diagram the box marked 'employed workers' can be regarded as the total of employing establishments in the LLM. Individual establishments have a number of departments and occupational grades with labour flows taking place between them. Employees enter at a particular level, or 'port of entry', and may leave at the same or at a higher level (or at a lower level in a small number of cases). The administrative rules and procedures which govern the pricing and allocation of labour constitute the 'internal labour market' (see Doeringer and Piore, 1971). These strategies are used to bring about equilibrium between the internal and external labour market.

The starting point on which to hang the following empirical work is a model of the organisation in a labour market context. The model proposed has been derived from the work of Holt and David (1966), Holt (1971a; 1971b), and Deaton and Thomas (1977). It has been expanded in the light of research into labour shortages carried out by Lester (1955), Hunter

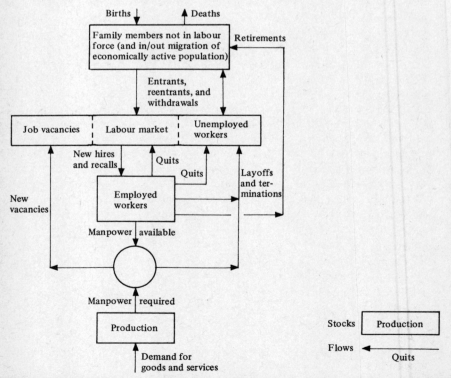

Figure 8.1. Flows and stocks of workers and jobs in the local labour market. Source: Carmichael (1978), adapted from Holt (1969).

(1978), and MSC (1978; 1979a; 1979b; 1979c), and extended to take account of labour surpluses (ILO, 1962). In particular, it goes further than the work of Deaton and Thomas by considering whole employing organisations, rather than single occupations, and by attempting a more explicit quantification of behaviour.

The LLM is 'driven' by demand for goods and services, and at the level of the individual organisation this results in a demand for a certain quantity of labour services (man-hours) from the employed work force. The size of the work force is regulated in part by flows out of the labour stock, in the form of retirements or quits (employee decisions), or layoffs and terminations (employer decisions). Further regulation is achieved by altering the number of new hires. An organisation is assumed to have a desired stock of employees (E^*) and an actual stock of employees (E). When these two are equal a stock balance exists $(E = E^*)$. At a point in time an organisation can be experiencing a manpower surplus $(E > E^*)$ or a manpower shortage $(E < E^*)$. Starting from equilibrium, an imbalance can arise, for example, owing to:

(a) a change in product demand, leading to a change in desired employee stock;
(b) improved technology, or rationalisation, leading to a change in desired employee stock;
(c) a change in labour inflows, leading to a change in actual employee stock;
(d) a change in labour outflows, leading to a change in actual employee stock.

Faced with an imbalance, the firm (that is, its managers) considers adjustment to restore equality between actual and desired employment by use of a variety of 'instruments'. These can be classified according to their main area of intended effect, namely desired total labour services, average hours worked per employee, labour outflows, and labour inflows. Some thirty-eight instruments have been identified as applicable either to one or to both situations of manpower imbalance. This is a wide range of possibilities, which provides a substantial caveat to traditional theories of price adjustment to disequilibrium in labour allocation between or within firms. These are listed in table 8.1, according to their main area of intended effect.

At its conceptual limits the notion of imbalance can be taken to mean the position where a firm, with actual and desired employment equal at a point in time, loses a single employee (for example, a quit). In this situation, the managers would evaluate the vacancy created to see whether it needed filling. If it did, then the firm would adjust, say, by recruiting one more employee. This would restore equilibrium after a slight time lag (that is, raise actual to meet desired employment). If it was decided not to fill the vacancy, desired employment would in effect have been revised downwards to meet the new level of actual employment. In practice this may be an overrestrictive definition of imbalance.

Table 8.1. Possible methods of adjusting to a manpower imbalance.

Adjustment instrument[a]	Manpower shortage[b]	Manpower surplus
Desired total labour services		
Capital investment	+	(+)
Subcontracting	+	−
Stocks	−	+
Transfer production from another location or occupation	na	+
Transfer production to another location or occupation	+	na
Productivity	+	−
Transfer employees from another location or occupation	+	na
Transfer employees to another location or occupation	na	+
Organisation and methods (including regrade labour)	+	na
Output	−	+
Orders	−	+
Average hours worked per employee		
Overtime hours	+	−
Short-time working	−	+
Overtime payments	+	(−)
Length of working week (basic)	+	−
Make-work practices	−	+
Outflows of labour		
Retirement age	+	−
Career prospects	+	−
Performance standards	−	+
Redundancy (voluntary/involuntary)	na	+
Lay-off	na	+
Conditions of work	+	(−)
Release temporary employees	na	+
Temporary Employment Subsidy[c]	na	+
Inflows of labour		
Hiring standards	−	+
Selection procedures and rules	−	+
Search area	+	−
Recall	+	na
Wages/salaries (basic)	+	(−)
Nonwage benefits	+	(−)
Training capacity, number	+	−
Training capacity, length of course	+	−
Recruitment	+	−
Convenience of hours	+	−
Employ part time/temporary/seasonal employees	+	na
Employ retired personnel	+	na
Liaison with public employment service	+	−
Work Experience on Employers Premises	+	−

[a] The adjustment instruments have been listed according to their area of primary intended impact. Some instruments may have a secondary impact. Those bracketed instruments are ones where the actions indicated are feasible, although in practice they are extremely unlikely to be used. The list has been derived from a variety of sources mainly concerned with responses to labour shortages. These included Lester (1955), ILO (1962), Deaton and Thomas (1977), Hunter (1978), MSC (1978; 1979a; 1979b; 1979c), and MSC/NEDO (1979). The list has also been extended.

[b] The symbol + means start, increase, improve, widen, etc. The symbol − means stop, decrease, worsen, narrow, etc. na means 'not applicable'.

[c] Scheme now finished.

8.3.2 Factors influencing adjustment

The nature of the employer–employee relationship means that the organisation's managers are unlikely to have a free choice in the adjustment instruments they use (Oi, 1962, regarded the labour factor of production as being 'quasi-fixed' in the short run, rather than variable). The constraints surrounding instrument choice can be classified as follows:

Financial. This can exist as the direct cost of adjustment, as the indirect costs incurred before and after adjustment, and as the transaction costs of hiring and disposing of employee services.

Physical. This is where physical limitations (such as space, storage life) present a finite limit to adjustment. This acts principally on stockholding, but also on capital investment for expansion or new equipment.

Technical. This arises from indivisibilities in production, for example, manning requirements on a machine, or the complementarity of processes.

Organisational. These are imposed by one section of management on another section, affecting the perception of manpower imbalances and the decisions leading to adjustment. The status of the personnel function vis-à-vis production or finance, and the status of the plant or office within the organisation are both important.

Legal. In Great Britain the employer–employee relationship derives its framework from the law, as enshrined in a parcel of acts relating to equal pay, sex discrimination, contracts of employment, employment protection, health and safety, race relations, etc. A structure of arbitration committees and industrial tribunals exists. The Employment Protection Act of 1975 in particular has had an important restraining effect on the removal of employees, and consequently on recruitment quality (Daniel and Stilgoe, 1978; Clifton and Tatton-Brown, 1979).

Industrial relations. Related to the legal constraints is the ability of trades unions and staff associations to exert modifying pressure on employers, particularly through collective bargaining and the 'strike threat'. National bargaining may prevent local 'fine-tuning' of wages and conditions. Incomes policy is also a formal constraint on employer behaviour.

Psychological. From the employee perspective the rapid transmission of demand fluctuations to the labour force reduces job security, and may increase wastage as a result. From the employer perspective uncertainty about future events may prevent a decision as to whether an imbalance is permanent or temporary, in turn affecting the decision to adjust.

External. This is a miscellaneous category relating to LLM conditions. Relevant factors here include labour-supply structure (age, sex, occupation, industry), wage structure, housing and transport infrastructure, LLM demand conditions, and the availability of local training facilities.

Other factors affecting adjustment behaviour, apart from the listed constraints, are:
(a) perception of the imbalance (permanent/temporary, visibility);
(b) perception of the potential instruments (knowledge, search behaviour);
(c) product-market conditions (competitive/monopolistic);
(d) internal labour-market structure (occupational variations, spatial considerations).

    Perception of the imbalance is crucial. Where an organisation has a personnel department and effective manpower and sales information systems an imbalance is more likely to be noticed quickly, or even to be anticipated, and a decision should be possible as to whether it is temporary or permanent. The severity of the effect of imbalances (such as lost production, delayed orders) will affect whether it is noticed. In consequence, response to a shortage is more likely than response to a surplus. Where imbalances are not frequently encountered, knowledge of the range of adjustments possible may be poor and choice is likely to be determined by any past experience [MSC (1979a) showed that employer response to chronic labour shortages often seems ad hoc and based on a poor understanding of the problem]. Only if these fail will wider search behaviour begin. Large organisations with well developed personnel functions should have a greater awareness of potential instruments. Product-market conditions play an important part in adjustment behaviour in that firms facing competitive conditions will be under more pressure to adjust quickly and correctly to restore efficient resource utilisation. In the public sector, for example, the need to adjust may not be as pressing. Finally, an organisation's internal labour market will reduce adjustment possibilities if it is highly structured. This is not usually the case in Britain (see MacKay et al, 1971; Bosanquet and Doeringer, 1973; Mace, 1979), although in large organisations there is a greater tendency towards structured internal markets. Sharp differentials in skill between work groups will act against easy adjustment through transfers of production or personnel.

    This framework for studying employer labour-market behaviour implies efficient operation. However, an organisation may be experiencing 'slack', either at a point in time or continuously (see Cyert and March, 1963). This means that the manpower resource will not be used at its most productive. As a result many small imbalances will not be recognised or will be ignored, either because they are readily absorbed or because they are of too little consequence in relation to the other problems facing the organisation.

8.4 Employment change in a local labour market
8.4.1 The local labour-market economic background
In Britain satisfactory establishment-level manpower analysis is not possible from published statistics. This is because the 1947 Statistics of Trade Act

prevents disclosure of the limited data that do exist (in particular, the Annual Census of Employment and the Census of Production). Consequently recourse is made to a range of sources, such as personal interviews and questionnaire surveys. Most of these approaches experience difficulties, particularly in obtaining representative and valid results. This study is no exception, and the following sections rely on a variety of data sources (described in the appendix).

All the data refer to a single LLM, Swindon, on the borders of the South East and South West Economic Planning Regions. For the purposes of this exercise, its boundary was defined according to the Smart (1974) method, using 1971 Census of Population Journey to Work data (see figure 8.2). The area was chosen primarily for its very high level of self-containment—in 1971, 94% of the employed people living in the area also worked there, and 93% of the people working there also lived there. Table 8.2 presents some basic background economic details.

The data shown in table 8.2 for the LLM actually relate to the Swindon Employment Exchange area, rather than the Census-defined LLM. This is because Census of Population data are not available beyond 1971, and because they are not published for Rural Districts. The two areas do not coincide in space (see figure 8.2) but their structures are sufficiently similar to be representative (see Carmichael, 1980). The only major difference

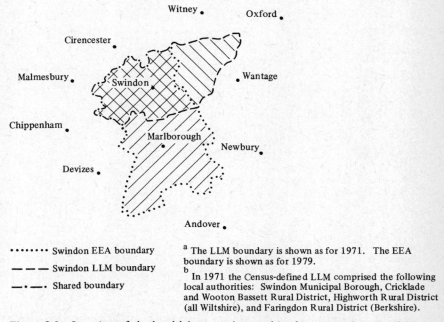

.... Swindon EEA boundary   [a] The LLM boundary is shown as for 1971. The EEA
                                     boundary is shown as for 1979.
— — — Swindon LLM boundary
                                     [b] In 1971 the Census-defined LLM comprised the following
—·—· Shared boundary   local authorities: Swindon Municipal Borough, Cricklade
                                     and Wooton Bassett Rural District, Highworth Rural District
                                     (all Wiltshire), and Faringdon Rural District (Berkshire).

Figure 8.2. Location of the local labour market used in the case study. Local labour market and Employment Exchange area boundaries are both shown[a,b].

between the two is that the Census-defined area is larger, having some 14% more employees in 1971.

The LLM experienced a rate of growth of total employment faster than the national rate over the 1961 to 1971 period. The fastest local growth period was 1961 to 1966. Within the total employment trend, male employment grew by +3% and female employment grew by +40%. Female employment growth rates were high both in the production and in the service sectors, with the former experiencing almost all its growth between 1961 and 1966, whereas service growth was more evenly distributed. Male production employment was almost static throughout the 1961 to 1971 period, whilst male service employment increased by +10% between 1961 and 1966 and was fairly stable between 1966 and 1971.

Recent changes in the rate of unemployment suggest that after 1976 the comparatively favourable position of the LLM relative to the nation worsened. This was hinted at in the 1971 to 1976 employment-change data by the slowing rate of growth, with the 1973 to 1976 period showing almost no net change. The local rate of unemployment was traditionally below the national rate. However, in January 1975 the position changed, and by early 1978 the local rate was over $\frac{1}{2}$% higher than the national rate. By February 1980 the local position was relatively better once again, with a rate of unemployment of 5·7% when the national rate equalled 6·0%.

Table 8.2. Local labour-market background economic data. (Source: Department of Employment.)

Statistics	LLM[a]	Great Britain
Total employment, 1976	74170	–
Rate of growth of total employment, 1961–1971[b]	+14·1%	+2·9%
Rate of growth of total employment 1971–1976[c]	+4·2%	+1·8%
Percentage of total employment which is male, 1976	60%	59%
Percentage of total employment in service industries, 1976	55%	57%
Rate of unemployment, February 1972	3·7%	4·1%
Rate of unemployment, February 1978	6·9%	6·2%

[a] All data refer to Swindon Employment Exchange area.
[b] Based on National Insurance Card estimates.
[c] Based on Annual Census of Employment (all 1976 employment data are derived from this).

8.4.2 Establishment-level employment change
The principal Local Authority in the LLM conducts an annual survey of local employers (see the appendix). From the returns to this survey it was possible to create a time series of employment data for ninety-two local employers, relating to January 1976, 1977, and 1978. This was a compromise between coverage of firms and length of unbroken series.

Total employment in this series was 24565 in 1976 (equivalent to 29% of estimated LLM employment) with 63% in production industries (only 42% of the 1976 Employment Office total was in this sector).

Table 8.3 shows the distribution of the ninety-two firms according to total employment trend in each of the years 1976–1977 and 1977–1978. A variety of performance is evident, with 55% of firms increasing their total employment in the first year compared to 53% in the second. Total employment was decreased by 35% of firms between 1976 and 1977, compared with 33% of firms between 1977 and 1978. However, only 34% of firms expanded in consecutive years and only 12% decreased in consecutive years. The production sector had double the proportion of members in the continually expanding group than the service sector; service-sector firms experienced a more equal distribution of trends. Those firms experiencing an employment increase would have had engagements greater than separations, and would therefore have been more likely to experience manpower shortage than manpower surplus. Those firms experiencing decline in total employment would have had more separations than engagements, and would therefore have been more likely to experience manpower surplus. Faster rates of total employment change would tend to result in larger, and possibly more severe, imbalances. These trends apply to total employment; however, occupation groups within an organisation need not be changing their size in the same direction as the total. In general, groups with the lowest rate of employment change were the most important, 49% of employers in 1976–1977, and 55% in 1977–1978, belonging to them. Service-industry rates of change tended to be lower (see table 8.4).

Between January 1976 and January 1978, total employment at the ninety-two firms in the time series rose by 1477 (+6·0%). The components

Table 8.3. Trends in total employment by industry group; time-series firms, 1976–1977–1978. (Source: Local Authority Employment Surveys.)

Employment trend		Number of firms		
1976–1977	1977–1978	production	services	total
+	+	22	9	31
+	0	1	2	3
+	−	8	9	17
0	+	1	4	5
0	0	2	–	2
0	−	–	2	2
−	+	10	3	13
−	0	2	6	8
−	−	3	8	11
Total		49	43	92

of this change were as follows:

male	⌈ nonmanual	19% (22%)	⌉ nonmanual 24% (40%)	
	⌊ manual	49% (51%)		
female	⌈ nonmanual	5% (18%)		⌉ manual
	⌊ manual	27% (9%)		76% (60%)

The figures in brackets show the proportions of 1976 employment in each category. All the contributions to change were positive. The largest was by male-manual, the smallest by female-nonmanual. Female contributions were most out of line with their share of total employment.

Table 8.4. Rate of change of total employment by industry group (time-series firms, 1976-1977-1978). (Source: Local Authority Employment Surveys.)

Rate of change (%)	Proportion of cases (%)					
	production		services		total	
	1976–1977	1977–1978	1976–1977	1977–1978	1976–1977	1977–1978
+ 0·1-9·9	28·6	32·7	27·9	27·9	28·3	30·4
⩾10·0	34·7	34·7	18·6	9·3	27·2	22·8
Subtotal	63·3	67·4	46·5	37·2	55·5	53·2
− 0·1-9·9	16·3	16·3	25·6	34·9	20·7	25·0
⩾10·0	14·3	6·1	14·0	9·3	14·1	7·6
Subtotal	30·6	19·4	39·6	44·2	34·8	32·6
0 0·0	6·1	10·2	14·0	18·6	9·8	14·1
Total	100·0	100·0	100·1	100·0	100·1	99·9
Base number of cases	49	49	43	43	92	92

Table 8.5. Average employment and employment change by sex, occupation, and industry groups (time-series firms, 1976-1978). (Source: Local Authority Employment Surveys.)

Industry group		Production	Services	Total
Average employment 1976	Total	314·9	212·4	267·0
	Male nonmanual	53·2	62·6	57·6
	Male manual	205·3	59·1	137·0
	Female nonmanual	23·3	77·0	48·4
	Female manual	33·1	13·7	24·0
Average change in employment 1976–1978	Total	35·3	−5·9	16·1
	Male nonmanual	6·2	−0·6	3·0
	Male manual	18·4	−4·3	7·8
	Female nonmanual	3·6	−2·3	0·8
	Female manual	7·1	1·4	4·4
Number of firms		49	43	92

Between January 1976 and January 1978 the average net total number of jobs gained at these firms was 16 (production equalled plus 35, services equalled minus 6) (see table 8.5). However, a small number of employers had a major effect on net employment change. Four of the firms in the series experienced absolute change equivalent to greater than ±10% of the total net increase of 1477 jobs. Three firms together gained 1110 jobs whilst one firm lost 251 jobs, equivalent to +13%, +20%, +43%, and −17% of total net employment change. These firms were not the largest in the series.

Together this information shows that large production firms had the best employment-creation performance. Also evident are the differences in performance of individual firms within sectors, and this holds within industries. An analysis of aggregate local performance even at an industry-order level, misses a great deal of variety. Following on from this it was also evident that the fortunes of the area were greatly affected by the behaviour of a small number of organisations. These 'key firms' need not be the largest employers, and it is not clear that they will remain the same from year to year because of changes in product demand and technology [cf Erickson (1974) and his concept of the 'lead firm']. Only in a dominated LLM is a single large firm likely to be a key firm continuously [2].

8.4.3 Establishment labour turnover

So far, establishment-level data have been used to examine employment change; however, these can be further disaggregated. The greater the level of disaggregation the more behavioural the analysis becomes, or in other words, aggregate trends are the net result of individual behaviour, and in the summation much of the reasoning behind actions gets lost.

Aggregate personnel data were made available by four firms in the LLM, covering a range of time periods. The four organisations were: A, a local authority; and three manufacturing companies making: B, electronic components; C, swimwear; and D, specialist electronic circuits. Total employment in each of these was as follows:

Firm	Total (1978)	% male (1978)	% change (1977–1978)	
A	1553	73	+0·8	March 1977 and 1978
B	306	31	−7·3 ⎤	
C	616	14	+16·2 ⎥	January 1977 and 1978
D	642	49	−14·6 ⎦	

These might be regarded as typical medium and large sized organisations. Only one, the local authority, had a majority of male employees. Between January 1977 and January 1978 total employment in the local authority was almost stable, implying an equality of inflows and outflows; total

---

[2] Lever (1979) arbitrarily defined domination as one nontertiary employer accounting for 12·5% of total LLM employment. Out of his 301 defined British LLMs, 95 were dominated, including Crewe, Doncaster, Luton, and Yeovil.

employment in firms B and D declined sharply, implying an excess of outflows over inflows; and total employment in firm C increased, implying an excess of inflows over outflows. Tables 8.6 and 8.7 show accessions and separations from these organisations, in terms of average monthly flows and crude accession and separation rates[3]. These support the

Table 8.6. Monthly average engagements and separations at four organisations, 1974–1978. [Source: Company personnel records (aggregate).]

Measure	Year	Organisation			
		A	B	C	D
Monthly average engagements (number)	1974	24·1	–	–	–
	1975	11·3	–	–	–
	1976	4·5	6·8	–	22·2
	1977	8·0	1·5	25·8	11·6
	1978[a]	13·6	1·2	7·3	–
Monthly average separations (number)	1974	11·0	–	–	–
	1975	7·1	–	–	–
	1976	5·8	6·0	–	9·2
	1977	8·3	3·6	15·4	11·8
	1978[a]	7·6	1·8	9·7	–

[a] Estimated from partial data.

Table 8.7. Crude accession and separation rates at four organisations, 1974–1978. [Source: Company personnel records (aggregate).]

Measure	Year	Organisation			
		A	B	C	D
Accession rates (%)	1974	–	–	–	–
	1975	16·5	–	–	–
	1976	6·6	24·8	–	39·9
	1977	12·0	5·7	32·3	19·9
	1978[a]	20·2	4·6	14·6	–
Separation rates (%)	1974	–	–	–	–
	1975	10·3	–	–	–
	1976	8·4	22·1	–	16·5
	1977	12·6	13·5	31·7	20·4
	1978[a]	11·3	7·3	19·3	–

[a] Estimated from partial data.

[3]
$$\text{Accession rate} = \frac{\text{number of new members added during a period}}{\text{average number of members during the period}}.$$
For separation rate substitute 'number of members leaving during a period' in the numerator. This measure has several problems with its interpretation (see Price, 1975) but has been chosen for its ease of computation and the lack of any aggregate length-of-service data.

previous contentions about labour flows—for example, in 1977 firm C had monthly average engagements of 26 and monthly average separations of 15, whilst total employment grew by 16%. The common pattern in these tables is of a greater level of labour-market activity in the earlier part of the period, owing to better macroeconomic conditions and a higher level of demand in the LLM. This general pattern holds for each firm. However, crude rates between firms show considerable variation. For example, in 1977 accession rates ranged from 6% to 32%, and separation rates ranged from 13% to 32%.

In the two organisations where the personnel records were sampled, leavers tended to be younger, female, in low-status occupations, and to have a shorter length of service than stayers[4]. The indication was that each organisation had a substantial core of long service employees and a smaller number of people who left relatively quickly. In the local authority (organisation A), 87% of stayers had a length of service greater than two years, compared to 57% of leavers. In the manufacturing firm (organisation B), 95% of stayers had a length of service greater than two years, compared to 55% of leavers. The mean and median lengths of service in each organisation varied substantially, indicating a highly skewed distribution (see table 8.8). The mean figures illustrate considerable attachment to employers and jobs. For stayers, this was eight years in the local authority, and about nine-and-a-half years in the manufacturing firm.

Reasons for leaving showed some variation. In firm B, 29% of leavers were made redundant, 18% left for personal betterment, 16% because of pregnancy, and 10% left the district. The remaining reasons were largely voluntary. The redundancy was the termination of an evening shift, taken on to meet a Christmas boom in demand. The high positions of 'pregnancy' and 'leaving the area' were the consequence of a largely female work force. For the local authority, A, 47% left for another job, 14% left for domestic reasons, and 10% each retired, reached the end of their temporary contract, and left for personal reasons. In firm C, 72% of

Table 8.8. Mean and median lengths of service in two organisations (1974–1978). (Source: Company personnel records.)

Organisation	Group	Length of service (months)	
		mean	median
A Local authority	stayers	94·8	68·0
(staff)	leavers	58·9	30·0
B Manufacturing firm	stayers	115·4	80·7
	leavers	67·9	30·0

[4] Stayers were those people sampled who were in employment with the relevant organisation in May 1978. Leavers were those people sampled who had ceased employment with the relevant organisation between 1974 and 1978. The precise dates of coverage varied slightly between the two organisations.

leavers were resignations (classified as 'unavoidable') and the remainder left either for reasons of unsuitability or of discipline. No information was available for firm D.

These results illustrate the great importance of voluntary separations, as also shown by MacKay et al (1971) and Daniel (1974). However, it should be noted that occupational variations will exist, with lower level occupations having a higher propensity to face involuntary leaving (dismissal, redundancy, ill health, etc). This is particularly the case with unskilled manual workers. The importance of voluntary quits also implies that to maintain equilibrium of desired and actual employment, an organisation's labour-market activity is likely to be mainly concerned with replacement recruitment (that is, acting on labour inflows), although effort may be put into reducing labour outflows. (See Dunnell and Head, 1975, for a description of employer recruitment behaviour.) The next section presents an empirical examination of the adjustment framework.

8.5 Employer responses to manpower imbalance
8.5.1 Perceptions of imbalance
An attempt was made, using a variety of information, to quantify employer labour-market behaviour in the case study LLM. These sources included company personnel records and a postal survey of employers. The personnel records were most useful in illustrating detailed changes in company employment structure, but it was not possible to relate these changes directly to adjustment behaviour. The survey was most useful in outlining the range of employer behaviour and only this is reported here, although the use of personnel records is discussed briefly in the appendix, which also gives details of the survey sampling and response. One aim of the postal survey was to measure the responses to manpower imbalances made by employers, and the reasons for choosing these. The questions were worded to convey to sample firms the ideas of labour requirements and any deviations from these [5].

However, only 49% of respondents had experienced a manpower shortage between January 1976 and August 1978, 26% a manpower surplus, and 14% both. These are lower proportions than are to be expected—for example, a literal interpretation of the model as presented in section 8.3 should mean that a single employee separation caused a manpower shortage, or that the loss of a small order caused a manpower surplus. This implies that the outlined model of adjustment was overspecified. Although the model rejected any notion of cost-minimising behaviour, a degree of rationality was implied. It was assumed that employers could identify a

[5] The principal Yes/No filter question was worded "In the period since 1 January 1976 has your establishment experienced a situation where the number of persons employed has been less than (or "greater than" in the case of a manpower surplus) the number required?"

precise level of labour demand and would act efficiently by taking action when actual employment deviated from this.

In explaining these figures two points are relevant, both illustrating the inefficiency of manpower utilisation in some organisations. First, a survey of National Institute of Economic and Social Research industrial panel firms in December 1976 showed that, on average, firms could increase their output by 8% with their present hours, by 12% with additional over-time, and by 22% with additional employees (NIER, 1977). There were wide variations around these averages, with a quarter of respondents saying that no increase was possible with present hours, and a fifth saying that a minimum of a 20% increase was possible with present hours. The highest potential increases were in such industries as chemicals, clothing and foot-wear, and construction. These results were supported by aggregate statistical analyses. Thus, given that a similar situation existed locally, this would mean that small variations in actual employment could simply be absorbed, unless key-workers were involved and/or serious side effects resulted. Other than this the changes would not be regarded as imbalances.

The second point relates to manpower planning practice. Just over three-quarters (77%) of the Swindon survey respondents stated that 'they attempted to estimate future manpower requirements'. When those employers using managerial judgement alone were excluded from the analysis, only a half of the respondents engaged in estimation. The propensity to estimate increased with firm size. The most important methods used were a market or sales forecast (by 78% of employers), managerial judgement (62%), and a fixed financial establishment (24%). By time horizon, estimation was distributed 32% six months or less, 35% seven to twelve months, and 46% over twelve months.

A national survey of manpower planning found a higher incidence and greater sophistication of planning (Thakur, 1975). However, this can be explained by the fact that 90% of the firms sampled employed over one thousand people, organisations where best-practice manpower planning would be expected. In contrast, MacKay et al (1971) were more critical of company practice. It might be expected that organisations using sophisticated manpower-planning methods would be much more conscious of manpower utilisation problems, helping to minimise overmanning and keeping desired and actual employment closely in line.

The overall implication is that in many firms the relationship between desired and actual employment is 'flexible', with the former not being known precisely and small fluctuations between the two therefore being disregarded. In this context the proportion of survey firms in Swindon recording periods of imbalance is not surprising. Consequently the model of adjustment should be modified, so that desired employment takes on a range of values within which actual employment could fluctuate, according to slight changes in wastage or output demand, without a technical imbalance being recognised.

8.5.2 Responses to manpower shortage

In the Swindon survey thirty-six respondents had experienced one or more periods of manpower deficit between January 1976 and August 1978. Of these, 47% were in production industries, compared with 32% of nonshortage respondents. Of those firms recording a shortage, 83% attempted to estimate future manpower requirements compared with 71% of nonshortage respondents; they also used more formal estimating methods. It is likely that this would have created a greater awareness of their manpower position. However, the firms may also have had a greater need for manpower planning because of a greater susceptibility to imbalance.

Further questioning focused on each firm's most recent shortage (the average number of cases recorded was $1 \cdot 6$, a quarter of which were regarded either as continuous or seasonal). Adjustment to the noncontinuous cases can be assumed to have been generally successful because they are historical. The shortages most frequently affected skilled manual jobs, although all occupation groups were represented. A variety of reasons were given for the shortages (mean equal to $1 \cdot 3$), the main one being an increase in product or service demand (63% of employers). Changes in labour supply (20%), changes in labour wastage (14%), and lack of skills available locally (9%) were much less important. The shortages varied in size (59% involving between one and five employees, 24% between six and ten, and 18% over ten), and lasted for a range of time periods (46% less than four weeks, 34% between one and six months, and 20% over six months).

All respondents took some action to cope with their most recent shortages but there was a great variety of behaviour, with each organisation using an average of $3 \cdot 7$ methods. This figure was higher for those organisations in production industries and those employing over one hundred employees. All those instruments used are listed in table 8.9. This can be compared with the list of possible instruments (table 8.1). Only three of the possible methods were used by more than one-third of employers—increase overtime working (by 69% of employers), increase recruitment (54%), and employ temporary or seasonal labour (34%). Overall the distribution of main areas of intended effect was as follows:

desired total labour services	27%	
average hours worked per employee	22%	of all mentions.
labour outflows	1%	
labour inflows	50%	

Very little effort was made to reduce labour outflows, and the main focus of attention was on labour inflows. This may reflect the fact that an employer has more control over inflows, it being easier to modify company than employee behaviour. Cross-analysis of adjustment instrument and reported cause of the shortage showed that each adjustment had been used in response to a variety of stimuli, and each stimulus had been adjusted to using a variety of instruments. For example, twenty different instruments had been used in response to shortages caused by an increase in output demand, although increased overtime and recruitment accounted for one-third of all cases of use; or increased overtime was used in response to increases in output demand in half its cases and in response to another six stimuli in the remaining cases.

Similarly, a break down by occupation group showed that each instrument had been used for a variety of affected occupations. Between manual and nonmanual groups the proportion of all mentions accounted for by each instrument was similar, although rankings varied. The largest deviations were the higher usage for nonmanual occupations of 'employ temporary or seasonal labour', 'transfer employees from another location', 'widen the recruitment search area', and 'increase numbers training'. For manual occupations the largest positive deviations were in the use of 'increase

Table 8.9. Instruments used to adjust to labour shortage. (Source: Questionnaire survey to employers.)

Instrument	Main area of effect[a]	Number of mentions
Increase overtime working	average hours	24
Increase recruitment	labour inflows	19
Employ temporary or seasonal labour	labour inflows	12
Increase subcontracting	total labour	10
Raise productivity	total labour	8
Employ part-time labour	labour inflows	8
Widen recruitment search area	labour inflows	7
Increase numbers training	labour inflows	5
Increase overtime payments	average hours	5
Delay orders	total labour	4
Increase basic wages/ salaries	labour inflows	4
Transfer employees from another location	total labour	4
Lower hiring standards	labour inflows	4
Increase capital investment	total labour	3
Reorganise production methods	total labour	3
Decrease stocks of output	total labour	1
Employ retired personnel	labour inflows	1
Improve career prospects	labour outflows	1
Improve nonwage benefits	labour inflows	1
Increase length of training	labour inflows	1
Slacken selection procedures	labour inflows	1
Work Experience Programme	labour inflows	1
Transfer production to another location	total labour	1
Transfer production to another occupation	total labour	1
Make hours more convenient	labour inflows	1
Total		130

[a] The abbreviations in the 'main area of effect' column refer to the following areas: total labour—desired total labour services; average hours—average hours worked per employee.

Table 8.10. The principal instruments most frequently used to adjust to labour shortages: comparative findings[a].

Rank	Six Employment Service Division districts (source: MSC, 1979a)		
	nonmanual	manual	total[b]
1	increased overtime	increased overtime	increased overtime
2	raised wages	raised wages	raised wages
3	train or retrain existing staff	subcontracted	subcontracted
4	redesigned job	increased recruitment of trainees	increased recruitment of trainees
5	regraded staff	increased automation	train or retrain existing staff

	West Central Scotland (source: Hunter, 1978)		
	technical (nonmanagerial)	skilled	semi and unskilled
1	increased training in firm	using more overtime	using more overtime
2	using more overtime	increased training in firm	increased training in firm
3	improving working conditions[c]	improving working conditions	use of part time workers
4	increased apprentice intake[c]	increased apprentice intake[d]	improving working conditions
5	subcontracting work requiring shortage labour	subcontracting work requiring shortage labour[d]	use of seasonal or temporary labour

	West Midlands (source: MSC, 1979b)		
	degree level jobs	skilled manual	total
1	improved wages, conditions, etc	widened the range of sources used to identify applicants	widened the range of sources used to identify applicants
2	widened the range of sources used to identify applicants	improved wages, conditions, etc	train up existing less skilled employees
3	train up existing less skilled workers	train up existing less skilled workers	improved wages, conditions, etc
4	adopted more flexible working arrangements	invested in labour saving equipment	increased overtime levels
5	increased intake of apprentices or other trainees	increased overtime levels	invested in labour saving equipment

Table 8.10 (continued).

Rank	National (Source: MSC, 1978)	Reading (Source: MSC/NEDO, 1979)	Central Region (Source: MSC, 1979c)
	total	total	total
1	used more overtime	advertised vacancies in the media	increase overtime
2	liaised more closely with ESD	used the public employment services	increase intake of new apprentices or trainees
3	tried different ways of attracting recruits	increased overtime	increase in-plant training of existing employees
4	used temporary or contract labour	increased training of existing employees	instal more efficient capital equipment
5	upgraded workers	improved pay and conditions	improve pay and conditions

[a] The descriptions of the instruments used have been taken directly from the particular studies concerned.
[b] Two-thirds of employers also widened their recruitment search area, in answer to a separate question. This would have ranked in the first five instruments.
[c] Rank 3 equal.
[d] Rank 4 equal.

subcontracting', 'delay orders', and 'increase overtime payments'. However, it should be remembered that 'increase overtime working' and 'increase recruitment' dominated each group, accounting for about one-third of all instruments mentioned.

A number of recently published studies have also tried to measure the adjustments made by employers in response to recruitment and/or retention problems. These can be regarded as a special case of the manpower deficit or shortage as defined in this study. One of the studies was national (MSC, 1978), and the others were conducted in six areas of the Employment Service Division (MSC, 1979a), in West Central Scotland (Hunter, 1978), in Reading (MSC/NEDO, 1979), in the West Midlands (MSC, 1979b), and in the Central Region of Scotland (MSC, 1979c). Table 8.10 attempts to summarise the main adjustment instruments used. This should be interpreted carefully as it is difficult to relate accurately the different studies, due mainly to slight differences in question wording, and in sampling. Despite this, it can be seen that 'increased overtime working' most frequently ranked first. This is the most immediate adjustment, although if a shortage persists its use will be purely ameliorative. Also, if a high level of overtime is already being worked its increase may not be a feasible adjustment; for example, 45% of the case-study LLM survey respondents stated that their employees were working overtime on a regular basis. In the Reading engineering study, 'increased overtime working' ranked third, behind 'advertise vacancies in the media' and 'used the public employment services'. In the West

Central Scotland study, 'increased training' was more frequently used than 'increased overtime' as an adjustment to technical staff vacancies, probably because such nonmanual employees rarely work official overtime. Other instruments recurring in table 8.10 were 'increased training' or 'increased recruitment of trainees', 'widened recruitment search', 'increased sub-contracting', 'improve wages and conditions', and the 'use of part time, temporary, or retired workers'.

The present study of Swindon LLM, as well as covering a wider range of instruments and trying to set these in an integrated framework of behaviour, is also unique in trying to establish reasons for choice. Each employer gave an average of 1·8 reasons for choosing the adjustment instruments used. The most important reasons were 'immediate effect', mentioned by 77% of employers, and 'reversible at a future date', mentioned by 40% of employers. The presence of 'few constraints' or 'no undesirable side-effects', a 'predictable effect', and 'low cost' were all mentioned by less than a quarter of employers. It is important to notice the overriding importance of speed here and the lesser importance of constraints and cost. Particular instruments were used by different employers for different reasons, meaning that no single instrument could be classified as immediate, reversible, etc. Only one organisation stated that the instrument they had used was not the one they would normally have used in the manpower shortage situation.

Half of the employers experiencing a manpower shortage stated that constraints were operating to limit their freedom of choice of instrument. This is less important than was suggested in the original model. By far the most frequently mentioned constraints were financial, which suggests that many of the constraints discussed earlier (such as legal, technical, physical) are accepted and regarded as part of the normal operating environment by many firms, and are not actually regarded as constraints. This is a view taken by Hunter (1978) in regard to labour-shortage adjustment, and by Daniel and Stilgoe (1978) in regard to the impact of employment-protection legislation.

8.5.3 Responses to manpower surplus
Nineteen respondents to the Swindon survey stated that they had experienced a manpower surplus between January 1976 and August 1978. Of these, 53% were in the production sector, compared with 35% of 'nonsurplus' employers. Of these 'surplus' employers, 95% tried to estimate future manpower requirements, compared with 65% of 'non-surplus' employers. This greater incidence of planning was similar to the shortage situation, and again more formal estimating methods were used.

An average of 1·3 incidences of manpower surplus were recorded by each employer. The majority of the most recent cases had affected semi/unskilled manual employees, in contrast to the skilled-manual worker bias in manpower shortage; the skilled-manual category was the second most important. Reasons for the surpluses were predominantly a decrease in output demand (58% of 'surplus' employers), and apart from this only technological change was mentioned by more than one employer. All the surpluses were small, involving twenty or less employees. Almost three-quarters lasted for one to six months. In contrast with manpower shortages, fewer surpluses were short run, perhaps indicating the greater success of adjustment to surplus in the long run, but the lesser impact of or the greater reluctance to use short-run ameliorative instruments. It also corresponds to the idea that the effects of shortages are more visible to employers (for example, lengthened delivery dates, reduced output, lost orders).

Two employers did not take compensatory action to correct their surpluses. One said this was because the imbalance was known to be only temporary, and the other because it was felt to be too small. The remaining firms used an average of 2·6 instruments, fewer than in the shortage case. Again this figure was higher for those organisations in production industries, and those employing over one hundred employees. Those instruments used are listed in table 8.11. This can be compared to the list of possible instruments given in table 8.1.

Only two of the possible methods were used by more than one-third of employers—introduce redundancy and reduce overtime (both by 50% of employers). Overall the distribution of main areas of intended effect was

Table 8.11. Instruments used to adjust to labour surplus. (Source: Questionnaire survey of employers.)

Instrument	Main area of effect[a]	Number of mentions
Introduce redundancy	labour outflows	8
Reduce overtime working	average hours	8
Transfer employees to another location	total labour	5
Introduce short-time working	average hours	3
Reduce overtime payments	average hours	3
Reduce subcontracting	total labour	3
Suspend recruitment	labour inflows	2
Reduce numbers training	labour inflows	2
Tighten selection procedures	labour inflows	2
Introduce temporary lay-off	labour outflows	2
Temporary Employment Subsidy	labour outflows	1
Release temporary employees	labour outflows	1
Increase stocks of output	total labour	1
Total		41

[a] The abbreviations in the 'main area of effect' column refer to the following areas: total labour—desired total labour services; average hours—average hours worked per employee.

as follows:

desired total labour services	22%
average hours worked per employee	34%
labour outflows	29%
labour inflows	15%

of all mentions.

Here the main areas of effect were more evenly represented than in the shortage case, and labour outflows now ranked second. As in the shortage case each instrument was used in response to a variety of causes, for example, twelve instruments were used in response to a decrease in output demand, although 'reduce overtime' and 'introduce redundancy' accounted for almost 40% of all cases of use. The variation in use was less than in the shortage case. Despite this it is apparent that employers respond to similar stimuli in different ways.

By occupation group the differences in adjustment to manpower surplus were more striking than in the shortage case. The most important methods for nonmanual jobs were 'introduce redundancy', 'reduce overtime working' and 'transfer employees to another location'; the most important for manual jobs were 'reduce overtime working', 'introduce redundancy' and 'reduce subcontracting'. The largest deviations between the two groups were towards 'introduce redundancy' and 'suspend recruitment' in the nonmanual case, and towards 'reduce subcontracting' and 'reduce overtime working' in the manual case.

An average of 2·1 reasons were given by employers for choosing the adjustments they did. Of the employers, 67% said 'immediate effect', 47% said 'reversible at a future date', and 33% said 'predictable effect'. 'Low cost', 'no undesirable side-effects', and 'few constraints' were each mentioned by fewer than a quarter of manpower surplus employers. 'Immediacy' and 'reversibility' ranked one and two both in the shortage and in the surplus case. Again, particular instruments were used for different reasons by different employers. Only two employers stated that the adjustments they had used were not the ones they would normally have used in a manpower surplus situation.

Almost three-quarters (73%) of employers experiencing a surplus and acting on it stated that there were constraints affecting their freedom of choice of action. This was much bigger than in the shortage case, but it was not surprising given that of employers with trades union members amongst their work force (55% of all survey respondents) 27% faced manning agreements, 22% faced recruitment restrictions, 20% faced training restrictions, and 71% faced dismissal restrictions. The most frequently mentioned constraints were industrial relations and financial; legal, technical, and organisational were seen as much less important.

8.6 Summary and conclusions

This study has followed the disaggregated approach to labour-market analysis recommended in section 8.2, taking as its focus the local labour market (LLM), the individual employer, and the short-run horizon. The main emphasis was on outlining the range of employer labour-market strategies, that is the ways in which firms' managers attempt to maintain a balance between actual and desired employment. This was set in the context of information about organisation employment performance. The findings, although based only on information supplied by seventy-four employers in a single LLM, and a number of other sources, enable some inferences to be drawn about internal labour-market adjustment and the model put forward for studying this. The problems faced in relation to data will need to be faced in any microlevel LLM study, and in this sense the present paper is not unique.

The model proposed that firms had a known, precise level of labour demand, derived from output demand. Any deviation of actual employment from this level would create a manpower imbalance, either a surplus or a shortage, to which employers would respond. This response would involve using 'adjustment instruments', chosen from a very wide range, which were classified as acting upon desired labour services, hours worked per employee, labour inflows, or labour outflows. However, the choice of these instruments was restricted by a number of factors. Actual constraints existed on the use of each instrument, according to eight main categories. Choice was further affected by perception of the imbalance and of the available instruments, as well as by product-market conditions and by internal labour-market structure. The model still implied that employers would act efficiently by responding to an imbalance. The main data source used related to a single LLM, Swindon. Until recently this had an employment performance better than the national average. Employment change at ninety-two local employers for the 1976–1977–1978 period was reported. This showed a great variety of trends, but with production firms generally having the better employment-creation prospects. The fortunes of the area were vulnerable to the performance and associated behaviour of a few firms. Within the total employment change most leaving was voluntary, putting employers in the position of responding to this.

On a literal interpretation of the adjustment model, all firms would have been expected to record either a manpower shortage or a manpower surplus in the survey period. However, only a half reported a shortage and a quarter reported a surplus. Rather than simply not adjusting to imbalances, they were not being recorded. Inefficient utilisation of labour was the main reason postulated for this. In many firms the relationship between desired and actual employment is flexible, with the former not being known precisely and any small fluctuations between the two being disregarded.

Where imbalances were reported their main cause was generally an increase or decrease in output demand. Both in the case of shortage and of surplus a wide range of adjustments were used, although these did not coincide with particular affected occupations or with particular causes. In the shortage cases most adjustment was on labour inflows, with virtually none on labour outflows. The balance of activity was more even for surpluses. The evidence is that changes in output demand only translate into external labour-market effects after a time lag, and with a sustained rise or fall in demand. In situations both of shortage and of surplus, immediacy of effect was the main reason for choosing an adjustment instrument, followed by reversibility at a future date. Few constraints and low cost were much less important reasons. Constraints were recognised as operating by only a half of employers in the manpower shortage case, possibly because any actual constraints were regarded as part of the normal operating environment. However, in the manpower surplus case, constraints were much more explicit, particularly those concerning industrial relations and finance.

The model of manpower imbalance outlined stands up to empirical examination. The overall conclusion to be drawn is that most employers satisfice in their labour-market behaviour, rather than optimise. Although there are suggestions of pragmatism, particularly in the reasons given for choice of recruitment channel and of adjustment instrument, and of habitual behaviour. However, it is not clear that all employers are using the most efficient labour-market strategies open to them. Possible reasons for this are imperfect understanding of the nature of manpower imbalance and restricted knowledge of the alternatives available, combined with the pressure of operational problems other than manpower. It is not clear what status manpower problems carry when set in relation to other problems facing organisations.

The themes of this paper require further development using a larger and more robust data base. Comparative work also needs to be carried out, looking at different types of LLM. More stress would need to be placed on reasons for behaviour and on the time element in the adoption of instruments. Further emphasis would need to be given to the precise utilisation of labour within organisations.

Neither the macroscale nor the microscale of analysis are mutually exclusive. However, it is possible that they can only be integrated within a framework of LLM accounts which is both comprehensive and dynamic. The creation of these accounts presents formidable data problems, even at the national level, which are unlikely to be resolved in the near future. Until they are, the two approaches are best regarded as complementary, both having a role to play in increasing the understanding of labour-market operation. The micro, employer-based approach is appropriate to organisations such as the Manpower Services Commission. This is because it focuses on the level at which labour-market policies are intended to work.

The model presented here is a possible framework for studying employer behaviour, and could be expanded into an explicit manpower-policy context.

Acknowledgements. The fieldwork reported in this paper was conducted whilst the author was a postgraduate student in the Department of Geography, London School of Economics and Political Science. A grant was received from the Central Research Fund of the University of London to cover the cost of the postal survey. Many people provided information about the LLM, and several colleagues made helpful comments on the draft version of this paper. I gratefully acknowledge their assistance and advice but must stress that they bear no subsequent responsibility.

Finally, the views presented in this paper are those of the author and do not necessarily represent those of the Manpower Services Commission.

References

Ball R M, 1980 "The use and definition of travel-to-work areas in Great Britain: some problems" *Regional Studies* **14** 125-139

Bosanquet N, Doeringer P B, 1973 "Is there a dual labour market in Britain?" *Economic Journal* **83** 421-435

Brechling F P R, 1967 "Trends and cycles in British regional unemployment" *Oxford Economic Papers* **19** 1-21

Carmichael C L, 1978 "Local labour market analysis: its importance and a possible approach" *Geoforum* **9** 127-148

Carmichael C L, 1980 *The Labour Market Behaviour of Employers: A Case Study of Swindon* Ph D thesis, University of London

Chisholm M, Oeppen J, 1973 *The Changing Pattern of Employment. Regional Specialisation and Industrial Localisation in Britain* (Croom Helm, London)

Clifton R, Tatton-Brown C, 1979 "Impact of employment legislation on small firms" Research Paper 6, Department of Employment, London

CDP, 1977 *The Costs of Industrial Change* Home Office (Urban Deprivation Unit), London

Cyert R M, March J G, 1963 *A Behavioural Theory of the Firm* (Prentice-Hall, Englewood Cliffs, NJ)

Daniel W W, 1974 *A National Survey of the Unemployed* Broadsheet 546, Political and Economic Planning (now Policy Studies Institute), London

Daniel W W, Stilgoe E, 1978 *The Impact of Employment Protection Laws* Broadsheet 577, Policy Studies Institute, London

Deaton D, Thomas B, 1977 *Labour Shortages and Economic Analysis: A Study of Occupational Labour Markets* Warwick Studies in Industrial Relations (Basil Blackwell, Oxford)

DEm, 1977 *Employment in Metropolitan Areas* Unit for Manpower Studies, Department of Employment, London

Dennis R D, 1978 "The decline of manufacturing employment in Greater London: 1966-74" *Urban Studies* **15** 559-574

Doeringer P B, Piore M J, 1971 *Internal Labour Markets and Manpower Analysis* (D C Heath, Lexington, Mass)

Dunnell K, Head E, 1975 *Employers and Employment Services: A Survey Carried Out for the Employment Service Agency* SS 1012, Social Survey Division, Office of Population Censuses and Surveys, London

Erickson R A, 1974 "The regional impact of growth firms: the case of Boeing 1963-8" *Land Economics* **50** 127-136

Frost M E, Spence N A, 1979 "Urban and regional unemployment in Britain. The timing of unemployment response" WR-5, Departments of Geography, London School of Economics and Political Science and University of London, King's College

Goodman J F B, 1970 "The definition and analysis of local labour markets: some empirical problems" *British Journal of Industrial Relations* **8** 179–196

Gudgin G, 1978 *Industrial Location Processes and Regional Employment Growth* (Saxon House, Teakfield, Farnborough, Hants)

Hall P, Gracey H, Drewett R, Thomas R, 1973 *The Containment of Urban England* (Allen and Unwin, London)

Holt C C, 1969 "Improving the labour market trade-off between inflation and unemployment" *American Economic Review* **58** 135–146

Holt C C, 1971a "Job search, Phillips' wage relation, and union influence: theory and evidence" in *Microeconomic Foundations of Employment and Inflation Theory* Eds E S Phelps and others (W W Norton, New York) pp 53–123

Holt C C, 1971b "How can the Phillips Curve be moved to reduce both inflation and unemployment?" in *Microeconomic Foundations of Employment and Inflation Theory* Eds E S Phelps and others (W W Norton, New York) pp 224–256

Holt C C, David M H, 1966 "The concept of job vacancies in a dynamic theory of the labour market" in *The Measurement and Interpretation of Job Vacancies* (The National Bureau of Economic Research, New York) pp 73–110

Hunter L C, 1978 *Labour Shortages and Manpower Policy* Manpower Studies 2, Manpower Services Commission (HMSO, London)

ILO, 1962 *Unemployment and Structural Change* International Labour Organisation, Geneva

Kerr C, 1954 "The balkanisation of labour markets" in *Labour Mobility and Economic Opportunity* Eds E W Bakke and others (MIT/John Wiley, New York) pp 92–110

Lambeth IAS, 1977 *Local Employers Study* IAS/LA/16, Department of the Environment, London

Lester R A, 1955 "Adjustments to labour shortages: management practices and institutional controls in an area of expanding employment" RR-91, Industrial Relations Section, Department of Economics and Sociology, Princeton University, Princeton, NJ

Lever W F, 1979 "Industry and labour markets in Great Britain" in *Spatial Analysis, Industry and the Industrial Environment. Volume 1. Industrial Systems* Eds F E I Hamilton, G J R Linge (John Wiley, Chichester, Sussex) pp 89–114

Lloyd P E, Mason C M, 1978 "Manufacturing industry in the inner city: a case study of Greater Manchester" *Transactions of the British Institute of Geographers* **3** 66–90

Mace J, 1979 "Internal labour markets for engineers in British industry" *British Journal of Industrial Relations* **17** 50–63

MacKay D I, Boddy D, Brack J, Diack J A, Jones N, 1971 *Labour Markets Under Different Employment Conditions* University of Glasgow Social and Economic Studies, Number 22 (Allen and Unwin, London)

Massey D B, Meegan R A, 1979 "The geography of industrial organisation: the spatial effects of the restructuring of the electrical engineering sector under the Industrial Reorganisation Corporation" *Progress in Planning* volume 10(3) (Pergamon Press, Oxford)

MSC, 1978 *Training for Skills: A Programme of Action* Manpower Services Commission, London

MSC, 1979a *Report on Hard-to-Fill Vacancies* Manpower Services Commission, London

MSC, 1979b *Labour Shortages in the West Midlands Region* Manpower Services Commission, London

MSC, 1979c *Skill Shortages in Manufacturing Industry in Central Region* Manpower Services Commission Office for Scotland, Edinburgh

MSC/NEDO, 1979 *Engineering Skill Shortages in the Reading Area* Manpower Services Commission, London

NIER, 1977 *National Institute Economic Review* Number 87, February, 45-51

Oi, W Y, 1962 "Labour as a quasi-fixed factor" *Journal of Political Economy* **70** 538-555

Price J L, 1975 "The measurement of turnover" *Industrial Relations* **6** 33-46

Salt J, 1976 *Local Unemployment in the U.K. in the 1970's* Paper presented at the Regional Studies Association Annual Conference, July 1976 (Regional Studies Association, London)

Smart M W, 1974 "Local labour market areas: uses and definition" *Progress in Planning* Volume 2(4) (Pergamon Press, Oxford)

Thakur M, 1975 "Manpower planning in action" Information Report 19, Institute of Personnel Management, London

Appendix

Local labour-market data sources used

Local authority employment surveys

The Corporate Planning Division of one of the local authorities in the LLM instituted a survey of employment at local firms in January 1971. This has been repeated annually, with the exception of 1975. The aim is to provide information about current employment and about future labour requirements, as an input to the planning process. A postal approach has been used since January 1972. The sample began as 175 organisations and had risen to 310 by 1978. Response rates have varied between 62% and 77%. However, the response by individual firms has been erratic. Between 1972 and 1978, three hundred and thirteen different organisations responded, but only twenty-eight had replied to each of the six surveys, and only ninety-two had replied in 1976, 1977, and 1978.

Postal questionnaire survey of employers

Interviews were conducted with four organisation personnel managers as a pilot study for the postal questionnaire. This was concerned with labour-market behaviour, and was sent to a sample of two hundred and twenty-four employers in the LLM, each of whom had more than twenty employees. The sample was drawn from the list of respondents to each Local Authority Employment Survey and a list of firms supplied by another local authority. Seventy-four questionnaires were returned complete and were analysed (33% effective response rate) after one written and one telephone reminder. Nonrespondents tended to be in the production sector. Production respondents tended to be larger organisations, and service respondents tended to be smaller, than their counterparts in the sample as a whole. Total employment in the seventy-four respondents was estimated to be equivalent to some 18% of the LLM total in 1978.

Company personnel records

A random sample of forty employers, stratified by size, was drawn from the list of employers included in the 1978 Local Authority Employment Survey. These were written to, asking for access to their personnel records. Only two of the forty were willing to assist and kept suitable records. The main reason for noncooperation was confidentiality of the records.

In the two participating organisations, a manufacturing company and a local authority (staff records only), random one in two samples of all 'live' records at the end of May 1978 and of all 'dead' records between 1974 and 1978 were drawn. Information was abstracted from these personal files and was coded into seventeen variables.

Aggregate personnel information was supplied by these and by two other organisations (both in manufacturing industry).

Labour-market theory and spatial unemployment: the role of demand reconsidered

P C Cheshire

9.1 Introduction

In every complete decade since the Second World War unemployment in the United Kingdom has approximately doubled, so it is not surprising that it has been a topic of growing concern. As the ranks of the unemployed have swelled, the rate of growth of the unemployment industry has been even faster; government agencies and special programmes have multiplied; contract research has boomed and academic interest has flourished.

What does, perhaps, need some explanation is the emphasis that this growing interest in unemployment has taken. In this study, I shall concentrate on the academic literature and the more widely publicised contract research, though the emphasis of government programmes has been similar. This emphasis is on what might be characterised as market imperfections and institutional causes of unemployment, not on the consequences of the level of excess demand.

The role of excess demand has been comparatively neglected both in the literature dealing with unemployment at a national level and where the focus has been on unemployment in local labour markets. At a national level much academic research has been concentrated on whether or not increased levels of unemployment benefit, especially Earnings Related Supplement (ERS), were a factor causing higher unemployment. Most of this literature cites Gujarati (1972) as having first proposed a causal link between the change in benefits and higher unemployment[1]. Since then, serious articles have appeared on this theme; some, for example, Taylor (1972), Foster (1973), Cubbin and Foley (1977), or Sawyer (1979)

[1] In fact a link had been hypothesised but been demonstrated to be of little quantitive importance by a number of earlier writers. Bowers et al (1970), and Bowers et al (1972), examined aggregative data and showed that benefit levels, whilst they might have had some impact on overall unemployment were quantitatively of little significance. In a strangely neglected piece, published just a few months later, Mackay and Reid (1972) had shown from survey data that the search activity of workers receiving ERS and/or Redundancy Payments was all but identical to that of workers not in receipt of such payments. Grossing the effects of those differences up to national levels showed that the change in benefits and redundancy payments together could not account for more than a small fraction of the overall increase in unemployment at that time. This is the only direct evidence bearing on the controversy known to the present writer. All other evidence is either what might be called inferential or, in the case of the evidence in favour of the suggestion that increased unemployment has resulted from higher benefit payments, the existence of statistically significant associations between variables. In the case of Gujarati (1972) the 'variable' was simply a dummy for when unemployment started to increase.

dispute the role of benefit levels, particularly ERS, in higher unemployment; others, most notably Maki and Spindler (1975) and Spindler and Maki (1979) argue that higher benefit levels have at least played a significant role. The reality is probably as diagnosed by the Department of Employment's enquiry, the findings of which were published in the *Gazette*, DEm (1976); these were that increased benefit levels have played some significant part in increasing unemployment against other indicators but that their role has been quantitively unimportant. In 1976 the estimate was in the order of an extra 20000 unemployed at most. Thus the question appears to be a policy issue. Is a small increase in average unemployment levels an acceptable price for society to pay to reduce average income loss resulting from unemployment and perhaps, by financing a small increase in job search, achieve a small increase in average job satisfaction?

Another area of study has concentrated on the question of labour hoarding and dishoarding. Taylor (1972; 1974; 1976; 1979) has made a substantial contribution here, though his contributions have addressed themselves perhaps more to the general question of labour hoarding and its measurement, than to the specific question of explaining the increase in unemployment since 1966. Other contributions have been made by Leslie and Laing (1978), McKendrick (1975), and Knight and Wilson (1974). This literature, particularly the writing of Taylor, and of Knight and Wilson, has tended to demonstrate a significant dishoarding of labour by employers since 1966. In the case of Taylor (1972), and Knight and Wilson, this has been cited as evidence against the role of increased benefits. Knight and Wilson relate the increase in dishoarding to the effects of the Redundancy Payments Act (1965) in reducing employee resistance to being laid off. A later suggestion was that the Act may also have had the effect of increasing layoffs of workers of less than two years service, two years being the minimum period necessary before becoming eligible for redundancy payments. Thus the Act is seen as being a causal factor in higher unemployment not as a result of the effect of the payments received by redundant workers on their job search activity but by being instrumental in increasing the flow of workers into the pool of unemployed.

Another area in which contributions have been made to the debate on national unemployment is the recording phenomenon; how far is the increase in unemployment the result of an increase in the proportion of all unemployed recording as such (see Evans, 1977), and how far is the increase in unemployment against vacancies the result of an increased incidence of vacancy recording by the restructured employment services (see Bowers, 1976).

Comparatively little attention appears to have been given in the academic literature on national unemployment to the problems of structural unemployment or technological unemployment, except briefly in the early

1970s and in the unrelated literature, mainly by futurologists and other noneconomists, on the effects of microprocessors on employment[2].

The emphasis in research on local unemployment has been quite different. Not surprisingly, purely national factors, such as changes in benefit levels, have been entirely ignored. More surprising has been the heavy concentration on factors which have been ignored at a national level, especially various forms of structural unemployment, often called 'mismatch' in the local unemployment literature, and various forms of what labour economists would call 'geographic structural' or 'geographic frictional' unemployment. As at the national level, relatively little attention has been given to spatial differences in excess demand or to the impact in local labour markets of changes in the national level of excess demand.

In the context of local labour markets, two particular issues appear to have attracted research. One is the role of differences in personal characteristics either of the local labour force or of the unemployed in determining differences in unemployment rates; the other is the role of housing tenure in influencing mobility and hence unemployment, especially the role of local authority housing. Both Metcalf (1975) and Metcalf and Richardson (1976) used personal characteristics of the labour force with various indicators of local demand to try and explain interurban and intraurban unemployment variations. McGregor (1977) used personal characteristics, including being housed in a 'problem' estate, to explain within-sample variation in unemployment duration. Gleave and Palmer (1979a) and McCormick (1979) found that variations in the proportions of the labour force in an area being in local authority housing appeared to influence spatial variations in unemployment.

Reasons for the comparative neglect of the role of excess demand, both at the level of the national and the local labour market, are not immediately obvious. At the national level it may in part be the result of the rising influence of monetarist theory with its stress on price flexibility and the natural rate of unemployment, and denial of an important role for deficiency of aggregate demand. Yet the remaining influence of Keynesian theories and the rising interest in problems of disequilibrium both provide a macroeconomic theoretical framework within which to examine problems of negative excess demand. It may be that since most of the specific work on unemployment has been done by labour economists or micro-orientated economists, the role of excess demand has tended to be regarded as exogenous. It may be that the role of excess demand has been thought so obvious that it has not merited research in its own right.

At the local market level of enquiry the explanation seems more straightforward. Several studies have been of specific individual or sets of

---

[2] One exception to this is the article by Stoneman (1975), who concluded that the effects of computers on employment were not likely to be large.

local labour markets at a single point of time; for example, the Inner Area Studies (1977a; 1977b) or McGregor (1977). Such an enquiry does not lend itself to an examination of the role of excess demand. In addition, investigators interested in problems of local unemployment may not give emphasis to the level of excess demand in the national labour market or even in the local one, since that may be regarded as beyond the control of local decisionmakers. A further factor in some cases, for example, that of the Inner Area Studies (1977a; 1977b), may simply be a lack of an analytical labour-market framework within which to assess the role of excess demand.

The purpose of this chapter is to try and rectify this omission. Within the framework of explicit labour-market theory and empirical findings, the intention is to examine the ways in which both the level of excess demand in the national labour market and spatial variations in the level of excess demand affect local labour markets, particularly unemployment. The reasons for doing this are first, the writer's belief that the level of excess demand is not only by far the most important determinant of the overall level of unemployment both in national and in local labour markets, but the prevailing level of excess demand affects many other features of labour markets as well. Second, whatever the reasons for the lack of explicit emphasis in research on the level of excess demand, the fact is that there has been a lack of emphasis, so it is proper to try to offset this imbalance, even if it can only be to some small extent. In the process of doing this an attempt will be made to try and draw together some of the research of the last ten years and relate those findings to the role of excess demand.

9.2 Spatial adjustment mechanisms in labour markets

As has been argued elsewhere (Cheshire, 1979), the degree to which a particular local labour market is affected by specific spatial variation in the level of excess demand is a function of its degree of independence of other local labour markets. This is because of variations in adjustment costs. Job changing is a major phenomenon. As Department of Employment figures over the last two decades show, the annual total of job moves is in the order of one-third to one-half of the total number of employees in employment. As Hunter and Reid (1968) showed, about two-thirds of job moves involve a change of industry. The volume of this turnover, its relatively low or negligible cost to the worker, and the fact that in general we can expect the net flow to be into spatial/economic areas of greater job opportunities, together imply that between sets of contiguous labour markets there will be relatively little friction in the adjustment process. Spatial variations in excess demand between such labour markets will thus quickly tend to disappear. Since job mobility is itself a positive function of the level of excess demand, however, the efficiency of this adjustment process must be expected to vary according to the overall level of excess demand in the set of contiguous local labour markets that make up a regional or, ultimately, national labour market.

Where a local labour market is independent of other local labour markets, measured in terms of potential across-boundary job changes without residential relocation relative to total employment in the local labour market, adjustment to spatial variations in job opportunities reflecting spatial variation in excess demand will be far more costly, and consequently frictions will be greater and variations more persistent. Since the volume of gross migration flows and job mobility is a positive function of excess demand for labour in any set of independent local labour markets, the efficiency of this adjustment process, too, will vary with excess demand.

If this is accepted as a simple description of the spatial adjustment process between local labour markets, there are, apart from the implications for the diagnosis of interurban and intraurban variation in unemployment rates, implications for the strength of the case for regional policy. There are, in addition, implications for the way in which local labour markets should be defined.

One of the arguments for regional policy is that the social returns from employing unemployed labour exceed the private returns; consequently there is a social benefit derived from diverting growth from full employment regions to regions where there is negative excess demand for labour. If the prevailing level of excess demand in the national economy falls, so that there is negative excess demand for labour in all regions, this argument presumably ceases to apply. The efficiency of the adjustment process to regional variations in excess demand is itself a function of the prevailing level of excess demand in the national economy, however; both because, as suggested above, interregional labour flows are reduced as excess demand falls and because interregional flows of jobs in the opposite direction are also a positive function of the prevailing level of excess demand (see Moore and Rhodes, 1976). Thus as the national level of excess demand falls, although the pure efficiency argument for regional policy may be weakened, the equity argument is strengthened. Given that political pressures are more likely to be generated by equity questions, especially spatial equity questions, than efficiency considerations, this may at least in part account for the very much reduced political demands for regional policy in the 1950s and the increasing concern with it during the 1960s.

The implications of the suggested spatial adjustment process for the definition of local labour markets are complex. The traditional means of drawing boundaries around spatial labour markets has been to plot commuting contours. The arguments above, however, strongly suggest that these commuting flows reflect not some natural order but the spatial pattern of demand for labour interacting with transport costs and systems, and other determinants of residential location relative to employment location. Since the spatial pattern of demand is volatile, the pattern of flows, and thus commuting contours, will be subject to economic forces;

effectively one function of commuting flows is as an equilibrating mechanism in the spatial adjustment of demand to supply in labour markets.

Another implication is that not only are the boundaries of local labour markets, drawn with respect to commuting flows, ultimately arbitrary, but that the very idea of a local labour market formulated in terms of a unique geographical definition is ultimately arbitrary. The definition of a local labour market is in principle a matter to be determined by the problem under investigation or the policy variable being considered.

If, for example, the problem is to identify unemployment resulting from a deficiency of aggregate demand, the arguments above suggest that a large area, which will be relatively self-contained and independent, is most appropriate. A small area, where a significant proportion of workers can in principle take jobs in other contiguous labour markets will not, if the arguments above are accepted, exhibit a stable or purely local level of excess demand. Because of its high degree of interdependence with surrounding areas the level of excess demand in such a market will primarily reflect factors at something approaching a regional level. If the local labour market is part of a larger metropolitan area, this problem will be reinforced by economic segregation, both in terms of residence and of employment.

If, however, the problem was to examine, say, structural and frictional unemployment, the appropriate local labour market might be considerably smaller. If frictional unemployment is defined as unemployed workers for whom appropriate jobs exist, then such jobs are only appropriate if they are within travel-to-work distance for the particular worker. Similarly, structural unemployment is usually defined as unemployment existing when jobs are available within travel-to-work distance but for which the unemployed workers are not qualified. Both such types of unemployment suggest a local labour market of a considerably smaller geographical extent than a region.

A further complication arises because the actual distance corresponding to travel-to-work distance is itself not unique but varies with the characteristics of the worker involved. Actual travel-to-work distances vary significantly with income; for example, table 9.1 shows distance of residence from work place compared with income for workers at Heathrow Airport. The sample was large, so each income class had 950 or more members and the pattern with ten independent observations is clearcut; the better paid workers live further from work. There is a possibility of bias if these figures are taken as representative of all workers because of the high income elasticity of demand for environmental quality and, perhaps, because of the cheap flights available to airline staff, who are strongly represented amongst the better paid and some of whom use the airlines to commute extreme distances (for example, from Cornwall, the Channel Islands, and Cheshire). Nevertheless, it is consistent with a more general positive association between income and commuting distance, so, in principle, the implication is that the geographical extent of the local labour market (still excluding residential relocation) varies with income and occupation. Thus the appropriate sized labour market within which to measure frictional unemployment of accountants, with a potential travel-to-work distance of 50 miles, might be 8000 square miles; for an unskilled building worker, with a potential travel-to-work distance of $7\frac{1}{2}$ miles, it would be 175 square miles.

These arguments are not to suggest that defining and analysing local labour markets is futile. Much very useful work has been done, most recently and perhaps most painstakingly by Lever (1979). Rather it is to suggest no single definition is universally appropriate; in the light of how spatial labour markets adjust and the spatial constraints acting on agents within them, all definitions are ultimately arbitrary. Cutoff points for commuting distances are arbitrary; and given the spatial adjustment mechanism of job relocation between contiguous local labour markets the chosen definition of spatial independence is arbitrary. In addition, given that mechanism, any chosen commuting contour will reflect the current spatial distribution of excess demand, which is subject to change. Although not rendering the definition and analysis of local labour markets futile, these factors do suggest previously unrecognised conceptual problems beset the familiar approach[3] of partitioning unemployment between demand deficiency and various categories of nondemand deficiency. The most appropriate geographical labour market within which to identify demand deficiency unemployment is likely to be too large for the appropriate definition of categories of nondemand deficiency unemployment.

The immediate implications are that the most appropriate size of local labour markets will vary with the purpose for which the definition is intended. Since, in the present context, interest is focused on the role of

Table 9.1. Commuting distances and income.

Annual income class	Percentage of class living		
	less than 2 miles from work	2–5 miles from work	more than 5 miles from work
Under £2000	32	31	37
£2000–£2999	32	21	47
£3000–£3999	28	22	50
£4000–£6999	5	15	80
£7000 and over	4	6	90

Source: EAG (1974) data.

[3] For a recent summary of this literature and refinement of the approach, see Gleave and Palmer (1979b).

excess demand, then the analysis points to the use of geographically large areas made up of many contiguous and interacting local labour markets, but between which job relocation will be relatively insignificant as an adjustment mechanism. Spatial adjustment will consequently depend primarily on migration. Since this is costly and there is substantial inertia, demand differences will be relatively persistent[4].

9.3 Regional labour markets in the 1970s

The stability of regional unemployment rates relative to the national rate was, as table 9.2 shows[5], maintained during the decade of the 1970s. The ranking of regions has remained remarkably constant. The spread of regional unemployment, as measured by the standard deviation of the regional rate relative to the national rate, has similarly retained a consistent pattern through time. As national unemployment rises so the standard deviation

Table 9.2. Regional unemployment rates relative to that for Great Britain[a].

Region	1969	1970	1971	1972	1973	1974	1975	1976	1977	1978	1979	1980[b]
SE	0·62	0·62	0·58	0·56	0·58	0·61	0·70	0·77	0·77	0·72	0·67	0·65
EA	0·72	0·77	0·90	0·71	0·69	0·77	0·88	0·89	0·89	0·84	0·80	0·77
SW	0·98	1·00	0·92	0·87	0·86	1·00	1·16	1·14	1·11	1·06	0·98	0·95
WM	0·79	1·01	1·02	1·04	0·83	0·84	1·03	1·06	0·94	0·93	0·98	1·03
EM	0·77	0·78	0·92	0·82	0·80	0·86	0·91	0·86	0·83	0·85	0·84	0·88
Y/H	0·98	1·11	1·17	1·09	1·08	1·03	0·98	1·00	0·93	0·99	1·00	1·05
NW	0·97	1·06	1·18	1·33	1·40	1·35	1·37	1·27	1·22	1·25	1·28	1·29
N	1·86	1·80	1·66	1·62	1·78	1·78	1·50	1·35	1·36	1·45	1·54	1·50
Wales	1·55	1·43	1·31	1·35	1·29	1·50	1·38	1·31	1·29	1·40	1·49	1·41
S'land	1·49	1·63	1·79	1·73	1·78	1·56	1·30	1·27	1·35	1·37	1·44	1·43
SD	0·42	0·38	0·37	0·39	0·44	0·39	0·26	0·21	0·22	0·26	0·31	0·30

[a] These data refer to all workers excluding school leavers and adult students registered as unemployed in June; not seasonally adjusted.
[b] Seasonally adjusted.
Key: SE–South East; EA–East Anglia; SW–South West; WM–West Midlands; EM–East Midlands; Y/H–Yorkshire and Humberside; NW–North West; N–North; S'land–Scotland; SD–standard deviation.

[4] It is recognised that the arguments as presented here are imprecise. Demand differences can persist between any set of freestanding urban areas surrounded by sparsely populated hinterlands. But as was pointed out in the text, the arguments suggest all definitions are ultimately arbitrary and hence that fixed on is partly a matter of convenience. Since statistics are available at a regional level, and regional labour markets are geographically large enough to be substantially independent of each other, it is convenient in what follows to conduct the analysis at a regional level.
[5] This method of showing the regional dispersion of unemployment is open to the objection that together the regions compose the nation (see Johnston, 1979). The simplicity of the method seems to the present author to outweigh this defect, however.

of the relative regional rates declines; the absolute dispersion, however, widens. If we compare 1969 with 1976, the national unemployment rate doubled and the standard deviation of the relative regional rates halved. This is proportionately a greater reduction in the dispersion of relative regional rates than occurred between June 1966 and June 1969[6], when unemployment also approximately doubled.

Within this general picture there have been some minor changes. The North West appears to have suffered a real relative decline rather than a cyclical fluctuation. It now seems appropriate to classify this region in terms of unemployment with Wales, the North, and Scotland as a depressed region; within this group Scotland has shown some improvement. Despite publicity given to the decline in the fortunes of the West Midlands, in relative unemployment terms, its position does not appear to have altered during the 1970s although its sensitivity to cyclical decline has continued. There has been some deterioration from the early 1960s, however. The South West and East Anglia, the two regions showing strongest growth in Regional Gross Domestic Product (see *Economic Trends*, 1976, 1977, 1978, and 1979), appear to have shown a relative improvement in unemployment, especially since 1976.

Table 9.3. Regional unemployment/vacancy ratios relative to those for Great Britain[a].

Region	1969	1970	1971	1972	1973	1974	1975	1976	1977	1978	1979	1980[b]
SE	0·49	0·48	0·43	0·38	0·42	0·45	0·55	0·63	0·59	0·53	0·48	0·48
EA	0·68	0·77	0·96	0·59	0·53	0·67	0·86	0·87	0·94	0·86	0·70	0·66
SW	0·88	0·82	0·64	0·63	0·64	0·80	1·01	1·02	1·18	1·04	0·89	0·90
WM					0·72	1·09	2·19	2·08	1·68	1·58	1·63	1·84
EM					0·96	0·90	1·08	1·01	0·88	0·95	0·96	1·00
W/EM[c]	0·83	1·21	1·28	1·29	0·81	1·01	1·74	1·65	1·35	1·32	1·37	1·50
Y/H	1·05	1·25	1·44	1·32	1·36	1·23	1·19	1·13	1·00	1·27	1·32	1·77
NW	1·04	1·17	1·51	2·29	2·10	1·90	1·86	1·73	1·81	1·98	1·89	1·96
N	2·69	2·36	2·16	2·16	2·36	2·39	1·26	1·21	1·42	1·72	2·05	2·07
Wales	2·20	1·70	1·49	1·51	1·93	2·26	1·64	1·39	1·39	1·58	1·57	1·54
S'land	2·19	2·70	3·56	3·31	3·00	2·36	1·04	0·95	1·20	1·29	1·54	1·19
SD	0·80	0·74	0·93	0·95	0·93	0·78	0·43	0·36	0·35	0·44	0·53	0·57

[a] These data refer to all unemployed workers, excluding school leavers and adult students; vacancies are for adults registered at employment offices. Figures for June, not seasonally adjusted.
[b] Seasonally adjusted.
[c] Vacancy figures were not published for the separate Midlands regions prior to 1973.
Key: see table 9.2.

[6] Not shown in table 9.2; for a discussion in general terms see NIER (1971).

In table 9.3 similar data are presented for the ratio of unemployment to vacancies[7] in each region as a measure approximating slightly more closely to that usually associated with pure excess demand for labour (but see below). The general pattern is similar to that for the relative rates of regional unemployment alone. The dispersion of these, too, appears to be sensitive to the overall cycle. But while the ranking of the more prosperous regions has remained consistent, there do appear to have been marked changes in the relative positions of some of the other regions. Unfortunately vacancy statistics, unlike unemployment statistics, were not published separately for the East and West Midlands prior to 1973 but it would appear that, even allowing for its extra sensitivity to the overall cycle, the West Midlands labour market, based on this measure, has deteriorated very significantly relative to the rest of the country. In terms of the ratio of unemployed to vacancies, since 1975 the West Midlands has ranked alongside the North and North West as one of the three most depressed regions in Britain. Even more marked has been the transformation of the relative position of the Scottish labour market. Though unemployment remains relatively high in Scotland, in terms of its ratio of vacancies to unemployment, Scotland has moved from being substantially the worst region in Britain to near the national position. It is now closer to a still relatively prosperous region like the East Midlands than it is to Wales, the next worst region. This change, brought about more by a relative increase in vacancies than a decline in relative unemployment, may be a labour-market reflection of the significant restructuring both in spatial and in occupational terms of the Scottish economy partly as a result of North Sea oil.

9.4 The role of excess demand in regional unemployment

How, then, does the level of excess demand for labour relate to the evidence so far presented? It has been conventional for a decade or more to categorise unemployment into demand deficiency and nondemand deficiency, or structural and frictional unemployment[8]. For almost as long, the present author has suspected that important interaction existed between the level of excess demand and conventional measures of local labour-market efficiency, or structural and frictional unemployment, measured using relationships between unemployment, U, and vacancies, V. Some grounds for these suspicions were voiced in Cheshire (1979). In this study it is intended to consider an alternative and, it will be argued, more important route by which such interaction occurs.

In the past fifteen years or so, general economic theory bearing on unemployment has been concentrated into two different lines of approach.

[7] The arguments concerning the interpretation of the vacancy statistics are thought to be too well known to be repeated here.

[8] Again for a recent summary of this literature see Gleave and Palmer (1979b).

Monetarist models have analysed a world in which information is complete, and adjustment mechanisms, though subject to expectations, tend to work relatively efficiently. Attention in these models has been on the 'natural' rate of unemployment derived from the equilibrium determined by the interaction of demand and supply in the labour market as functions of the real wage. These models have been partially complemented by labour-market research stressing the economics of information and search; the seminal work here is that of Phelps (1970) and Holt (1970a; 1970b). The second major approach has been in terms of the dynamics of disequilibrium and the implications of uncertainty. The literature here, initiated in the work of writers such as Clower (1965), Leijonhufvud (1968), and Barro and Grossman (1971), has tended to be at a high level of abstraction.

The earlier applied work of Oi (1962), however, to an extent straddles these two approaches. Oi's arguments relating to labour as a quasi-fixed factor of production, although microeconomic, are concerned with disequilibrium. As we all know, in the long run in which all factors of production are variable, fixed costs as well as variable costs must be covered and so they also affect the amount of a factor employed. Oi's simple insight was that there are fixed costs attached to varying labour inputs; labour is not a purely variable factor. His respecification of labour costs is

$$C_q = \sum_{t=0}^{\tau} W_{qt}^e (1+\phi)^{-t} + C_q^h + C_q^{tr} , \qquad (9.1)$$

where C_q is the total discounted cost of hiring a particular type or quality of worker, q; W_{qt}^e is the expected wage in the tth period for that quality of worker; ϕ is the rate of discount; τ is the expected period of employment; C_q^h are the hiring costs, and C_q^{tr} the training expenses.

It follows from the formulation of labour costs in this way that, with the normal competitive assumptions, the short-run equilibrium conditions differ from their long-run equivalents directly with the element of fixed costs associated with the particular quality of worker. The fact that profit maximisation implies decisionmaking with respect to employment in time t, on the basis of expected future prices and wage rate, introduces uncertainty into the model which reinforces the conclusions.

In terms of cyclical fluctuations in aggregate employment, the implications are that ceteris paribus, qualities of labour with the highest 'degree of fixity' will experience the lowest relative changes in employment following any given change in product demand. Or, in other words, the incentive, for example, to hoard skilled labour in a cyclical downturn and to work such labour overtime in the upturn, will be greater than is the case with unskilled labour. But this is a purely cyclical disequilibrium argument; if product demand moves to a new level at which it is expected to stay permanently, the cost-minimising labour input will be adjusted to the long-run level where the value of the worker's total marginal product must cover not only his wages, but also his 'periodic rent', which represents the fixed employment costs in each period.

Testing this prediction produced the answer that indeed, in the sense implied, employment fluctuations of different qualities of workers did seem to vary systematically with a measure of labour fixity in the way predicted.

There is, however, one small and one more-significant modification that can be suggested to Oi's formulation of wage costs. In deciding in an equilibrium context whether to hire another unit of a particular class of worker, the hiring costs in time t and the training costs throughout the worker's training period are the relevant costs. In a context of short-run disequilibrium, however, when product demand has temporarily fallen, the relevant costs are the *expected* hiring and training costs in time $t+1$ when demand rises.

We may get round this by assuming that hiring and training costs of a given quality of worker do not vary systematically with time. The Oi formulation, however, provides a theoretical foundation for the existence of internal and external labour markets, and also some analytical basis for employers' decisionmaking in the short run on the adjustment of labour inputs by changing hours per worker or the number of workers employed. But although hiring and training costs may not vary systematically with time, they *will* vary negatively with the unemployment rate of a particular quality of worker which is expected to prevail in the external labour market.

If unemployment of a particular class of skilled worker is high, hiring and recruitment costs will be correspondingly lower. In a market with substantial positive excess demand, employers may have to pay agency fees, search in other local labour markets, advertise and, above all, wait, before they can recruit. In markets with substantial negative excess demand, suitable workers may be readily available without extensive search or expenditure by the employer and without delay. Training costs should be expected to behave in the same way. The higher the unemployment rate, other things being equal, the greater the probability that an employer can directly recruit an already skilled worker from the external market and so the lower will be an employer's expected training costs. In high unemployment markets, even where the skills of a particular worker may be, to an important degree, firm specific, the employer may regard training costs as being lower since there will be a higher probability of recruiting an unemployed worker who has previously worked in the job.

The general argument extends to the choice of manhours versus workers. As several writers have suggested, given short-run output fluctuations, not only may labour hoarding occur but the concept of labour hoarding can be extended to 'paid-for' and 'unpaid-for' labour hoarding (see Taylor, 1979, for a recent summary; also Knight and Wilson, 1974). We may assume that workers, offered less hours of work than they would choose if not constrained, will have a higher quit rate than workers whose hoarded services are paid for by the employer[9]. In addition, their quit rate will be sensitive to the unemployment rate in the external labour market. Thus the employers' cost-minimising choice between 'paid-for' versus 'unpaid-for' hoarding will, too, be a function of the expected unemployment rate in the external labour market, with a higher proportion of labour hoarding being paid for in low-unemployment labour markets.

The costs of employment can thus be rewritten as

$$C_q = \sum_{t=0}^{\tau} W_{qt}^e (1+\phi)^{-t} + C_q^h - c_q^h(U_q^e) + C_q^{tr} - c_q^{tr}(U_q^e) , \qquad (9.2)$$

where U_q^e is the expected long-run level of unemployment for workers of quality q, and c^h and c^{tr} are coefficients relating hiring and training costs negatively to expected unemployment in the external labour market. For empirical purposes it would seem reasonable to approximate U_q^e by the mean unemployment rate over the previous cycle for that class of worker in the particular local external labour market. We may thus rewrite a worker's periodic rent, R, as

$$R_q = \frac{C_q^h - c_q^h(U_q^e) + C_q^{tr} - c_q^{tr}(U_q^e)}{\sum_{t=0}^{\tau}(1+\phi)^{-t}} . \qquad (9.3)$$

So, as mean unemployment rates of a particular quality of worker rise, the worker's periodic rent falls and employers treat it increasingly as a variable factor of production.

The implications for regional labour markets are that employers in high unemployment regions should hoard less labour on average, so that, for any given change in output, there should be a larger change in employment in high unemployment regions than in low. In addition, labour hoarding that does occur in high unemployment regions may be proportionately more in the form of 'unpaid-for' than 'paid-for' hoarding. In as far as this is true, the differential elasticity of man-hours with respect to output should be greater between high and low unemployment regions than the elasticity of employment with respect to output.

9.5 Empirical evidence

The most obvious way to test these hypotheses on regional labour-market data would be to adapt the short-run employment-function approach originating in the work of Brechling (1965) and Ball and St Cyr (1966), and which uses regional data for employment, total man-hours, and output. Whilst the author was collecting data to try such a test, however,

---

[9] In fact, in low-unemployment local labour markets, putting a group of workers on short time can probably be regarded as a management technique for shedding labour costlessly.

the article by Bell and Hart (1980) appeared. For different motives these authors had tested an ideal model by using the best available data (the regional manufacturing output data used by Bell and Hart were still not known to the author, who was attempting to use regional income accounting data).

Bell and Hart were interested primarily in regional econometric modelling, and were using recently available statistics to "construct a model of the regional demand for labour services". They were somewhat puzzled by their results, which showed marked and highly significant differences between the grouped data for regions with and without significant Development Area (DA) status. Taking an orthodox view of the arguments of Oi, already referred to, they first looked at skill differences between the regional labour forces of Scotland, the North West, North Yorkshire and Humberside, and Wales (the DAs) on the one hand, and the South East, East Anglia, West and East Midlands (the not DAs or NDAs) on the other. They considered whether more rigid working practices, lower profitability, or regional policy itself might be the cause of the differences found. But they concluded, having examined skill differences between the NDAs and DAs, that "Whether these differences alone are sufficient to explain our results, ... is difficult to assess".

In the interests of economy, rather than rework the data analysed by Bell and Hart, their results are partially reproduced here (table 9.4). The equation they were using was derived with some small modifications from the short-term employment function models of Ball and St Cyr (1966), Brechling (1965), Fair (1969), and Ehrenberg (1971). The employment equation fitted took the following form,

$$E_{it}^m = g_i + \gamma_1 Q_{it} + \gamma_2 K_{it} + (1 - \eta_i) E_{i(t-1)}^m + \epsilon_{it} . \tag{9.4}$$

Table 9.4. Regional short-run employment function estimates, 1970–1975.

Regional grouping	NDA	NDA	DA	DA
Dependent variable	E_{it}^m	H_{it}	E_{it}^m	H_{it}
Constant	0·013	3·743	−0·073	3·642
	(0·58)	(115·59)	(−1·27)	(66·43)
E_{it-1}^m	0·917		0·876	
	(72·26)		(45·98)	
Q_{it}	0·068	0·008	0·110	0·022
	(5·51)	(1·96)	(6·18)	(3·08)
K_{it}	−0·012	−0·003	−0·013	−0·009
	(−6·20)	(−1·58)	(−4·91)	(−4·70)
$E_{it}^{m*} - E_{it}^m$		0·098		0·027
		(4·61)		(1·23)
R^2	0·99	0·55	0·99	0·51
F	47665·8	10·74	4941·6	9·18
Residual sum of squares	0·0035	0·0069	0·0081	0·0073

Figures in brackets are t values. Source: Bell and Hart (1980), table 1.

All variables are specified in logarithms; E_{it}^m is the number of full-time adult males employed in region i at time t in manufacturing, Q is the manufacturing output, K is the net capital formation, γ_1 measures the elasticity of employment with respect to output, and $(1 - \eta)$ measures the average adjustment lag.

The hours equation took the following specification,

$$H_{it} = d_i + \delta_{1i}Q_{it} + \delta_{2i}K_{it} + \rho_i(E_{it}^* - E_{it}) + \epsilon_{it} , \qquad (9.5)$$

where H is average weekly hours of full-time men in manufacturing, and E^{m*} denotes an equilibrium value of E^m. Both equations contain a constant and an error term. Because of data shortage, with net manufacturing output only available on a regional basis for the period 1970 to 1975, a combined cross-section–time-series procedure was adopted with data pooled on the basis already indicated.

It will be seen immediately that the estimated elasticity of employment with respect to output is almost twice as great in the high unemployment regions as it is in the low. The implied speed of adjustment to employment to output was faster in the high unemployment regions than the low, though still, at an estimated seven years, remarkably slow. The estimated elasticity of average hours with respect to output is almost three times as great in the high unemployment regions as in the low but the elasticity of average hours with respect to deviations of employment levels from equilibrium levels is very low; indeed the coefficient is not significantly different from zero. This appears to imply that, relative to the low unemployment regions, overtime is not used as a means of offsetting a perceived shortfall of workers in high unemployment regions; rather there is recourse to the slacker external market. However, as suggested above, variations in hours are used by manufacturing employers in high unemployment regions as a response to variations in output. When product demand falls, workers are put on short time, that is, there is unpaid-for hoarding, whereas in low unemployment regions labour hoarding is more likely to be paid for by the employer. Bell and Hart tested to see whether the observed differences between the DAs and not DAs were statistically significant and found that they were.

These results seem to provide evidence, as strong as could be reasonably expected, supporting the development of the Oi hypothesis suggested above. In spatial labour markets with different long-run expected levels of unemployment, employers have different attitudes to labour hoarding; employment will be more sensitive to output changes in high unemployment regions than in low, and employers will have more recourse to the external labour market in such regions. This finding can be related to the analogous findings of Knight and Wilson (1974), Taylor (1972; 1974; 1976), relating to differences over time.

Now, if differences in long-run expected unemployment rates between regional labour markets primarily reflect differences in the spatial pattern of demand, as the analysis of the spatial adjustment mechanism above suggested, there are further consequences for the operation of regional labour markets.

If we use a simple adaptation of the Holt model (Holt, 1970b), referred to above, which states

$$a = \frac{UV \, \text{prob}(UV)}{T} \, , \tag{9.6}$$

where

a	is the flow of hires and recalls (that is, accessions) from all sources expressed as a percentage of the labour force;
T	is the average market search time, that is, the average time to find and evaluate a potential employee/job offer;
prob(UV)	is the probability a particular U–V contact will result in an accepted job offer;
U, V	are the unemployment, vacancy rates;

we derive the following relationship between unemployment and vacancies:

$$U = \frac{aT}{\text{prob}(UV)} V^{-1} \, . \tag{9.7}$$

If we assume voluntary turnover is directly from job to job and so does not add to the stock of recorded unemployment[10], and if employers, where unemployment is high, are more ready to fire workers when product demand falls and hire them when demand rises, because average unemployment rates affect hiring and training costs in the way suggested, then this will affect the value of a in the local labour market. Where average unemployment is higher, a will be larger. Consequently, the high unemployment labour-market UV curve—in this case defined for a region since that seems most appropriate when the effects of excess demand differences are being examined—will be further from the origin. This implies that there will be interaction between the level of excess demand prevailing in a region and the measure of labour-market efficiency most commonly used. Regional labour markets with lower long-run levels of excess demand for labour will necessarily appear to be less efficient. This would extend not just to estimates of the level of unemployment at which it was estimated unemployment would be equal to vacancies, but to individual measures such as structural unemployment, 'mismatch', or frictional unemployment.

The intuitive interpretation of the above is that in labour markets with higher unemployment, since with temporary fluctuations of product demand less labour is hoarded and more is released onto the external market, there will tend to be more search at any given level of excess demand. But this

[10] This implies an increase in disappointed job changers, that is, people leaving jobs and not expecting to pass through unemployment but whose expectations are disappointed, would similarly cause the U–V relationship to shift outwards.

additional search is the result of the long-run level of excess demand itself being lower. It is not a primary cause of labour-market inefficiency. That higher unemployment regional labour markets tend to have higher estimated levels of nondemand deficiency unemployment is well known.

9.6 Conclusions
The analysis and evidence discussed here suggest yet a further route for interaction between the level of excess demand in a labour market and the apparent level of nondemand deficiency unemployment in that market. The underlying causal factor is again the level of excess demand. Furthermore, if accepted, the analysis would appear to apply equally to variations in the long-run level of excess demand for labour within a labour market through time. It might quite appropriately explain the findings of Knight and Wilson (1974), for example, rather than the somewhat ad hoc explanations relating to the Redundancy Payments Act suggested by them.

This is not to suggest that factors other than the level of excess demand have no role in explaining unemployment levels within a spatial labour market. Apart from factors connected with the spatial structure of metropolitan areas, other spatial factors (such as spatial structure and transport facilities), information networks, skill structures and changes in them, and cultural and institutional factors affecting mobility and adaptability may reasonably be regarded as independent causes of unemployment. The purpose of this study, however, has been to reemphasise the preeminent role of the level of excess demand in determining both the absolute level of unemployment and, between spatially independent labour markets such as the British Regions, spatial differences in unemployment.

References
Ball R J, St Cyr E B A, 1966 "Short term employment fluctuations in British manufacturing industry" *Review of Economic Studies* 33 179-207
Barro R J, Grossman H I, 1971 "A general disequilibrium model of income and employment" *American Economic Review* 56 82-93
Bell D N F, Hart R A, 1980 "The regional demand for labour services" *Scottish Journal of Political Economy* 27 140-151
Bowers J K, 1976 "Some notes on current unemployment" in *The Concept and Measurement of Involuntary Unemployment* Ed. G D N Worswick (Allen and Unwin, London) pp 109-133
Bowers J K, Cheshire P C, Webb A E, 1970 "The change in the relationship between unemployment and earnings increases: a review" *National Institute Economic Review* number 54, 44-63
Bowers J K, Cheshire P C, Webb A E, Weeden R, 1972 "Some aspects of unemployment and the labour market, 1966-71" *National Institute Economic Review* number 62, 75-88
Brechling F P R, 1965 "The relationship between output and employment in British manufacturing industries" *Review of Economic Studies* 32 187-216
Cheshire P C, 1979 "Inner areas as spatial labour markets: a critique of the inner area studies" *Urban Studies* 16 29-43

Clower R, 1965 "The Keynesian counter revolution: a theoretical appraisal" in *The Theory of Interest Rates* Eds F H Hahn, F P R Brechling (Macmillan, London) pp 103-125

Cubbin J S, Foley K, 1977 "The extent of benefit-induced unemployment in Great Britain: some new evidence" *Oxford Economic Papers* **29** 129-140

DEm, 1976 "The changed relationship between unemployment and vacancies" *Department of Employment Gazette* October 1976, 1093-1099

EAG, 1974 *Economic Effects of Heathrow Airport on the Local Area*, Economist's Advisory Group Report of a survey of employees in the Heathrow area by a private consultant

Economic Trends, 1976 numbers 272, 277; 1977 numbers 284, 289; 1978 number 296; 1979 numbers 308, 313

Ehrenberg R G, 1971 *Fringe Benefits and Overtime Behaviour* (D C Heath, Lexington, Mass)

Evans A W, 1977 "Notes on the changing relationship between registered unemployment and notified vacancies: 1961-1966 and 1966-1971" *Economica* **44** 179-196

Fair R C, 1969 *The Short Run Demand for Workers and Hours* (North-Holland, Amsterdam)

Foster J I, 1973 "The behaviour of unemployment and unfilled vacancies: Great Britain, 1958-1971—a comment" *Economic Journal* **83** 192-201

Gleave D, Palmer D, 1979a "Mobility constraints and unemployment mismatch: an analysis of structural changes in the housing market and their consequences on job migration" paper presented to *Urban Economics Conference*, Manchester

Gleave D, Palmer D, 1979b "Spatial variations in unemployment problems: a typology" paper presented to the *European Congress of the Regional Science Association*, London; Papers of the Regional Science Association, forthcoming

Gujarati D, 1972 "The behaviour of unemployment and unfilled vacancies" *Economic Journal* **82** 195-204

Holt C C, 1970a "Job search, Phillips's wage relation, and union influence; theory and evidence" in *Microeconomic Foundations of Employment and Inflation Theory* Ed. E S Phelps (W W Norton, New York) pp 53-123

Holt C C, 1970b "How can the Phillips curve be moved to reduce both inflation and unemployment" in *Microeconomic Foundations of Employment and Inflation Theory* Ed. E S Phelps (W W Norton, New York) pp 224-256

Hunter L C, Reid G L, 1968 *Urban Worker Mobility* (OECD, Paris)

Inner Area Studies, 1977a "Liverpool, Birmingham and Lambeth" *Summaries of Consultants' Final Report* Department of the Environment (HMSO, London)

Inner Area Studies Final Reports, 1977b *Change or Decay?* H Wilson, L Womersely, *Unequal City* Llewelyn-Davies, Weeks, Forestier-Walker and Bor, and *Inner London* Shankland Cox Partnership; Department of the Environment (passive author) (HMSO, London)

Johnston R F, 1979 "On the relationship between regional and national unemployment trends" *Regional Studies* **13** 409-416

Knight K G, Wilson R A, 1974 "Labour hoarding, employment and unemployment in British manufacturing industry" *Applied Economics* **6** 303-310

Leijonhufvud A, 1968 *On Keynesian Economics and the Economics of Keynes* (Oxford University Press, New York)

Leslie D, Laing C, 1978 "The theory and measurement of labour hoarding" *Scottish Journal of Political Economy* **25** 41-56

Lever W F, 1979 "The operation of local labour markets in Great Britain", paper presented to the *European Congress of the Regional Science Association*, London

McCormick B, 1979 " 'Council' housing, labour mobility and the spatial distribution of unemployment: theory and evidence", paper presented to *Urban Economics Conference*, Manchester (available from Department of Economics, University of Southampton, mimeo)

McGregor A, 1977 "Intra-urban variations in unemployment duration: a case study" *Urban Studies* **14** 303-313

Mackay D I, Reid G L, 1972 "Redundancy, unemployment and manpower policy" *Economic Journal* **82** 1256-1272

McKendrick S, 1975 "An inter-industry analysis of labour hoarding in Britain, 1953-72" *Applied Economics* **7** 101-117

Maki D, Spindler Z A, 1975 "The effect of unemployment compensation on the rate of unemployment in Great Britain" *Oxford Economic Papers* **27** 440-454

Metcalf D, 1975 "Urban unemployment in England" *Economic Journal* **85** 578-589

Metcalf D, Richardson R, 1976 "Unemployment in London" in *The Concept and Measurement of Involuntary Unemployment* Ed. G D N Worswick (Allen and Unwin, London) pp 203-220

Moore B, Rhodes J, 1976 "Regional economic policy and the movement of manufacturing firms to development areas" *Economica* **43** 17-31

NIER, 1971 "The economic situation: annual review" *National Institute Economic Review* number 55, 18-19

Oi W Y, 1962 "Labour as a quasi-fixed factor" *Journal of Political Economy* **70** 538-555

Phelps E S (Ed.), 1970 *Microeconomic Foundations of Employment and Inflation Theory* (W W Norton, New York)

Redundancy Payments Act, 1965 Public General Acts—Elizabeth II, 1965, chapter 62 (HMSO, London)

Sawyer M C, 1979 "The effects of unemployment compensation on the rate of unemployment in Great Britain: a comment" *Oxford Economic Papers* **31** 133-146

Spindler Z A, Maki D, 1979 "More on the effects of unemployment compensation on the rate of unemployment in Great Britain" *Oxford Economic Papers* **31** 147-164

Stoneman P, 1975 "The effects of computers on the demand for labour in the U.K." *Economic Journal* **85** 590-606

Taylor J, 1972 "The behaviour of unemployment and unfilled vacancies: an interchange" *Economic Journal* **82** 1352-1365

Taylor J, 1974 *Unemployment and Wage Inflation with Special Reference to Britain and the U.S.A.* (Longman, London)

Taylor J, 1976 "The unemployment gap in Britain's production sector 1953-73" in *The Concept and Measurement of Involuntary Unemployment* Ed. G D N Worswick (Allen and Unwin, London) pp 146-167

Taylor J, 1979 "The theory and measurement of labour hoarding: a comment" *Scottish Journal of Political Economy* **26** 191-201

The timing of unemployment response in British regional labour markets, 1963–1976 [†]

M Frost, N Spence

10.1 Introduction

The purpose of this study is to investigate, at two levels of scale, the possibility of unemployment levels within some areas of Great Britain reacting earlier or later than others to changes in levels of national activity. The two spatial scales consist of approximate subregional units, obtained by aggregating Department of Employment local office areas (see appendix), and the smaller Department of Employment 'travel to work' areas, which are defined in an attempt to delimit reasonably self-contained labour-market areas (Smart, 1974). For these areas the two series of male and female unemployment rates were collected on a bimonthly basis for the seventy-seven bimonthly points between June 1963 and February 1976. This data collection was associated with a larger project whose objectives were to investigate links between public policies, changing spatial economic structure, and resultant variations in unemployment characteristics. The timing of unemployment response is clearly an important component of such characteristics, particularly in a period which has seen substantial changes in the economic structure of the country and has also seen considerable increases in the general level of unemployment in this country, associated with major fluctuations in unemployment rates during the 1970s. It is the timing implications of these fluctuations that are reported here.

If an area consistently reacts earlier than others it is usually termed a 'leading' area, whereas conversely, if an area regularly reacts later than other areas or the national series, then it is described as a 'lagging' area. The study of the spatial distribution of such 'leads' and 'lags' is well developed, particularly with respect to the use of unemployment rates as the indicators of responses in an area's economy. In general, these studies may be grouped into two categories. The first deals with differences in response time as one component in a more extensive description of unemployment change. Thus, in Brechling's original work (Brechling, 1967) and the subsequent use of similar methods (King and Clark, 1978; Jeffrey and Webb, 1972; NRST, 1975), the models are specified in order to allow for the possible existence of leads and lags in response patterns which would otherwise spoil the specification and estimation of the relationships. The second category of studies is more explicitly concerned with using unemployment changes in an area as an indicator of local

† This chapter is based on research undertaken with the support of a Social Science Research Council Grant (1976) *Regional Unemployment Variations and Changing Economic Structure in Great Britain*. This support is gratefully acknowledged.

economic conditions, and studying the response patterns of these as a guide to the passage of economic impulses through the structure of urban and rural places. In this category, work such as that of Bassett and Haggett (1971) and King et al (1969) draws heavily upon the bases of central place and growth-pole theory to establish and interpret the transmission of such impulses from higher to lower order places both in time and space. Clearly the pattern of leads and lags is very important in studies such as these for confirming the ordering of centres and the relationships between them and their hinterlands.

Studies from both of these categories have revealed the existence of response-time differences in several countries. Brechling identified a slight tendency in a British standard region context for Scotland and the North to show an identifiably lagged response to national unemployment changes with a lag period of around three months. In Canada and Australia similar methods have revealed some pronounced tendencies for the peripheral areas of their respective economies to react in a delayed fashion to national events. In these cases lags of one or two months were identified. In US studies, lags of up to five months were suggested in some towns of the Mid-West, whereas in studies of South-West England it appeared that some of the smaller centres reacted about one to three months before Bristol.

Thus there is some background material on which to base a search for differences in response timing in a British context. However, certain problems exist when building upon the foundation of other studies. The most basic of these is that in most of the existing literature leads or lags are treated as essentially statistical concepts, with few attempts being made to relate them directly or indirectly to the economic mechanisms which cause them. On the basis of evidence from studies of national economic cycles (Vining, 1946; Borts, 1960), speculations have been made that leads or lags are of structural origin, being the result of the particular industrial mix that is found in any area. This is not necessarily consistent with other arguments put forward from a central place viewpoint, that leads and lags are generated by the operation of some form of economic dependence of smaller centres upon larger ones. This dependence is sometimes interpreted in terms of the transmission of information or of directives which take some time to operate, thus creating a wave-like effect filtering through the economy. Either way, there appear to be no studies which have attempted to identify the mechanisms at work or, better still, to include them and test them in a model of unemployment change. Instead, all of the studies rely on the descriptive statistical identification of lag effects, and this has a number of consequences.

First, the identification and indeed the definition of a lag in standard time-series statistics requires it to be an essentially symmetrical phenomenon. In other words, if the rate of unemployment in an area starts to rise two months before the national onset of a particular recession, to be identified as a leading area its unemployment rates must start to fall two months before the rest of the country as well. No allowance can be made for situations where a region is 'first in–last out' of a recession, which has sometimes been put forward as the position of the development areas in a British context.

Second, to be identified satisfactorily in statistical terms the response pattern of an area must be a regular event, regardless of the nature or causes of a particular recession or boom in the economy. Given the fact that national recessions do have different industrial impacts according to their detailed causes, this makes any testing of the 'structural' argument rather difficult, and it illustrates the need for a more problem-based approach.

It may be argued that these restrictions are simply statistical common-sense, and that the terms lead or lag in themselves imply this level of consistency. However, the purpose of illustrating these features of a statistical analysis of response timing is to show that it is not completely free of internal restrictions and that there may be aspects of response timing, of an irregular but possibly interesting nature, that would not be revealed in such an approach. Nevertheless, in the absence of any clear notions of the causes of regional leads and lags, a statistical approach must be at least a starting point in a study such as this, and a number of different tests were applied to the unemployment series in an attempt to identify any regularities, or even dissimilarities, in the timing of unemployment responses.

10.2 Lags in 'Brechling-type' relationships

The first method used to analyse the components of the unemployment series, and to allow some scope for the specification of lead and lag effects, was that originally proposed by Brechling (1967), the subsequent use of which has been referred to in the introduction to the chapter. In this, the relationship specified is as follows:

$$U_{it} = \beta_{i0} + \beta_{i1} U_{N, t \pm k_i} + \beta_{i3} t + \beta_{i4} t^2 + (\beta_{i5} Z_1 + ... + \beta_{i9} Z_5) + \epsilon_{it} , \qquad (10.1)$$

where

U_{it} is the rate of unemployment in region i at time t,
$U_{N,t}$ is the national rate of unemployment at time t,
$(Z_1 ... Z_5)$ are seasonal dummies (in this case for a bimonthly series),
ϵ_{it} are residuals of region i, and
k_i is the lag effect for region i.

The method used to identify leads or lags in this setting is a fairly crude one, statistically. It is to experiment with a certain number of leads or lags applied to the relationship between the subregion and the national series, and to accept the lead or lag term which produces the highest R^2 value associated with the full equations outlined above. This was attempted in the current study for leads or lags for up to six points within three time periods, the results of which are shown in table 10.1. In this first trial, the whole series for males and the whole series for females were used to identify leads or lags.

The second trial was conducted on the first forty points of each series, and the third trial on the remaining thirty-seven points in the series. This division was made in order to separate the considerable fluctuations in level found in the 1971–1972 and 1974–1976 recessions from the more moderate early part of the series. This allowed the identification of any differences in leads or lags operating over the two periods and was partly necessitated by the almost total absence of lags shown in the results for the whole series. In these results only Clydeside (54) shows any signs of a slight lag, and even then the R^2 difference involved is so small that it could well have arisen from slight random or otherwise uninterpretable features of the series. This result is not consistent with the previous findings that have already been outlined. However, the British studies in question were generally using earlier time series, so that the current absence of response-timing differences might represent some feature of change in the behaviour of the spatial economic system of the country. In particular it seems plausible to suggest that the events of 1971–1972 and 1974–1976 were of such an extreme nature, in unemployment terms at least, that their impact was felt almost immediately throughout the economy. In these terms they could be thought of as catastrophic events rather than cycles. Thus the series was split into two sections, the division being aimed at separating the 'normal' early part of the period from the 'catastrophic' later part. When the relevant results in table 10.1 are examined, they do not reveal much useful material. No situations are

Table 10.1. Subregional lags from the Brechling (1967) regression equations (R^2 values).

Subregion	Male	Subregion	Female
June 1963–February 1976			
54	Lag 0 = 0·88, Lag 1 = 0·90		none[a]
June 1963–December 1969			
25	Lag 0 = 0·93, Lag 1 = 0·94	17	Lag 0 = 0·90, Lag 1 = 0·91
29	Lag 0 = 0·98, Lag 1 = 0·99	32	Lag 0 = 0·83, Lag 1 = 0·84
41	Lag 0 = 0·94, Lag 1 = 0·96	37	Lag 0 = 0·90, Lag 1 = 0·91
		45	Lag 0 = 0·93, Lag 1 = 0·95
		53	Lag 0 = 0·92, Lag 1 = 0·93
February 1970–February 1976			
3	Lag 0 = 0·92, Lag 1 = 0·93		none
4	Lag 0 = 0·96, Lag 1 = 0·97		
17	Lag 0 = 0·88, Lag 1 = 0·91		
19	Lag 0 = 0·91, Lag 1 = 0·93		
25	Lag 0 = 0·94, Lag 1 = 0·95		
53	Lag 0 = 0·88, Lag 5 = 0·96		

[a] No nonzero lag correlations greater than correlations at lag zero found.

found where subregional changes preceded the national series, only examples where the subregions lagged behind national events, in all but one case by only one lag (two-month period). Even in the cases which are reported the R^2 differences are small, the only exceptional area being South West Wales (53) where there is a considerable lag identified together with a sizable increase in the associated R^2 value. In the context of the other results the behaviour of this single subregion in this second part of the period appears to be something of a freak, and unrepresentative of the behaviour of the system as a whole.

Thus it is concluded from these results that, although response-timing differences may have once existed between different regions of the country, no interpretable effects of this can be found in the series between June, 1963 and February, 1976. Furthermore, it appears that this absence is not simply the product of the dramatic events that have occurred since 1971 in the economy, but reflects a general consistency of response timing that runs throughout the series. However, in research of this type it is difficult to show that a phenomenon does not exist and, in this context, there must be some slight doubt over the technique employed to identify the lags used here.

In particular, the use of the national series as a bench mark against which to compare the performance of the individual subregions does seem to be rather crude. The argument over this goes to the roots of the mechanisms of lag generation in the economy. If any part of a structural argument of lag formation is accepted, then it follows that, just as the response timing in an area will be determined by its industrial mix, the national series will be a complex mixture of timings reflecting the sum of the subregional structures and their consequent response patterns. So to compare the pattern of change for a subregion with the national change may not give the clearest indication of response-timing differences, since at least some of the pattern of that subregion will inevitably be included in national events (see Johnston, 1979). The alternative to this is to compare subregions with one another in the hope that differences between them will be more clearly revealed.

10.3 Subregional cross correlations
The method used here was to correlate each subregion with every other subregion in the country at up to twelve leading or lagging points. In this essentially exploratory work only the results for the male series were calculated as a test for the existence of lags. The male series are generally regarded as more reliable figures than those for females and they do display clearer cyclical movements, thus making lag identification easier. The series involved were first deseasonalised using seasonal dummies and then first differences were taken in order to reduce the possibly distorting influence of autocorrelation within the series for each of the regions.

The net results of the 91 500 cross correlations performed in this exercise are shown in table 10.2. In this table all of the leading or lagging correlations which are greater than the value for no response-time difference (zero lead–lag) are shown: a lag meaning that the subregion listed first (on left) lags behind the second listed subregion by the stated period. Conversely, a lead indicates that the subregion entered first precedes the second in its pattern of change. The overall impression from these results is that they confirm the finding of the previous test that there is virtually no evidence to suggest that, between subregions, response-time differences exist that can be identified as a regular lead or lag effect during the period used in the study. The differences that appear in table 10.2 are generally small or are the results of a reversal of sign with considerable lags (17 and 53), and these are difficult to interpret in any useful way. Few of the important subregions appear in these results which are simply insufficiently consistent or general to allow any overall structure of leading or lagging within the subregions to be identified.

However, it is difficult to abandon the search for lags, particularly when it is known that other researchers have found them. Thus, although it might be accepted that the subregions showed no signs of response-time differences, it could be argued that this was a result of their areal definitions producing an averaging effect that submerges the evidence of anything as delicate as a two- or three-month lag effect. So a further set of tests were conducted, this time at the level of travel-to-work areas.

Table 10.2. Subregional cross correlations (male series, deseasonalised and first differences taken).

Subregions correlated

9 with 14	Lag 1 = 0·361	Lag 0 = 0·338
9 with 16	Lag 3 = 0·383	Lag 0 = 0·320
9 with 17	Lag 3 = 0·324	Lag 0 = 0·048
9 with 49	Lag 1 = 0·485	Lag 0 = 0·322
9 with 55	Lead 8 = 0·309	Lead 0 = 0·235
9 with 59	Lead 3 = 0·278	Lead 0 = 0·271
9 with 61	Lead 3 = 0·309	Lead 0 = 0·227
17 with 32	Lag 10 = −0·234	Lag 0 = 0·233
19 with 55	Lead 2 = 0·396	Lead 0 = 0·367
53 with 57	Lag 7 = −0·403	Lag 0 = 0·398

10.4 Travel-to-work area response-time analysis
Grouping of the Department of Employment's 1974 (Smart, 1974) travel-to-work areas for a comparable series between 1963 and 1976 produced a set of 428 areas. Clearly, with 428 areas instead of the 61 subregions, a more selective and structured approach was necessary to investigate the possible existence of leads and lags. First, it was decided to examine the components of interregional differences rather than small-scale intraregional

variations, in accordance with Bassett and Haggett's (1971) division of the two effects. Thus a selection was made of the main urban centres of the country with a range sufficient to allow the inclusion of centres with contrasting characteristics from varying regional environments. The reason for this is primarily related to the objective of the study as a whole, which is rather more concerned with broad-scale regional events rather than with the details of small-scale local changes. It also reflects in part the basic fact that the large urban centres contain the major concentrations of unemployed people and this has a considerable influence on patterns of national change and on relevant policies. The final list of selected centres was London, Manchester, Birmingham, Tyneside, Leeds, Glasgow, Cardiff, Bristol, and Nottingham.

It was also decided that particular care should be taken to apply suitable methods to the identification of response-time differences between these areas. Again, it was accepted that a clearer test of response-time differences would be produced if the cities were compared with one another, rather than directly with the national series. However, a more sensitive statistical procedure was sought and, in particular, one which overcame more effectively the problem of autocorrelation running through the series for each area than the taking of first differences. This problem and its consequences are discussed at some length in the time-series literature (Bartlett, 1966; Box and Jenkins, 1970; Bennett, 1979). The method selected for this study was to estimate an impulse-response function between pairs of cities, having first used an autoregressive-integrative-moving-average (ARIMA) filter to transform the series and remove the effects of autocorrelation. This method is described in detail by Box and Jenkins and is not outlined algebraically here.

Once again the analysis was conducted for males, with the whole series being used to estimate the relevant response lags together with the filter respecified and the lags reestimated for the first period of forty points and the second period of thirty-seven points. This analysis differs from the

Table 10.3. ARIMA analysis of major city response (male series, Tyneside as output).

Input	Response lag		
	1963–1976	June 1963–December 1969	February 1970–February 1976
Leeds	0	1	0
London	0	3	0
Bristol	0	3	0
Cardiff	0	3	0
Birmingham	0	0	0
Nottingham	0	4	0
Manchester	0	4	0
Glasgow	0	0	0

correlation tests recorded in the previous section in that the method requires the specification of an input and an output series, because in order to estimate the impulse-response function weights, the input series filter is also applied to the output series. Also, once this has been done only response lags may be identified. Thus on the evidence of previous research by Brechling (1967), and others, the northern areas of Glasgow and Tyneside were selected as output series, and Leeds and Birmingham were also added to the test to check for possible differences between London and the South East and the remainder of the country. From these analyses over all three periods, only the results for Tyneside show any nonzero response lags. These results are shown in table 10.3. They reveal no lags over the series as a whole, but some identifiable lag effect of a variable length between areas in the first period from June, 1963–December, 1969. This shows a one-period lag for the relationship with Leeds, with three periods separating the response to changes in London, Bristol, and Cardiff, four periods with Manchester and Nottingham, but no lag with Birmingham or Glasgow.

Standing alone as the sole evidence of lag effects operating in this system of major cities, these results clearly deserve further investigation, particularly as the lag is not present either in the whole series or in the later period. Some interesting evidence on this, and on the whole concept of spatial lags in response, is provided in the graphs of figure 10.1. These show plots for Tyneside, Manchester, Glasgow, Leeds, and Birmingham and are the raw material behind some of the results of table 10.3. There are clear differences between these graphs. One feature that stands out is the difference in response-time between Tyneside and Manchester over the period from October 1966–December 1970. Although the turning point is similar in both series, at June, 1966, their behaviour after this is very different. In the case of Manchester the initial rise soon terminates in a period of relative stability, whereas in the case of Tyneside there is a much stronger general trend. This may partly be the result of mine closures in the late 1960s and goes some of the way towards explaining the results of table 10.3. Thus, although Tyneside responded at a similar initial time to the upturn of unemployment in the winter of 1966–1967, it appears that, statistically at least, its response continues for much longer in comparison with Manchester, although in reality it may be responding to a completely different set of economic forces. Note also here that the pattern for Leeds, which contains a small part of the Yorkshire coalfield, is very similar at this period, with a much smaller lag value estimated.

However, another aspect of the comparison in behaviour at the beginning of this series is where Tyneside and Glasgow appear to recover rather slowly from the 1963 recession. The correspondence of these two areas over this early period could explain the lack of an estimated lag between them, in spite of the fact that Glasgow shows no subsequent 'coal-mining hump'. It could also serve to confirm the strong lag identified in the early period with respect to Manchester, which shows an apparently earlier recovery. There are two conclusions from these issues that are raised by the graphs of figure 10.1. The first is a commonsense point; that it is statistically dangerous to estimate lags from the effects of about one-and-a-half cycles, which is the case with the first half of this series. The second is that there appears to be a good deal of inconsistency in the patterns and nature of response to major recessions and recoveries shown by these large cities. If the example of Glasgow is extended, it can be seen that it appears to recover late in 1963, to respond to the recession in 1966–1967 exactly in phase, to react early to the major 1971–1972 recession, to recover from it in phase with the other cities, and to react weakly and rather late to the current recession. A similar point can be illustrated if the series for Tyneside and Manchester are compared. Here in 1963 Tyneside's recovery seems to lag behind that of Manchester, the upturn of 1966 shows Manchester reacting rather faster but certainly to a much smaller extent. The 1971–1972 recession sees Manchester showing a later response together with a later recovery, although associated with a pronounced peak in unemployment. The latest recession shows Manchester reacting slightly later again to the onset of increased unemployment.

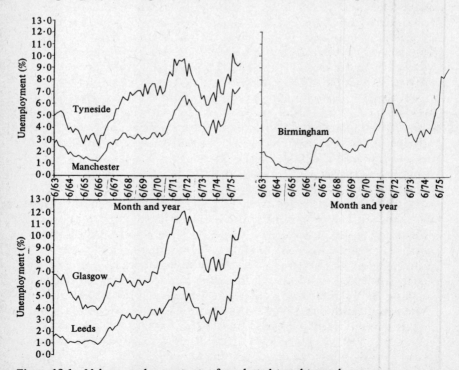

Figure 10.1. Male unemployment rates for selected travel-to-work areas.

Leeds can be likened to Tyneside except that it responds later, but to a greater degree to the most recent increases in unemployment levels.

Clearly, with this mixture of early and late responses associated with different levels of response, it is hardly surprising that the statistical results point to no consistent relationships between areas of the country and their response timing. Indeed, terms like 'lead' and 'lag' really have to be abandoned in this setting because it is clear that the processes at work are much more complicated than could be adequately summarised in such terms. The terms themselves are based on uniform cyclical movements, and the irregularities in response shown here are simply too inconsistent for these essentially regular terms to apply. Instead, new methods have to be used to attempt to identify some order in response patterns that is not necessarily cyclically consistent through time. One way to do this is to seek spatially ordered groupings that share similar response patterns and then to attempt to understand the nature of such groupings, together with any timing implications which such groups may have.

10.5 Analysis of regional cycles
Once we have abandoned the notion of numerically regular and consistent lead and lag effects, differential regional response patterns become much more complicated phenomena. This is because they become essentially features of irregularity in the unemployment performance of a region, features that may result from an infinite range of causes from systematic industrial to simply random effects. A method has to be adopted which will identify the 'regular' irregularities from amongst those that are purely specific to an individual region, at any individual point in time. The approach that is adopted here consists of several stages. First the regular trends and responses of each area to national events, through the series, are extracted using the Brechling-based relations set out in equation (10.1). With the lag term set to zero the residuals of this equation may be interpreted as a 'regional cycle' effect. This represents changes in the unemployment levels in an area that do not correspond to its average response to national events or to any simple trend component in the series, but will include response-timing differences, whether of a consistent or inconsistent type. The next stage in the method is to try to identify common features of response from amongst these 'regional cycles' that would point to specific areas of the country either overreacting or under-reacting, or alternatively reacting early or late to changes in national economic conditions. At the subregional level this may be achieved by factor analysis, at the travel-to-work-area level a modified approach is adopted.

10.5.1 Subregional analysis
In this analysis the seventy-seven residual values for males and females from each of the sixty-one subregions were separately subjected to a

Table 10.4. Factor analysis of subregional residuals (male series, rotated solution; female series, unrotated solution).

Region	Male factors			Female factors	
	1	2	3	1	2
Industrial North East:					
1 North	0·17	0·58	−0·55	0·75	−0·20
2 South	0·83	0·21	−0·19	0·65	−0·39
Rural North East:					
3 North	−0·41	0·84	0·02	0·09	−0·33
4 South	−0·54	0·73	0·06	0·10	−0·71
5 Cumberland and Westmorland	−0·48	0·11	−0·12	−0·42	0·43
6 North Humberside	0·21	0·49	−0·21	0·36	−0·08
7 South Humberside	0·11	0·23	−0·01	0·14	−0·09
8 Mid Yorkshire	−0·51	0·76	0·05	−0·33	−0·50
9 South Lindsey	−0·58	0·29	−0·01	−0·33	−0·20
10 South Yorkshire	0·88	−0·09	−0·22	0·80	0·13
11 Yorkshire Coalfield	0·32	0·76	−0·29	0·67	−0·01
12 West Yorkshire	0·05	0·34	0·50	−0·07	−0·48
13 South Cheshire	−0·19	0·19	0·09	−0·18	−0·48
14 South Lancashire	0·70	0·00	0·14	0·64	0·22
15 Manchester	0·93	−0·13	−0·02	0·47	0·23
16 Liverpool/Merseyside	0·75	0·39	−0·12	0·86	0·04
17 Furness	−0·28	0·13	−0·36	0·20	0·39
18 Fylde	−0·70	−0·28	0·01	−0·57	0·31
19 Lancaster	−0·37	0·17	0·61	−0·03	−0·37
20 Mid Lancashire	0·53	0·19	0·35	0·24	0·60
21 North East Lancashire	−0·02	−0·59	0·62	0·11	0·38
22 Nottingham/Derbyshire	−0·00	0·88	0·02	0·12	−0·43
23 Leicester	−0·58	−0·59	0·22	−0·87	0·20
24 Eastern Lowlands	0·29	0·37	0·67	−0·54	−0·31
25 Northampton	−0·85	−0·35	0·14	−0·31	−0·19
West Midlands:					
26 Central	−0·33	0·11	0·10	−0·47	−0·30
27 Conurbation	0·38	−0·83	0·01	−0·52	0·54
28 Coventry Belt	−0·22	−0·83	−0·05	−0·69	0·45
29 West Midlands: Rural West	−0·84	0·00	−0·05	−0·74	0·22
30 North Staffordshire	0·21	0·76	−0·02	0·18	−0·33
East Anglia:					
31 South East	−0·67	−0·02	0·60	−0·19	−0·31
32 North East	−0·65	0·14	0·61	−0·44	−0·10
33 North West	−0·01	−0·15	0·90	−0·19	0·28
34 South West	−0·75	−0·47	0·23	−0·40	−0·03
35 Greater London	−0·50	−0·74	−0·19	−0·79	0·09
36 Outer Metropolitan	−0·87	−0·42	0·02	−0·91	0·06
37 Essex	−0·79	−0·21	0·17	−0·47	−0·47
38 Kent	−0·84	0·41	0·12	−0·59	−0·53
39 Sussex Coast	−0·95	−0·01	0·01	−0·67	−0·37
40 Solent	−0·93	0·13	0·07	−0·90	−0·08
41 Beds, Berks, Bucks, and Oxon	−0·93	−0·22	0·07	−0·91	−0·05
South West:					
42 Central	−0·95	−0·05	0·10	−0·91	−0·07
43 Southern	−0·93	0·18	0·20	−0·85	−0·23
44 Western	−0·85	−0·16	0·02	−0·85	−0·02
45 Northern	−0·78	−0·46	0·11	−0·85	−0·30

Table 10.4 (continued).

Region	Male factors			Female factors	
	1	2	3	1	2
Industrial South Wales:					
46 Central and Eastern Valleys	−0·54	−0·52	−0·19	−0·54	0·57
47 West South Wales	−0·31	−0·67	−0·22	−0·10	0·63
48 Coastal Belt	−0·52	−0·58	−0·36	−0·42	0·08
49 North East Wales	−0·67	0·11	−0·01	−0·70	0·34
North West Wales:					
50 North Coast	−0·88	0·06	−0·06	−0·53	−0·32
51 Remainder	−0·35	−0·10	0·56	−0·30	0·12
52 Central Wales	−0·84	−0·28	−0·23	−0·65	0·11
53 South West Wales	−0·83	0·27	0·05	−0·75	−0·15
54 Glasgow/Clydeside	0·86	0·28	0·13	0·93	−0·00
55 Falkirk/Stirling	0·80	0·33	0·22	0·67	0·17
56 Edinburgh	0·55	0·69	0·13	0·66	0·17
57 Tayside	0·64	0·21	0·41	0·82	−0·11
58 Borders	−0·36	0·33	0·64	0·29	−0·44
Scotland:					
59 South West	−0·56	−0·18	−0·17	−0·67	0·24
60 North East	0·39	0·73	0·15	0·72	−0·26
61 Highlands	−0·63	−0·04	0·17	−0·62	−0·02
Original variance explained	39·5%	18·9%	9·0%	34·2%	10·2%

Q-mode factor analysis, the purpose of which was to reveal groups of subregions which shared similar patterns of residual variation in the model specified in equation (10.1). A summary of the results of both of these factor analyses is presented in table 10.4, with plots of the factor scores presented in figure 10.2, showing the first two male factors and the first female factor. Examining first the male results, the structure which emerges is a surprisingly clear one. The first factor, after rotation, explains nearly 40% of the total original variation of the set of residual values, and its associated loadings show a clear pattern of differentiation among the subregions. This pattern reveals an essentially north–south division of the country, with high positive loadings in the north and high negative loadings in the south. Thus, the Industrial North-East: South (2), South Yorkshire (10), Manchester (15), Glasgow/Clydeside (54), and Liverpool/Merseyside (16) all stand out with a strong positive relationship between their regional cycles and the derived factor. However, a large block of regions in the Outer Metropolitan (36) and Outer South-East regions, with parts of the South-West and Wales, all show consistently strong negative relationships with the same factor. It is interesting to note here that in his correlations of residuals, in a similar analysis, Brechling too identified for a much earlier period a tendency for a north–south division in his results, although with only standard regions he had too few areas to be able to develop this finding.

If the scores on the first factor are considered in figure 10.2, the source
of this clear patterning can be seen. These scores show a strongly cyclical
pattern, but are dominated by a considerable peak around the 1971–1972
recession and a considerable drop from this into the current recession.
This factor is certainly picking out those areas that overreacted to the
1971–1972 recession and have underreacted to current events, forming
such apparently uniform blocks of areas within the country. What is also
interesting, however, is that their behaviour since 1971, although more
accentuated, should broadly conform with the cyclical pattern that existed
prior to that date. It is as though there was a regular cycle of advantage–
disadvantage running through time in the economy, with first the north
and then the south experiencing a period of relative advantage followed by
one of relative disadvantage in terms of national events. This effect is, of
course, accentuated by the form of the model, where the national series,
as the sum of the subregions, serves as the base for comparison. In this
situation, any area that has relatively high unemployment must be matched,
allowing for magnitudes, by an area that is relatively low. This will make
any differential spatial effect appear as above, but nonetheless, to appear
as it does, the differential effect must exist, meaning that different areas
of the country responded differently to the various changes in the level of

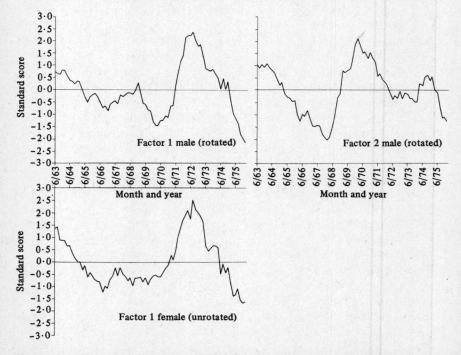

Figure 10.2. Factor scores resulting from a factor analysis of regression residuals.

economic activity over the period and that these differences in response had an ordered spatial pattern.

However, the structure of the differential response is not completely simple. There are some notable exceptions from the list of subregions showing close correspondence either in a positive or in a negative fashion with the first factor. The Industrial North-East: North (1), West Midlands: Central (26), Coventry Belt (28), and particularly Greater London (35) are missing from the list. They are much more closely related to a complex second factor. At first sight it is difficult to know whether to identify this as a West Midlands factor or a coalfield factor. Many of the coalfield areas show high positive loadings, including Rural North-East: North (3), Yorkshire Coalfield (11), Nottingham/Derbyshire (22), whereas the West Midlands areas (26 and 27) and Greater London (35) show high negative loadings. If the scores of figure 10.2 are examined some interpretation of this can be made, illustrating the danger of attempting to use this type of analysis to establish the economic mechanisms behind these ordered regional responses. The plots of figure 10.2 show the dominating events in this factor to be associated with a period before the 1971–1972 recession. The main trough in the scores centres on the period of 1966–1967, which was represented by a sharp rise in unemployment in the national series and in many subregions. The main peak occurs in 1969–1970, which in many areas was a period of slight upturn in economic conditions. Greater London and the West Midlands appear to have suffered severely from the 1966–1967 rise, but then to have experienced a sharp recovery in the later years of the 1960s. This is exemplified by the graph of Birmingham's travel-to-work-area unemployment in figure 10.3. Conversely, the coalfield areas did not seem to react sharply to the events of 1966–1967, but then to have been much affected by a series of closures which had substantial and long-lasting effects and which can be seen in the plot of Tyneside's rate in figure 10.1. The coalfield pattern of response therefore seems to be fairly easy to explain. What is difficult, however, is to explain why some of the main engineering centres of the country should show the opposite pattern of response. It would take an enormous imaginative step to link these two phenomena together, and this illustrates the need for caution in interpreting these results and attributing causal mechanisms to the products of simple description.

Before considering the third male factor, note that the Welsh coalfield areas do not show the same response patterns as those areas which have already been commented on. If anything, they appear to exhibit the opposite pattern from the evidence of the loadings, where Industrial South Wales: Valleys (46), West South Wales (47), and Coastal Belt (48) all show strong negative associations with the second factor rather than the expected positive associations. Some part of this may reflect the strength of the industrial links between South Wales and the West Midlands, but part also relates to the pattern of coalfield unemployment in which the

South Wales area appeared to suffer the effects of closures rather earlier than comparable English areas, a leading effect which disrupts the simple relationships that might otherwise exist.

If we now consider the pattern of loading of factor 3, the fall in explanatory power of this factor starts to become apparent. Between them, the first two factors account for 58·4% of the original variation of the full set of residuals, whereas factor 3 adds only a further 9%. It is clear from the loadings that the variation contained in factor 3 is of a more particular localised type and does not reflect large-scale differences through most of the economy. The centre for high loadings seems to be in East Anglia (31–33), with outliers occurring in widely dispersed areas from the borders of Scotland (58) to the eastern lowlands (24) and parts of Lancashire (19, 21). There is a suggestion here of a specifically rural

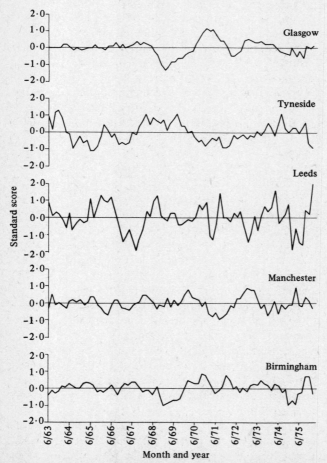

Figure 10.3. Final residuals after extraction of 'regional effects': males.

influence, but it is by no means general enough to be represented as a rural factor and as such it probably represents the limit of sensible general interpretation of the male factor analysis results.

The complementary female results permit some interesting comparisons. In general the level of explanation is rather lower, suggesting the intuitively plausible finding that female employment variations are likely to be more related to local conditions not amenable to national generalisation than is the case in the patterns of male response. However, in spite of this, one clear factor does emerge as the first factor, which, at 34·0% of original variance explained, is not very much less powerful than its male counterpart. It is interesting to note from figure 10.2 that its scores display a broadly similar pattern to that of the first male factor, particularly in the period since 1971. This confirms the generality of this differentiating pattern of response that was observed in the male characterisation. What also confirms the strength of the result for males is that the pattern of subregional loadings on this female factor seems to be quite closely related to the male pattern, with the additional feature that, with no distinct coalmining effect in female unemployment, some of the coalfield areas in northern England load highly on this factor.

The Industrial North East: North (2) and the Yorkshire Coalfield (11) now show strong positive loadings, although Nottingham/Derbyshire (22) still shows little relationship with this factor. Overall, however, the pattern of loadings on the two factors corresponds closely, particularly in the extensive block of negative loadings around London, the South East, and South West. Interestingly in this analysis, Greater London shows results much more similar to the rest of the South East, while the results of the West Midlands are far less distinctive than they were in the male results.

The second female factor resembles the third male factor in its explanatory power and in the problems associated with its interpretation. Here again there are isolated high loadings that occur in a dispersed fashion over the set of subregions. There seems to be no strong unifying force in the factor loadings or in the factor scores, suggesting that, as in the male case, at this low level of explanatory power the factor is identifying the chance coincidence of individual subregions rather than representing an interpretable source of response differentiation.

However, taking the results both of the male and of the female analyses together, the finding is clear that, at this level of scale, there is pronounced 'regional' ordering in the response time of areas to changes in national economic circumstances. This also means it is likely that the irregularities in response noted in the previous section may be unpredictable in temporal terms but have a regular spatial expression which may involve timing differences in the response of large areas of the country to national changes. Before discussing the possibility of timing differences existing in these broad response patterns, however, the analysis is extended to the more detailed level of the travel-to-work area.

Table 10.5. Correlations between travel-to-work-area residuals from Brechling (1967) regressions and the regional effect from the subregional factor analysis (males).

Factor 1

Greater than +0·60

5 Hartlepool	0·85	344 Leigh	0·83	370 Dumbarton	0·69
7 Middlesborough	0·91	345 Liverpool	0·75	375 Falkirk	0·76
46 Mexborough	0·62	346 Manchester	0·91	377 Glasgow	0·84
48 Sheffield	0·86	352 Rochdale	0·71	380 Kilmarnock	0·65
52 Dinnington	0·75	353 Shaw	0·67	382 Motherwell	0·90
66 Rotherham	0·88	355 Widnes	0·64	383 Paisley	0·86
275 Walsall	0·62	356 Wigan	0·78	385 Stirling	0·69
308 Coalville	0·68	364 Oldham	0·84	393 Cupar	0·69
334 Ashton-under-	0·79	366 Arbroath	0·66	394 Dundee	0·60
Lyne		368 Bathgate	0·76	395 Dunoon	0·64
337 Bolton	0·90			408 Kilsyth	0·62

Less than −0·60

18 Blyth	−0·67	144 Dereham	−0·74	216 Truro	−0·83
63 Louth	−0·68	150 Halesworth	−0·61	217 Wadebridge	−0·74
68 Skegness	−0·68	153 Huntingdon	−0·67	219 Weston-super-	−0·68
74 Aldershot	−0·78	156 Lowestoft	−0·65	Mare	
75 Braintree	−0·69	157 March	−0·60	220 Weymouth	−0·84
76 Brighton	−0·79	158 Newmarket	−0·63	225 Cardiff	−0·64
77 Canterbury	−0·71	166 Bournemouth	−0·84	228 Lampeter	−0·87
79 Chichester	−0·86	167 Bridgewater	−0·67	238 Pwellheli	−0·88
80 Crawley	−0·72	168 Bristol	−0·64	241 Wrexham	−0·65
81 Eastbourne	−0·87	170 Exeter	−0·75	246 Brecon	−0·69
82 Folkestone	−0·72	173 Plymouth	−0·84	247 Cardigan	−0·88
84 Guildford	−0·67	174 Redruth	−0·78	250 Colwyn Bay	−0·85
86 Hastings	−0·91	175 Salisbury	−0·90	252 Fishguard	−0·74
87 Hertford	−0·70	176 Shaftesbury	−0·60	254 Llandrindod	−0·64
88 High Wycombe	−0·79	177 Swanage	−0·74	Wells	
92 Oxford	−0·91	178 Tiverton	−0·78	257 Machynlleth	−0·73
93 Portsmouth	−0·91	179 Torbay	−0·88	258 Milford Haven	−0·72
94 Reading	−0·81	180 Trowbridge	−0·75	259 Monmouth	−0·75
98 Southampton	−0·65	181 Yeovil	−0·79	260 Newtown	
99 Southend	−0·78	182 Ashburton	−0·65	262 Rhyl	−0·64
100 Tunbridge Wells	−0·90	183 Barnstaple	−0·84	269 Kidderminster	−0·65
101 Watford	−0·74	185 Bideford	−0·74	270 Leominster	−0·83
103 Worthing	−0·89	187 Bridport	−0·81	281 Evesham	−0·72
105 Alton	−0·75	188 Bude	−0·79	282 Hereford	−0·64
106 Andover	−0·83	189 Camelford	−0·72	286 Ludlow	−0·61
107 Ashford	−0·66	194 Devizes	−0·82	287 Malvern	−0·73
108 Aylesbury	−0·79	195 Dorchester	−0·71	292 Ross-on-Wye	−0·83
111 Bedford	−0·80	198 Frome	−0·88	296 Stratford-on-	−0·71
113 Bletchley	−0·76	199 Gloucester	−0·66	Avon	
114 Buckingham	−0·66	200 Helston	−0·72	302 Northampton	−0·81
116 Clacton	−0·66	202 Ilfracombe	−0·70	317 Kettering	−0·81
121 Dover	−0·61	204 Launceston	−0·78	323 Melton Mowbray	−0·61
128 Petersfield	−0·69	205 Midsomer Norton	−0·79	327 Rushden	−0·64
129 Ramsgate	−0·77	208 Penzance	−0·69	329 Spalding	−0·68
135 Wolverton	−0·74	211 Street	−0·74	336 Blackpool	−0·62
138 Ipswich	−0·75	214 Taunton	−0·82	416 Newton Stewart	−0·77
139 North Walsham	−0·69	215 Tewkesbury	−0·69		

Table 10.5 (continued).

Factor 2

Greater than +0.50

1 Chester-le-Street	0·56	41 Yeadon	0·69	323 Melton Mowbray	0·58
6 Peterlee	0·56	43 Hemsworth	0·74	324 Newark	0·64
8 Tyneside	0·78	50 Bridlington	0·65	326 Retford	0·85
10 Whitehaven	0·67	53 Driffield	0·56	328 Sleaford	0·67
12 Alnwick	0·70	58 Harrogate	0·58	330 Sutton-in-	0·78
13 Amble	0·74	64 Maltby	0·72	Ashfield	
14 Ashington	0·52	69 Skipton	0·62	331 Swadlincote	0·62
16 Bedlington	0·56	71 Wakefield	0·73	333 Worksop	0·77
25 Malton	0·85	73 York	0·75	359 Congleton	0·62
26 Millom	0·56	119 Deal	0·55	365 Aberdeen	0·72
27 Morpeth	0·80	124 Lymington	0·66	370 Dumbarton	0·52
30 Pickering	0·58	195 Dorchester	0·61	373 Edinburgh	0·77
33 Seaton Delaval	0·79	207 Okehampton	0·78	378 Greenock	0·57
34 Thirsk	0·57	273 Stafford	0·59	381 Kircaldy	0·72
35 Whitby	0·67	274 Stoke-on-Trent	0·68	390 Campbeltown	0·71
36 Barnsley	0·82	278 Bridgnorth	0·79	402 Haddington	0·57
38 Castleford	0·88	279 Burton-on-Trent	0·63	413 Lesmahagow	0·65
39 Dewsbury	0·69	300 Chesterfield	0·68	423 Sanquhar	0·70
40 Doncaster	0·68	305 Alfreton	0·89	424 Shotts	0·63
		313 Heanor	0·57		

Less than −0.50

89 Letchworth	−0·69	225 Cardiff	−0·52	268 Dudley	−0·70
90 Luton	−0·51	226 Ebbw Vale	−0·66	283 Leamington	−0·70
104 Greater London	−0·73	231 Llanelli	−0·81	318 Leicester	−0·64
110 Basingstoke	−0·57	233 Neath	−0·71	335 Blackburn	−0·70
130 Royston	−0·51	234 Newport	−0·59	361 St Helens	−0·52
133 Stevenage	−0·51	235 Pontypool	−0·55	363 Accrington	−0·67
151 Haverhill	−0·65	237 Port Talbot	−0·60	367 Ayr	−0·53
153 Huntingdon	−0·53	266 Birmingham	−0·93	384 Perth	−0·57
168 Bristol	−0·57	267 Coventry	−0·70	397 Forfar	−0·50
196 Dursley	−0·82				

10.5.2 Travel-to-work-area analysis

The problem in this section of the analysis is that, whereas there were seventy-seven observations available for the analysis of sixty-one areas in the subregional section, there are still only seventy-seven values here for over four hundred travel-to-work areas (TTWs). Thus a compromise method was adopted. The first basis for this was the belief, outlined in the previous section, that the scores of the subregional factors represented important features of differentiation in response to national changes and that these patterns had a reasonably general expression throughout the economy. In other words they were of more fundamental importance and meaning than mere factor analytic freaks of the subregional analysis. Given this, the scores were used to represent this pattern of differentiation at the TTW level by standardising the residuals for each of the TTWs and regressing this standardised series against the relevant sets of factor scores —the first two factors for males, the first one for females. The coefficients in these relationships are the correlation coefficients between the residual series and the subregional factor scores, and are directly comparable with the subregional factor loadings.

The main correlations are shown in tables 10.5 and 10.6 for factors 1 and 2 for males and factor 1 for females. In all cases they extend very clearly the structure for the factors identified at the subregional level. In factor 1 for males, there is a remarkable contrast between parts of Lancashire and most of Central Scotland with practically all of Southern England and extensions into rural Wales. On this factor the East Midlands and rural parts of the West Midlands appear almost a transitional area between the blocks of the North and the South. Factor 2 for males brings out more areas in the East Midlands associated with coal mining together with the main coalfield areas of Yorkshire and the North East. Some Scottish areas appear here also, but it is interesting that the contrast with South Wales that was noted in the previous section persists here too.

Table 10.6. Correlations between travel-to-work-area residuals from Brechling (1967) regressions and the regional effect from the subregional factor analysis (females).

Factor 1

Greater than +0·60

5 Hartlepool	0·62	337 Bolton	0·76	377 Glasgow	0·94
7 Middlesborough	0·68	345 Liverpool	0·85	378 Greenock	0·67
8 Tyneside	0·73	348 Northwich	0·60	379 Irvine	0·70
9 Sunderland	0·79	353 Shaw	0·70	382 Motherwell	0·85
43 Hemsworth	0·72	356 Wigan	0·73	383 Paisley	0·91
46 Mexborough	0·60	365 Aberdeen	0·74	385 Stirling	0·71
48 Sheffield	0·65	370 Dumbarton	0·89	394 Dundee	0·84
66 Rotherham	0·86	372 Dunfermline	0·61	396 Eyemouth	0·67
311 Derby	0·60	373 Edinburgh	0·70	410 Lanark	0·69
				413 Lesmahagow	0·75

Less than −0·60

23 Kendal	−0·63	115 Chatham	−0·74	200 Helston	−0·76
37 Bradford	−0·72	128 Petersfield	−0·78	202 Ilfracombe	−0·64
79 Chichester	−0·75	135 Wolverton	−0·89	209 St Austell	−0·63
81 Eastbourne	−0·66	143 Cromer	−0·61	211 Street	−0·72
84 Guildford	−0·74	150 Halesworth	−0·60	212 Stroud	−0·75
86 Hastings	−0·69	155 Leiston	−0·67	213 Swindon	−0·74
90 Luton	−0·62	158 Newmarket	−0·69	214 Taunton	−0·77
92 Oxford	−0·83	166 Bournemouth	−0·72	215 Tewkesbury	−0·61
93 Portsmouth	−0·84	167 Bridgwater	−0·63	216 Truro	−0·76
94 Reading	−0·77	173 Plymouth	−0·80	220 Weymouth	−0·67
98 Southampton	−0·91	174 Salisbury	−0·75	221 Wimborne	−0·67
99 Southend	−0·76	177 Swanage	−0·71	239 Shotton	−0·76
100 Tunbridge Wells	−0·79	178 Tiverton	−0·66	247 Cardigan	−0·87
102 Weybridge	−0·72	180 Trowbridge	−0·77	249 Chepstow	−0·65
103 Worthing	−0·70	183 Barnstaple	−0·78	251 Denbigh	−0·65
104 Greater London	−0·80	187 Bridport	−0·67	253 Haverfordwest	−0·68
106 Andover	−0·79	188 Bude	−0·72	266 Birmingham	−0·64
108 Aylesbury	−0·69	194 Devizes	−0·61	267 Coventry	−0·68
113 Bletchley	−0·71	198 Frome	−0·70	268 Dudley	−0·66
114 Buckingham	−0·63			278 Bridgnorth	−0·61

In common with the subregional results the West Midlands: Central and Greater London, now joined by a few South East areas as well, are clearly related to this second factor, indicating that these somewhat unexpected results were not simply the effect of scale or boundaries in the first analysis.

In the female factor 1 results, the strength of the relationship between the TTW results and those identified in the subregions is similar to that found in the male lists. Again the clear division is between a relatively small number of northern areas of relatively high unemployment and a large number of predominantly southern and western areas with generally low overall rates. The results for females are not quite as clear as those for males but this situation again corresponds closely with the original results of the subregional factor analyses.

Thus these results confirm strongly the impression of the subregional findings that the pattern of differential unemployment response to national events is a very ordered one throughout most areas of the country. The strength of the correlations reveal that this is an important influence on the behaviour of individual areas in the changes of their unemployment levels. What the results do not necessarily reflect in themselves is that these regularities in response have any timing implications.

10.6 The timing implications of regional cycles

Two questions arise from the results of the factor analyses in the previous section. First, does the pattern of broad regional differentiation in response behaviour, identified by the preceding analyses, contain in itself irregularities in response to national changes that might account for the kind of irregular responses noted earlier in an examination of the raw data for selected TWWs in figure 10.1? Second, do the patterns of change which are not accounted for by the national, seasonal and this 'regional' effect still show persistent timing irregularities in response that are more general than simple random events affecting individual localities?

The first question is a difficult one to answer because the scores of figure 10.2 reflect differentiation between areas with respect to the *timing* and the *level* of response to particular events. Thus it could be argued that the positive scores at the beginning of the series reflect areas that were late to recover from the 1962–1963 recession. Whereas it could also be argued that these scores might just as well reflect an overreaction in level to that recession but not necessarily any response-time irregularity. Equally so, this trough in the scores centred around 1967 is later than the trough in the national unemployment series, but this could again reflect differences in the level of response to the 1966–1967 jump in unemployment rates rather than a difference in the timing of any response to that national increase. Thus it seems that the factor scores contain too much complicated information to allow the easy identification of early or late responses by the areas involved. That no dominant indications of leads or lags appear in these scores is only to be expected from the earlier results of this chapter.

However, the analysis does have a use in providing an additional control of
regional and local behaviour with respect to response-time levels, within
which the second question posed above can be more accurately examined.

A selection of the evidence relevant to the final stage in the examination
of timing irregularities in response can be found in figure 10.3, where
graphs are presented for the residuals (in standard score form) of the
relationship between the Brechling (1967) residuals for males for the TTW
areas discussed previously and the male factor scores. These residuals
should reflect as pure a local effect as can be obtained in this analysis.
Interestingly in most cases these residuals reveal a fairly high level of
ordering and some important individual features. In this respect the
graphs are typical of the results for all of the TTWs, which show persistent
and high levels of ordering in their residual values for this exercise. The
graph for Glasgow illustrates this well. In this it can be seen that most of
the irregularities commented upon earlier have been accounted for by this
two-stage analysis. There is little evidence to suggest that its response in
level or timing to the events of the first thirty points in the series is
different in any way to the normal response to the national and regional
changes which influence it. Equally there is a similar pattern towards the
end of the series. However, in the middle of the series the area was
affected by events that are clearly reflected in ordered values. There is a
drop in values centred on the period between 1968 and 1969 followed by
a distinct peak in 1970–1971. This latter feature is particularly interesting
because it reflects the tendency, noted in the previous interpretation of
this study, for Glasgow's unemployment to rise very early in the 1971–
1972 recession. In addition to this, the subsequent fall into negative
residuals suggests that the area recovered rather earlier too, showing
distinctly 'leading' tendencies. The opposite tendency was noted for
Manchester in the earlier comments and this too is reflected in these
residuals, where its negative values for the later 1970–1971 period reflect
its late response to the recession followed by a relatively late recovery,
shown on these graphs by a distinct sequence of positive values.

In both of the examples quoted above, the pattern of these residuals
has more than a simply local expression. Thus, in the case of Glasgow a
very similar pattern of residuals around this period can be found in the
series for Dumbarton, Edinburgh, Falkirk, Greenock, Kilmarnock, Paisley,
Motherwell, and Stirling. In Manchester's case a similar pattern is found
in Ashton-under-Lyne, Crewe, Liverpool, Northwich, Preston, Widnes,
Wigan, Chester, Macclesfield, and Oldham. It is clear that these features
are more than simply isolated local events. They represent 'subregional'
differences in response to supplement the 'regional' differences that were
identified in the factor analyses. A similar feature can be detailed in the
series for Birmingham around 1968–1969, where the negative residuals are
found in most of the West Midlands area. What is important is that these
more local effects do seem to contain within them distinct response-time

implications, sometimes indicating the early or the late response to particular events. Two additional features are also apparent. The first is that, even in the graphs of figure 10.3, it can be seen that not all areas are affected by these localised events. Leeds, for instance, shows a much more regular pattern of response which reflects a very close relationship with the national series and a relatively weak link with the regional factors. The second, and more important, feature is that even within areas like Glasgow or Manchester, where there is clear evidence of some irregular response, this is not a general feature of their behaviour. Thus it appears that their response to the 1971–1972 recession is out of phase with the rest of the country and with the other members of their regional grouping, but there is no evidence that strongly suggests they were out of phase at any other time between 1963 and 1976. This inconsistency of behaviour is difficult to explain in simple terms. Where areas like Wigan and Chester share similar patterns, it is clearly not the straightforward effect of industrial structure in their own areas. Here the lack of any clearly established insight into the mechanisms of local unemployment connections is very noticeable. However, even in descriptive terms these findings have importance, if only in a negative and cautionary setting.

10.7 Conclusions

The main conclusion from this study is that, at the subregional scale and for the main cities in the British urban system, there is no evidence to suggest that any area shows consistent tendencies for the timing of its unemployment responses to be different from that of other areas. This conclusion does not in itself negate other findings in this field, which have been based on larger series of data involving more cyclical events and with the additional component of a rural–urban difference built into the studies. This study is weak in respect of the small number of cycles contained in the period from 1963 to 1976, and it is different from other studies in that this period contains within it a substantial proportion after 1971 that could almost be described as traumatic in labour-market terms. It is thus difficult to use the evidence here in more than a questioning role. It seems that the notion of the existence of true lags or leads should be questioned at this level of scale and for current labour-market conditions. If it ever truly existed it seems to have been replaced by a pattern of irregular response, where areas display timing differences in their reactions to economic events that are significant for individual dates but are not consistent features of their cyclical behaviour. The main outcome of this irregular response seems to be relatively local concentrations either of early or of late changes in unemployment levels, within certain areas of the country, that are superimposed upon general tendencies for economic events to favour either the North or the South within the framework of national changes.

The causes of these irregularities remain, in this study, in the realms of speculation. It might be argued that the pattern of unemployment since 1967 or thereabouts has ceased to be a 'cyclical' event. In 1967, it responded to some sudden force for an upward shift, and subsequently, in 1971–1972 and 1974–1976, to sudden recessions in the economy that appear to have come to all areas at more or less the same time, producing different levels of response but having their effect at the same time as on the country. These were so sudden and deep as recessions that they are catastrophes rather than cycles, and the causes of accompanying spatial leads or lags are much more related to the features underlying regular production and consumption cycles in the economy, than they are to the recent extreme events associated with oil price rises and the like. There is, of course, no evidence on which to accept or refute this suggestion because of the paucity of information that exists with respect to the mechanisms of spatial lead or lag generation. If this study shows anything, then it is that more information is needed on these mechanisms before studies attempt to identify statistically leading or lagging areas within the economy. With an irregular pattern of response it is just luck and choice of terminal dates that will determine the outcome of any such attempt.

References

Bartlett M S, 1966 *An Introduction to Stochastic Processes* (Cambridge University Press, Cambridge)

Bassett K, Haggett P, 1971 "Towards short term forecasting for cyclic behaviour in a regional system of cities" in *Regional Forecasting* Eds M Chisholm, A E Frey, P Haggett (Butterworths, London) pp 389–413

Bennett R J, 1979 *Spatial Time Series. Analysis–Forecasting–Control* (Pion, London)

Borts G E, 1960 *Regional Cycles of Manufacturing Employment in the United States, 1914–1953* (National Bureau of Economic Research, New York)

Box G E P, Jenkins G M, 1970 *Time Series Analysis: Forecasting and Control* (Holden Day, San Francisco)

Brechling F, 1967 "Trends and cycles in British regional unemployment" *Oxford Economic Papers* 19 1–21

Jeffrey D, Webb D J, 1972 "Economic fluctuations in the Australian regional system" *Australian Geographical Studies* 10 141–160

Johnston R J, 1979 "On urban and regional systems in lagged correlation analyses" *Environment and Planning A* 11 705–713

King L J, Casseti E, Jeffrey D, 1969 "Economic impulses in a regional system of cities" *Regional Studies* 3 213–218

King L J, Clark G L, 1978 "Regional unemployment patterns and the spatial dimensions of macro-economic policy: the Canadian experience, 1966–1975" *Regional Studies* 12 283–296

NRST, 1975 *Cyclical Fluctuations in Economic Activity in the Northern Region: 1958–1975. Technical Report 1* Northern Region Strategy Team, Newcastle upon Tyne

Smart M W, 1974 "Labour market areas: uses and definition" *Progress in Planning* 2(4) (Pergamon Press, London)

Vining R, 1946 "Location of industry and regional patterns of business cycle behaviour" *Econometrica* 14 37–63

Appendix

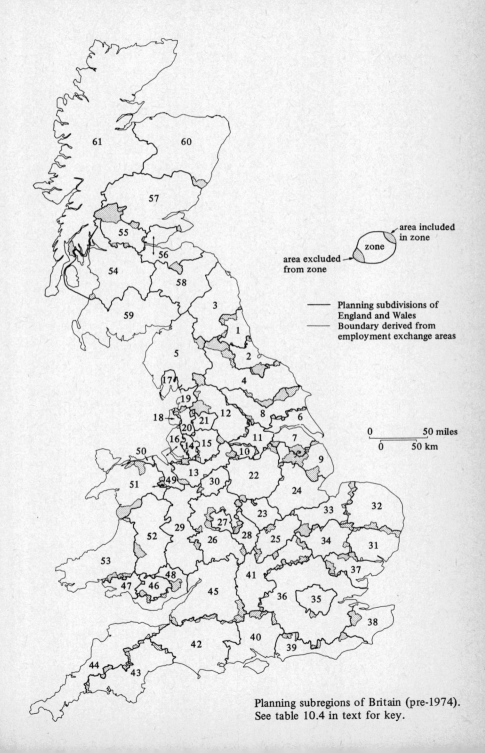

area included in zone

zone

area excluded from zone

—— Planning subdivisions of England and Wales

—— Boundary derived from employment exchange areas

| 0 | 50 miles |
| 0 | 50 km |

Planning subregions of Britain (pre-1974). See table 10.4 in text for key.

Index

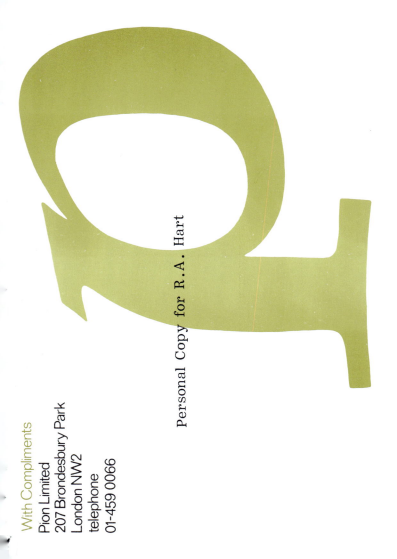

With Compliments

Pion Limited
207 Brondesbury Park
London NW2
telephone
01-459 0066

Personal Copy for R.A. Hart